Also by Ellen Goodman
Turning Points

CLOSE TO HOME

Ellen Goodman

SIMON AND SCHUSTER
NEW YORK

Published by Simon and Schuster
A Division of Gulf & Western Corporation
Simon & Schuster Building
Rockefeller Center
1230 Avenue of the Americas
New York, New York 10020
SIMON AND SCHUSTER and colophon
are trademarks of Simon & Schuster

Designed by Christine Swirnoff
Manufactured in the United States of America
Printed and bound by Fairfield Graphics, Inc.
        3 4 5 6 7 8 9 10

Library of Congress Cataloging in Publication Data

Goodman, Ellen.
    Close to home.

    I. Title.
AC8.G762   081   79-16007

ISBN 0-671-24883-9

This work was originally syndicated by
The Boston Globe Newspaper Company/Washington Post Writers Group

ACKNOWLEDGMENTS

For the past twelve years I've worked in one of the more hysterical and congenial newspaper offices in the country, the *Boston Globe*. It's been a good place to think.

The editor of the *Boston Globe*, Tom Winship, was the first person who suggested that I write a column. As I recall, I barged into his office, irate about some issue or other. Tom, in his own unflappable style, said, "Why don't you write a column about it?" I did, and I have ever since. He not only gave me the space, but also the support to fill it for the past several years. He has been both mentor and friend, and I thank him.

Aside from Winship, I also want to thank Bill Dickinson of the *Washington Post* Writers Group, which has syndicated my column for the past three and a half years. He is a man of sense and sensibility, or, as he would say, Kansas and Washington. Bill and Anna Karavangelos of the Writers Group have supported my opinions and tolerated my spelling with intelligence and good humor.

I am also, weekly, daily, grateful to all the friends and family whose brains I've picked and lives I've borrowed. But I especially have to thank my sister, Jane Holtz Kay, my "organizer" Micki Talmadge, and my best friends, Pat O'Brien, Otile McManus and Bob Levey, for being the sounding boards of my work.

to Katie

CONTENTS

CLOSE TO HOME

INTRODUCTION

When my daughter Katie was seven years old, I overheard her telling a friend, "My mommy is a columnist." "What's that?" asked the other little girl, reasonably enough. Katie thought about it awhile and finally said, "Well, my mother gets paid for telling people what she thinks."

All in all, that's not such a bad job description. The pieces collected in this book represent several years of "telling people what I think." They also represent two of the main qualifications for this business: nerve and endurance.

To write a column you need the egocentric confidence that your view of the world is important enough to be read. Then you need the pacing of a long-distance runner to write day after day, week after week, year after year. One journalist who dropped out of this endurance contest with a sigh of relief said that writing a column was like being married to a nymphomaniac: every time you think you're through, you have to start all over again. This was an unenlightened, but fairly accurate, analogy.

To meet my "quota," I need two opinions a week, although I assure you that some weeks I overflow with ideas, percolate opinions, while other weeks I can't decide what I think about the weather. Moreover, I have to fit these thoughts into a carefully reserved piece of newspaper property. I am allotted approximately the same number of words whether I am writing about life, love or the world-shattering problem of a zucchini that is sterile.

Despite these constraints, I tend to go through life like a vacuum cleaner, inhaling all the interesting tidbits in my path, using almost everything I observe, read or report. For me at least, this makes life more interesting and more integrated. I don't "go" to work or "return" to home life. The lines between the personal and professional sides of my life are far less rigidly drawn in this job than in virtually any other.

I suppose that is because I do write close to home.

I never wanted to be a package tour sort of columnist who covered thirteen countries in twenty-seven days. Nor do I want to write at arm's length about the Major Issues of Our Times. I think it's more important for all of us to be able to make links between our personal lives and public issues.

The most vital concerns can't be divided into internal and external affairs. What is more private a concern than the public policy decisions made about the family? What is more public a concern than the impact of divorce, or the new isolation, or the two-worker family? The ups and downs of presidential polls are no more crucial to our society than the way we raise our children.

As a writer, I've wanted to be seen as a person, not a pontificator. Why should people believe what I have to say if they know nothing about me? I don't want to present myself as a disembodied voice of authority but as a thirty-eight-year-old woman, mother, vegetable gardener, failed jogger and expert on only one subject: the ambivalence of life.

I see myself in these pieces, and in fact, as a fellow struggler. In that sense too I write close to home.

What else can I say about the collection? The pieces show that I am more comfortable observing—people, change, events—than judging. I am more concerned with the struggles between conflicting values than the struggles between conflicting political parties. I don't think there is anything undignified about being silly when all about me are grave.

And maybe these columns also show how much I like my work.

PART ONE

OUR TIMES

■ THE COMPANY MAN

He worked himself to death, finally and precisely, at 3:00 A.M. Sunday morning.

The obituary didn't say that, of course. It said that he died of a coronary thrombosis—I think that was it—but everyone among his friends and acquaintances knew it instantly. He was a perfect Type A, a workaholic, a classic, they said to each other and shook their heads —and thought for five or ten minutes about the way they lived.

This man who worked himself to death finally and precisely at 3:00 A.M. Sunday morning—on his day off—was fifty-one years old and a vice-president. He was, however, one of six vice-presidents, and one of three who might conceivably—if the president died or retired soon enough—have moved to the top spot. Phil knew that.

He worked six days a week, five of them until eight or nine at night, during a time when his own company had begun the four-day week for everyone but the executives. He worked like the Important People. He had no outside "extracurricular interests," unless, of course, you think about a monthly golf game that way. To Phil, it was work. He always ate egg salad sandwiches at his desk. He was, of course, overweight, by 20 or 25 pounds. He thought it was okay, though, because he didn't smoke.

On Saturdays, Phil wore a sports jacket to the office instead of a suit, because it was the weekend.

He had a lot of people working for him, maybe sixty, and most of them liked him most of the time. Three of them will be seriously considered for his job. The obituary didn't mention that.

But it did list his "survivors" quite accurately. He is survived by his wife, Helen, forty-eight years old, a good woman of no particular marketable skills, who worked in an office before marrying and mothering. She had, according to her daughter, given up trying to compete with his work years ago, when the children were small. A company friend said, "I know how much you will miss him." And she answered, "I already have."

"Missing him all these years," she must have given up part of herself which had cared too much for the man. She would be "well taken care of."

His "dearly beloved" eldest of the "dearly beloved" children is a hard-working executive in a manufacturing firm down South. In the day and a half before the funeral, he went around the neighborhood researching his father, asking the neighbors what he was like. They were embarrassed.

His second child is a girl, who is twenty-four and newly married. She lives near her mother and they are close, but whenever she was alone with her father, in a car driving somewhere, they had nothing to say to each other.

The youngest is twenty, a boy, a high-school graduate who has spent the last couple of years, like a lot of his friends, doing enough odd jobs to stay in grass and food. He was the one who tried to grab at his father, and tried to mean enough to him to keep the man at home. He was his father's favorite. Over the last two years, Phil stayed up nights worrying about the boy.

The boy once said, "My father and I only board here."

At the funeral, the sixty-year-old company president told the forty-eight-year-old widow that the fifty-one-year-old deceased had meant much to the company and would be missed and would be hard to replace. The widow didn't look him in the eye. She was afraid he would read her bitterness and, after all, she would need him to straighten out the finances—the stock options and all that.

Phil was overweight and nervous and worked too hard. If he wasn't at the office, he was worried about it. Phil was a Type A, a heart-attack natural. You could have picked him out in a minute from a lineup.

So when he finally worked himself to death, at precisely 3:00 A.M. Sunday morning, no one was really surprised.

By 5:00 P.M. the afternoon of the funeral, the company president had begun, discreetly of course, with care and taste, to make inquiries about his replacement. One of three men. He asked around: "Who's been working the hardest?"

OCTOBER 1976

WHO ARE THE
NEW CONSERVATIVES?

So we are all New Conservatives, are we? All New Moderates, and apathetic at that? So we are in retreat, back to basics like reading and writing, and 100 percent cotton, and politics without promises? At least, that's what we are told.

The trend setters have turned in upon themselves and reported a trend against trends. The political analysts, wallowing in disinterest, call us apathetic. The presidential candidates "casually" racing for convention delegates are trying to define us so that they can prove they reflect us. If they are boring, they swear we don't want flashiness. If they are devoid of plans, they say we don't want any promises. If they lull us to sleep, they say we don't want to be alarmed.

Everyone says we want a respite, a Fifties Revival—an Eisenhower, Shh-boom, June, Moon, Spoon, Croon kind of year—in which we all go to the seashore after we go to the polls.

Well, I don't buy that. I don't think we are happily hiding behind the hedges of our Main Streets and yearning for the days when Howdy Doody was the king of the airwaves. The fifties? Anyone who is nostalgic for the fifties deserves them. You could draw a better era out of a hat.

No, we are not in a retreat. The last decade hit us like adolescence, when our legs grew alarmingly out of proportion to the rest of us, and our voices suddenly cracked out of our former lives. It takes time for all of us to grow into some sense of a changed self, and it takes time for the rest of us to catch up and integrate comfortably. But we aren't about to resurrect Dress Codes and Church Latin and Feminine Mystiques and Postwar Patriotism. We aren't going back, because change isn't a seesaw but a spiral.

Once, in the sixties, author Angela McBride wrote that she thought a "married feminist" was a walking contradiction. Now she calls herself a walking dialectician. That's as good a term for these times as any. This is an era for walking dialecticians who hold conversations with themselves, or rather, among their many selves. The conversations begin, "On the one hand . . . on the other hand."

We try to resolve our conflicts. We want to reconcile our deep disillusionment with institutions and our deep need for stability. We want to resolve our distaste for the old repressive rules and our need for guidelines and traditions.

We aren't trying to fit ourselves and each other under the simple labels of the last decade: militant, hippy, hard hat, dropout, hawk, radical. Those words sound quaint. We are more concerned with accepting or at least recognizing our complexity: that we are a product of our private histories and public allegiance. The "hard hat" of the sixties is more likely to describe himself as a forty-five-year-old Italian-American church-going family planner with a mother who is on Social Security and a kid who has asthma.

Many of us want things that we will not accept as contradictory: a clean environment and full employment; meaningful work and college tuition; social justice and a balanced budget.

So, we are not the New Conservatives. We are the New Buts. We are Democrats, but . . . We are Republicans, but . . . We are working class, environmentalist, Baptist, unionist, patriotic . . . but. The only bloc vote that would win a majority this year is the "But" vote.

The real New Conservatives are the candidates. Not a risk taker among them. One offers us blind trust and another benign neglect, and a third promises no fancy stuff. They do not promise to lead; they promise not to mislead. They remind us of Marabel Morgan's injunction: "Support the Man, not the plan."

None of them has yet taken a chance that we might just respond to a politician who appealed to our own changed sense of self . . . more complex, more individual, still in process . . . a walking dialectician.

JUNE 1976

THE "SIXTIES KID"

She spied him right away as he jaywalked across Harvard Square. It was 26 degrees out and he was only wearing an old green army jacket and jeans. His shoes were soaked by the snow and his hands were stuffed into pockets instead of gloves.

That was Jack. He was thirty years old, six feet tall, skinny, scruffy, and he refused to dress for the weather. He looked like a boy who still had to be told to put on his boots. Perhaps he was afraid that if he wore a hat, he'd be mistaken as a serious applicant for adulthood.

She ran into him like this when he came into town occasionally to make some money or have his car fixed. Once or twice a year they ended up having coffee together.

The two had met briefly in the late sixties on some story about campus unrest. He was involved; she was reporting. At the time Jack had been a sophomore and she was already a mother. Then he dropped out—not only from college but from growing up—and the gap between their ages had widened.

Now it occurred to her, as they slid into the restaurant booth and ordered coffee, that somebody was always writing about the Sixties Kids. They wrote about the former radicals who were running things like government bureaucracies or businesses—the ones wearing ties and paying Social Security. They wrote about the ones who had moved to communes and stayed on to raise kids, who lived in country towns where the natives regarded them as neighbors now rather than hippies. But very few wrote about the burn-outs. Very few wrote about those who had suffered some psychic disease, a permanent loss of will. Like Jack.

Slowly, Jack told her about the past year. He talked as if he were reading a shopping list of events in no particular order of importance: His car was still working. He still had no furniture, no wife, and no children. He'd had a dog for a while, but no more. He was still painting houses for bread money—outside in the summer, inside in the winter.

Then, from the pockets of his green jacket, he emptied the more serious lint of his life. There was the quarterly letter from his parents pleading with him to go back to school. His unfinished childhood seemed to keep them in a state of painfully incomplete parenting. Behind the letter was a picture of the woman he had lived with last summer, and under that were some fuzzy directions to the house where he planned to spend the winter with friends. Only he couldn't remember whether the house was in Vermont or New Hampshire.

For some reason he irritated her. Thirty years old and he didn't know whether he was headed for Vermont or New Hampshire? States, statistics, plans, slipped through his mind as if through a sieve. She began badgering him. What were his goals now? "I'd like to keep my car running through the winter." Why are you still drifting? "I'm not drifting, I'm living my life."

The woman sipped her coffee. He wasn't the only Sixties Kid she knew. Others, like Jack, had lost the conviction that "it" made any difference; that "they" could make a difference. The distinctions between friends, ideals, politics, jobs, seemed no more important to them at this point than the choice of drinking black coffee or regular.

They did not seem to regard *anomie* as a disease of the spirit, but as a truth. They embraced their lack of purpose as if it were a benign response to a harsh world. They regarded struggle as foolish, differences as illusions. She knew this.

But suddenly she wanted to shake this Jack hard until something rattled out of him, a piece of engagement or anger. She wanted to squeeze his passivity out until it oozed through his damp shoes.

Why was she so mad? Because he had committed the sin of *accidie*—not becoming what he might have? Or because she felt in her gut that it was cowardly of him to quit in this way?

She had never been especially impressed by the heroics of the people convinced that they are about to change the world. She was more awed by the heroism of those who are willing to struggle to make one small difference after another. And he had attacked her heroes.

The two walked back out of the restaurant, onto the brick sidewalk. It had started snowing again. There were windchill factors being read on radios in the cars that drove by them. She wanted to say something important to Jack. As he turned to say goodbye, he stuffed his bare hands in his pockets, and she blurted out, "For Gawd's sakes, get some mittens!"

JANUARY 1979

THE NEW AMBIDEXTERS

The political expert explained it carefully over dinner. The country, he said, is turning to the right, but the New Right is farther to the left than it used to be. At the same time, the Left is farther to the right than it was in the Old Days when it was called the New Left.

By the time he was through chronicling the evolution of politics in America, I was totally unable to remember which hand I was supposed to cut my food with. Was it the right or the left, and was it important?

Now, I had read the Gallup poll, which said that 47 percent of the American people consider themselves to be right of center, and I had heard the accounts of the new conservative bash at the St. Regis hotel in New York last week. But, to be perfectly frank about it, I don't think that we can understand what's going on in politics in the classical terms of political anatomy. I don't think we are turning to the right, or to the left, for that matter. I think most of us are turning ambidextrous.

To sound more trendy about the whole thing, we seem to have become The New Ambidexters.

There is a much more widespread uncertainty, often a frustrating sense of the complexity of social issues. Every time someone offers a solution someone else offers a criticism. Most of us have become walking dialecticians, carrying our own debates in our arms. We are constantly arguing with ourselves—"on the one hand . . . on the other hand . . ." We are, in short, card-carrying members of the New Ambidextrous Party.

The New Ambidexters believe, for example, that on the one hand, government should provide services and, on the other hand, government should keep out of our lives. The New Ambidexters believe that the corporations have murderously gunked up the environment and put ruinous chemicals in our food, but that government regulations interfere too much with business.

The New Ambidexters believe that welfare mothers should get off the dole and go to work, and that mothers of small children should stay home with them. They believe that we've all become far too selfish, too "me-first," but that individuals have the right to lead their lives as they choose.

The Ambidexters simply hold onto a wide range of opinions

simultaneously, without always seeing them as contradictory. They want government to provide more and cost less. They want security and independence. They believe in responsibility and freedom.

The same people who rue the disruption of the family don't believe that people should be forced to stay in rotten marriages. The same people who believe in roots and community believe—on the other hand—in mobility and adventure.

Most of them, of course, weren't born ambidextrous. They have lived long enough to see the cost accounting of change.

They have seen that change, even the solutions, comes with a full attachment of new problems. When the government sets up a program to help those who can't work, they end up also helping those who won't work. When the government helps the aged who don't have families to depend on, they end up with more aged depending on the government instead of families. As divorce becomes more acceptable in society, there are more divorces for society to accept.

The Ambidexters don't want to go back to the thirties or the fifties. Few people want to remove the Social Security system or take away compensation for unemployment. They have no interest in returning to desperation. But when they look ahead to the future they weigh the issues in both hands.

The Ambidexters are aware that there are still serious social problems. They believe that government should Do Something. National health care. Day care. Welfare reform. But there are the other problems. Big government. Family responsibility. Taxes.

So, in view of the complexity of the situation, the one solution the Ambidexters seem to have agreed upon for the moment is to sit on their hands. The right hand, and the left.

DECEMBER 1977

THE LAST BOAT
TO THE MIDDLE CLASS

They'd caught it last year. The sort of buying panic usually seen in bargain basements and one-day sales. It was Margaret who called it a "panic." David, her husband, preferred to describe the feeling to me as anxiety.

But suddenly this couple in their early thirties were gripped with the notion that "the last boat to the middle class was leaving and we'd better get on it." The last boat was, of course, a house boat.

The couple, decent people who worry about their family and their town, read all the housing figures. In fact, like many of their friends, they memorized them.

The price of a new home in 1972 was $22,000, and now in 1978 it was $53,700. Older homes were only $6,000 less, on the average. They knew that people like their parents once spent 25 percent of their income on housing; now they were told that people spent 44 percent. But the news that impressed them the most was that the average cost was expected to rise by another $25,000 before 1981.

At that point, Margaret and David realized that savings had become too expensive. Housing costs in their northeastern city were rising faster than their average savings account. And so, they borrowed and collected all the financial scraps they could find into a bankbook. Then they leaped off the dock and grabbed for the side of the boat.

If some historian in the future wants to know why anyone bought a home during the late seventies, when the market went as wild as Wall Street in the twenties, they could do worse than if they looked up Margaret and David. This couple could tell them a lot about the self-fulfilling prophecy of the marketplace: Buy Now or Never. They could tell them a lot about the time when people congratulated themselves on their past housing investments with the line: "We could never afford our house if we went to buy it now."

And if those historians wanted to know why some people who once cared and petitioned about social causes began to care and petition about property taxes, perhaps they should research the depressing effect of the inflated housing market.

I don't know exactly why the notion of homeownership has such a grasp on the American imagination. Perhaps as descendants of land-less immigrants we turn our plots into symbols of stability.

But we are told that "ownership" is the American dream, and we believe it. Today the would-be-middle-class children of middle-class parents almost unanimously regard rent as money thrown away, and houses as investments. A house is the middle-class retirement plan, its equity, its legacy, its tax hedge. Its "real" estate.

And yet, more and more often, it's an albatross. David and Margaret have spent six months in their own six rooms. He isn't the only thirty-three-year-old homeowner who refers to himself half jok-ingly as "the first generation in my family to be downwardly mobile."

This leap onto the edge of their own property has been almost as stressful as their fear of being left behind. They will tell you that they have traded one anxiety for another. They are today what is called "house poor."

House-poor people, they say, spend nearly 50 percent of their after-tax income on their homes. House-poor people become perma-nent members of the two-worker family. House-poor people work for their land as much as any farmer. Never mind all that talk about the Now Generation; they have mortgaged the present for the future.

But equally important, David says without pride, "Our house has become our politics." House-poor people, he says, make hard choices. Just last week, they voted for "the roof over our heads" against costly improvements for their children's schools.

But if they start to worry about it—worry about the sort of national stinginess cycle that comes out of this housing inflation, worry about voting against the money to keep their towns as well trimmed as their hedges—they feel somewhat impotent. They can't vote against interest rates and purchase prices and bank loans.

Margaret and David still feel lucky just to have made the leap. Every Sunday they look at the real estate page, as if it were the stock market. Then they tell each other reassuringly that they were "right."

The market is still going up. And they are still holding on.

SEPTEMBER 1978

■ BEING ALONE

My friend Cassie is the sort of trendsetter they ought to hire over at *People.* Ever since she was eighteen, she's been a year or two ahead of the times.

When everyone else arrived at college with Villager blouses and circle pins which had to be discarded by Thanksgiving, Cassie came with black turtlenecked sweaters and tights. Cassie was married before anyone else, and divorced before anyone else. She had a Cuisinart and a schefflera when everyone else had a crêpe pan and a philodendron.

For these and other reasons, people have always thought of Cassie as an individualist, an eccentric. She, however, has always described herself as a premature conformist. She thinks of herself as someone who is following the crowd, but arriving a bit earlier.

Anyway, about a year ago, Cassie moved out of the last in a series of Meaningful Relationships and announced that she was now Into Being Alone. At the time, we both happily assumed that, at long last, Cassie was finding her own independent way through the world. But the fact of the matter is that, once again, she was just a bit ahead of things. This year, everyone who is anyone is Into Being Alone. People who were formerly "lonely." People who were previously "looking for the right relationship." People who were In Transition. Even people who were swinging singles. They are all Into Being Alone.

I am now quite convinced that Being Into Being Alone is this year's Alternative Lifestyle, having replaced Communes, the Soil, and Living Together. Alternative Lifestyles, the emotional fly-drive packages of our times, come equipped with a set of clothes, a choice of authors, a limited menu of sports and a discount coupon book of clichés.

In the last six months, I have heard more clichés about how to savor aloneness than how to save togetherness. There was one article that told me I don't need a date in order to wash my hair, and another that assured me I don't need a mate in order to cook a three-course dinner. Meanwhile, I keep reading about the Challenge of Living Alone as if a studio apartment in the city were three weeks on a rock with Outward Bound.

I do understand why some people prefer their own company.

When you live alone, you can be sure that the person who squeezed the toothpaste tube in the middle wasn't committing a hostile act.

The people who are new in the alone business, after years of being mated, are fascinated to find out exactly what they choose to do now that they aren't compromising. After a decade of Aspen and prime time, they may discover that they don't like skiing or television. They may find that they really prefer Russian dressing, not Italian, and like to keep the air conditioner on medium rather than high.

As for the people who've lived alone for years and liked it, a touch of Alone Pride is good for the ego.

But the problem is overkill. These Aloners remind me of the aggressive nonparent organizations which keep defending themselves after everyone's stopped attacking. They seem to go from espousing living alone as an option to extolling it as a positive choice to criticizing those who "need" other people: "What's wrong with them? Aren't they strong enough to be their own best friend?"

Eventually, those who are Into Being Alone limit themselves. To one. They learn that they deserve to cook a steak for themselves. They learn that they aren't lonely in a bubble bath. They learn that they can live alone. But they run out of material. They risk being permanently left with the only person they don't have to reach out to touch.

There is, however, hope. My friend Cassie says that this life-style usually lasts only a year. Eventually the fascination with the details of living alone—my key, my door, my refrigerator—begins to pale.

What happens next? I'm not sure. But Cassie, who is my Jeane Dixon about these matters, confided something to me last week. She's now Into Making a Commitment.

JULY 1977

THE CULT
OF IMPOTENCE

If they ever dig down through layers of future generations, looking for artifacts that tell something about mid-seventies America, let's hope they find John Lilly's isolation tank. It will tell them a great deal.

The California physician and psychoanalyst has designed an enclosed tank, with 10 inches of water heated to precisely 93 degrees and room for exactly one person. Why? As he told *People*, "Lying on your back, you can breathe quite comfortably and safely, freed from sight, sound, people and the universe outside. That way you can enter the universe within you."

Think what Greta Garbo could have done with that. Think what we do with it—"free" ourselves from other people and the environment, enter the "universe within."

The "isolation tank" is as good a symbol as any of a time when we are making a positive value out of our sense of impotence in the world, and a cult out of the fragmentation of society and missed connections of our personal lives. Over the last few years—driven by events more complex than the labels "Vietnam" and "Watergate"—we have turned inward, to the search for personal solutions. We are no longer convinced of the possibility of social change or even the capacity to "do good." Every change reverberates.

We have discovered that when you cure typhoid you get overpopulation and when you raise the standard of living you destroy the environment. It is no wonder that we "work on" an area that seems more within our control and power: ourselves.

This self-centering is not only a retreat from the world, but a by-product of the current condition of our lives. The newest definition of American individualism is aloneness.

In the years since 1960, the number of "primaries"—people living alone—has risen by 87 percent while the number of families has risen only by 23 percent. Fifteen million of us live alone. Fifty million of us are single, widowed or divorced. At least partially in response to this, the new therapies—from the isolation tank on—offer us ways to "get into ourselves." Those who aren't "doing their own thing" or "finding themselves" are "getting in touch with their feelings." The

West Coast greeting, "What are you into?" is most aptly answered with one word: myself.

In the hyperindividualism of a movement like est, we are trained to be self-reliant, totally responsible to and for our own lives. The range of the new therapies is characterized by a frenzied search inward. The "isolation tank" seems to suggest that the road to happiness, peace, fulfillment, understanding, is an internal route. As Dr. Lilly says, "If you are able to retire deep inside yourself, you can find the quiet place which nobody can penetrate. This way you can isolate yourself in your deep inner core."

But then where are you? Then what? The impulses to more self-awareness, self-exploration are positive ones—but not if they lead to a dead end of navel-gazing, a permanent retreat from others and the problems of the world. At a time when we seem in almost perilous need of personal connections and social solutions, the tendency toward the isolation-tank psychology can be a sad perversion of the old American individualism.

I am reminded of a brief exchange Peter Marin had with a man "into" mysticism, and which he repeated in a piece written for *Harper's* last year. He wrote:

"He was telling me about his sense of another reality. 'I know there is something outside of me,' he said. 'I can feel it. I know it is there. But what is it?'

" 'It may not be a mystery,' I said, 'Perhaps it is the world.' "

SEPTEMBER 1976

■■■■■ IT'S FAILURE,
NOT SUCCESS

I knew a man who went into therapy about three years ago because, as he put it, he couldn't live with himself any longer. I didn't blame him. The guy was a bigot, a tyrant and a creep.

In any case, I ran into him again after he'd finished therapy. He was still a bigot, a tyrant and a creep, *but* . . . he had learned to live with himself.

Now, I suppose this was an accomplishment of sorts. I mean, nobody else could live with him. But it seems to me that there are an awful lot of people running around and writing around these days encouraging us to feel good about what we should feel terrible about, and to accept in ourselves what we should change.

The only thing they seem to disapprove of is disapproval. The only judgment they make is against being judgmental, and they assure us that we have nothing to feel guilty about except guilt itself. It seems to me that they are all intent on proving that I'm OK and You're OK, when in fact, I may be perfectly dreadful and you may be unforgivably dreary, and it may be—gasp!—*wrong*.

What brings on my sudden attack of judgmentitis is success, or rather, *Success!*—the latest in a series of exclamation-point books all concerned with How to Make it.

In this one, Michael Korda is writing a recipe book for success. Like the other authors, he leapfrogs right over the "Shoulds" and into the "Hows." He eliminates value judgments and edits out moral questions as if he were Fanny Farmer and the subject was the making of a blueberry pie.

It's not that I have any reason to doubt Mr. Korda's advice on the way to achieve success. It may very well be that successful men wear handkerchiefs stuffed neatly in their breast pockets, and that successful single women should carry suitcases to the office on Fridays whether or not they are going away for the weekend.

He may be realistic when he says that "successful people generally have very low expectations of others." And he may be only slightly cynical when he writes: "One of the best ways to ensure success is to develop expensive tastes or marry someone who has them."

And he may be helpful with his handy hints on how to sit next to someone you are about to overpower.

But he simply finesses the issues of right and wrong—silly words, embarrassing words that have been excised like warts from the shiny surface of the new how-to books. To Korda, guilt is not a prod, but an enemy that he slays on page four. Right off the bat, he tells the would-be successful reader that:

- It's OK to be greedy.
- It's OK to look out for Number One.
- It's OK to be Machiavellian (if you can get away with it).
- It's OK to recognize that honesty is not always the best policy (provided you don't go around saying so).
- And it's always OK to be rich.

Well, in fact, it's not OK. It's not OK to be greedy, Machiavellian, dishonest. It's not always OK to be rich. There is a qualitative difference between succeeding by making napalm or by making penicillin. There is a difference between climbing the ladder of success, and machete-ing a path to the top.

Only someone with the moral perspective of a mushroom could assure us that this was all OK. It seems to me that most Americans harbor ambivalence toward success, not for neurotic reasons, but out of a realistic perception of what it demands.

Success is expensive in terms of time and energy and altered behavior—the sort of behavior he describes in the grossest of terms: "If you can undermine your boss and replace him, fine, do so, but never express anything but respect and loyalty for him while you're doing it."

This author—whose *Power!* topped the best-seller list last year —is intent on helping rid us of that ambivalence which is a signal from our conscience. He is like the other "Win!" "Me First!" writers, who try to make us comfortable when we should be uncomfortable.

They are all Doctor Feelgoods, offering us placebo prescriptions instead of strong medicine. They give us a way to live with ourselves, perhaps, but not a way to live with each other. They teach us a whole lot more about "Failure!" than about success.

OCTOBER 1977

INWARD BOUND

The sophomore had left college to "find herself," rather as if she were a set of misplaced keys. She had the notion that her mind was a collection of pockets and if she searched in each one of them long enough she would find the keys to unlock this self.

Months later, she told her parents that she was deeply into the independent study called "Who Am I?" And by now, surely, she had become a professional introspector. A very private eye.

The woman didn't know this sophomore very well; she was a friend of the parents. But she knew others her age who conducted their own missing persons bureau: others who had turned inward to see what they could find and had found self-discovery a totally absorbing sort of trip.

The woman wasn't opposed in principle to interior travels. She knew too many people who went through life without even stopping to interview themselves. They were wind-up toys. They did, therefore they were. Until they stopped. They never asked who or why.

Yet so many, so early, seemed so inward bound. They focused more energy on who they were than on who they might become. For every seventeen-year-old who actually "found" him or herself, there was another who simply lost experience. For every nineteen-year-old who got closer to his or her psyche, there was another who withdrew.

There was a young man she knew who spent his junior year in a dorm room rummaging through his mental pockets and never finding anything except lint. There was a twenty-two-year-old in her neighborhood whose horizons were still limited to the first person.

She wondered if there wasn't an age at which our pockets are waiting to be filled rather than sorted. Prolonged psyche-tripping at eighteen or nineteen seemed rather like writing an autobiography at ten or eleven. Sooner or later, you ran out of material.

There are people, more mystical than this woman, who believe that they were born with complete, coherent inner beings which only need to be uncovered and expressed. There are people, less mystical, who believe that they were born blank and then marked. Their selves are products of indelible chalk.

She had always figured that people were born with tendencies . . . potential . . . possibilities. But they "grew" selves. It wasn't the

34   CLOSE TO HOME

primal scene of birth that seemed most interesting, but the process of autobiography.

Some of the most self-aware people had taken their chances first and their temperature second. They didn't put introspection as a barrier before experience. They knew themselves in retrospect, through their histories. As an old and understanding man had said once in Detroit, "My life has been on-the-job training."

It was odd, but those who always tried to get their act together before they acted sometimes got stuck at the beginning. Those who thought of themselves as constantly improving sometimes learned more about their own character. This sophomore was still on her own internal trip. But perhaps she, too, would soon go and make some new material.

After all, most people don't find themselves; they become themselves. And life has a way of interrupting the most hypnotic private eye.

SEPTEMBER 1978

ANXIETY
IS THE CLASS UNIFORM

The college senior came up to the front of the room, wearing her anxiety like a hair shirt. The woman wasn't surprised to see it. She had been on enough campuses lately to know that anxiety is the class uniform. The students scratch their way to Commencement.

But this senior had been home for the weekend. Her parents had not understood what she was worried about. You have all these choices, they said, with pale-green edges to their voices. You are lucky, they said. The senior in anxiety had broken out in hives and she slammed the door between them. Now she stood in front of the woman, scratching.

You see, she said, if she didn't get into graduate school she didn't know what she would do. It would be, quite simply, The End. She wanted the woman to hand her some kind of prescription, a solution, some calamine lotion of experience.

Well, the woman had heard so much of this lately. There was the senior who was "desperate" for a job in television and the senior who "had" to go to medical school, and the senior whose life depended on getting a job in publishing, or architecture, or government.

The hair shirts were woven, she was told, out of the threads of the tight professional-school market and no-job market. Five years ago, seniors had difficulty deciding just what, if anything, they wanted to do. Now they simply competed for the available slots. They wanted to Get In—as if life were a final club and they had only one chance. It seemed to the woman that in their effort to be realistic, to be inalterably pragmatic, to be the certified public accountants of studentry, they had become incredibly unrealistic.

They believed, among other things, in one-track careers. The senior in front of her *had* to be accepted for a Ph.D. The Ph.D. ahead of her *had* to be an assistant professor. The assistant professor wanted only to get tenure. Meanwhile, somewhere, another tenured professor had acquired sideburns, a graduate student and a rash that woke him up in the middle of the night wondering what he had missed, and why he now had the fifty-year-old itch.

Recently, the woman had talked and mused with Matina Horner, the president of Radcliffe College, as humane and down-to-earth a person as sits in a president's chair. They had come around to the confusing subject of "contract careers." Dr. Horner had said: "I just don't think people are going to have one-track careers anymore. Society can't absorb it. There's going to be much more career shifting, second careers, third careers."

So, it seemed that just when students needed to be open to change, even serendipity, there they were, in their hair shirts, seeking the salves of a false security.

There was a certain bookkeeping attitude among students, and that was understandable. If you paid $20,000 for college, one male student had told her, then surely you should be guaranteed $5,000 more a year than someone who had not gone to college. He launched an anxiety attack against his college—because it wasn't a successful trade school. Relevancy wasn't a matter of social action. It was, he said, what looked good on a résumé. Scratch, scratch.

The woman knew that colleges were open to that kind of attack. But she hoped that they would not become so practically impractical.

What, after all, do college students need to know if they are going to have three careers? What is the best preparation for five decades? My answer: Just what college was supposed to teach people from the beginning. How to think. About themselves and their lives and whatever work they plunge into, sidle into, or fall into.

The woman wanted to tell the senior something like that. But she couldn't reach her through the hair shirt.

The senior was totally convinced that her life was a problem to be solved. She believed she absolutely *had* to solve it by the day after Commencement. And, wherever she went, she wore this uncomfortable conviction like a second skin.

MARCH 1978

TALK ABOUT PRIORITIES!

In the last year, Senator William Proxmire (D–Wisconsin), the man who brought hair transplants out of the closet, has proved that he's also handy with a pair of shears.

In his monthly "Golden Fleece" awards for the most "ridiculous or ironic" waste of government money, the senator has played on the ever-popular idea that big government wastes big money. In the process of pointing a finger at the rip-off of the month, he's also managed to mine a rich, or should we say "golden," vein of publicity.

In catchy press releases, we are told that we have spent half a million dollars to find out that monkeys clench their jaws when they're angry, and $84,000 to find out why people fall in love, and $102,000 to figure out if drunken fish are more aggressive than sober fish.

This is the sort of thing that makes some of us wince, some of us laugh and all of us sure that the chairman of the Appropriations Subcommittee is doing a bang-up good job, well done, give 'em hell, Bill.

Last week, in another elbow in the ribs of them fuzzy-headed academic types who think they can pull the wool over our eyes, he gave the award to the National Science Foundation for fleecing us of $47,100 "to study the effects of a scantily clad woman on the behavior of male drivers."

Now that's a real thigh-slapper, with a bit of titillation, and who among us doesn't enjoy a little laugh while we're over-balancing the budget? Well, Professor Robert A. Baron, for one.

Baron is the alleged "fleecer" who read about the award on page one of his West Lafayette, Indiana, newspaper last Tuesday. But he is not a fellow without a sense of humor and so he opened his Purdue University class the next morning saying, "Now that all of your worst fears about me have been confirmed . . ." The kids laughed.

This particular thirty-two-year-old is simply not a mad lecher given to sending out "scantily clad" students to distract the drivers of Indiana during National Safety Week. The fact is that his study bears little resemblance to the Proxmire satire. Baron is known—at least outside the Capitol—as a man who did some of the original and important research on violence in children's television. Since the late sixties he's been intrigued with the effect of the environment on human aggression. In those days, everyone was talking about the "long hot summer" effect on unrest in the cities, and he decided to study it.

He took his "hot money" from NSF and spent two and a half years boondoggling away in a 95-degree laboratory seeing if hot students would zap their colleagues with electrodes faster than cool students. The answer was yes, up to a point (or, rather, a degree).

Then, while other social scientists were off studying "The Signs of Slipping Virginity" at the University of Virginia, and "Why Male Moles Die after Mating" at Monash University in Australia, Baron moved on to try to figure out what "cools" violence, aside from air conditioning.

Enter the scantily clad maiden! After testing the capacity of humor, empathy and sexual arousal to defuse aggressiveness in the laboratory, Baron took $100 of the grant for a field study. The study was designed to show whether pedestrians with (1) mini-garb, (2) clown masks or (3) a pair of crutches could turn aside the wrath of the most hostile hot human known to mankind, the male driver.

Well, they all did distract the drivers, but they attracted the attention of the Proxmire brigade, which should stick to investigating the entertainment of military and civilian officials by defense contractors. Presumably, this was comic relief.

But, as chairman of the Joint Committee on Defense Production and of the Subcommittee on Priorities and Economy, the man should have known better. It's cheaper to study aggression than to support it.

Baron is no latter-day Jason. His $47,100 is hardly enough to refuel a B-1 bomber. His study costs less than the senator earned during the same time, and need we compare it to a $112 billion defense budget?

Talk about priorities and economy.

The fact is that the senator aimed his pot shot in the wrong direction. Slashing a bikini here and a drunken fish there is like trimming the split ends off a yak. Perhaps the Golden Fleece award for next month should go to the senator who knows a public relations sheep when he shears it.

MARCH 1976

PROTECTION FROM
THE PRYING CAMERA

Maybe it was the year-end picture roundup that finally did it. Maybe it was the double exposure to the same vivid photographs. Or perhaps it was the memory of three amateur photographers carefully standing in the cold last fall, calculating their f stops and exposures with light meters, trying to find the best angle, pointing their cameras at a drunk in a doorway. Or maybe it was simply my nine-year-old cousin playing Candid Camera at the family gathering.

But whatever the reason, it has finally hit me. We have become a nation of Kodachrome, Nikon, Instamatic addicts. But we haven't yet developed a clear idea of the ethics of picture-taking. We haven't yet determined the parameters of privacy in a world of flash cubes and telescopic lenses.

We "take" pictures. As psychologist Stanley Milgram puts it, "A photographer takes a picture, he does not create it or borrow it." But who has given us the right to "take" those pictures and under what circumstances?

Since the camera first became portable, we have easily and repeatedly aimed it at public people. It has always been open shooting season on them. With new technology, however, those intrusions have intensified. This year, someone with a camera committed the gross indecency of shooting an unaware Greta Garbo in the nude—and *People* printed it.

This year, again, Ron Gallela "took" the image of Jacqueline Onassis and sold it as if it belonged to him. This year, we have pictures of a crumpled Wayne Hays, an indiscreet Nelson Rockefeller and two presidential candidates in every imaginable pose from the absurd to the embarrassing.

We have accepted the idea that public people are always free targets for the camera—without even a statute of limitations for Jackie or Garbo. We have also accepted the idea that a private person becomes public by being involved in a public event. The earthquake victims of Guatemala, the lynched leftists of Thailand, the terror-stricken of Ireland—their emotions and their bodies become frozen images.

The right of the public to know, to see and to be affected is considered more important than the right of the individual to mourn, or even die, in privacy.

What happens now, however, when cameras proliferate until they are as common as television sets? What happens when the image being "taken" is that of a butcher, a baker or a derelict, rather than a public figure? Do we all lose our right to privacy simply by stepping into view?

Should we be allowed to point cameras at each other? To regard each other as objects of art? Does the photographer or the photographed own the image?

Several years ago, *Time* photographer Steve Northup, who had covered Vietnam, and Watergate, took a group of students around Cambridge shooting pictures. He quietly insisted that they ask every pizza-maker, truck driver and beautician for permission. His attitude toward private citizens was one of careful respect for the power of "exposure." In contrast to this, the average camera bug—like the average tourist—too often goes about snapping "quaint" people, along with "quaint" scenes: See the natives smile, see the natives carrying baskets of fruit, see the native children begging, see the drunk in the doorway. As Milgram wrote, "I find it hard to understand wherein the photographer has derived the right to keep for his own purposes the image of the peasant's face."

Where do we get the right to bring other people home in a canister? Where did we lose the right to control our image?

In a study that Milgram conducted last year, a full 65 percent of the people to whom his students talked in midtown Manhattan refused to have their pictures taken, refused to be photographed. I don't think they were camera shy, in the sense of being vain. Rather, they were reluctant to have their pictures "taken."

The Navahos long believed that the photographer took a piece of them away in his film. Like them, we are coming to understand the power of these frozen images. Photographs can help us to hold onto the truth of our past, to make our history and identity more real. Or they can rip something away from us as precious as the privacy which once clothed Greta Garbo.

JANUARY 1977

CLOTHES DON'T MAKE THE WOMAN

I have just read another of those articles that answers the searing 1970 question, "Whither the revolution?" with the depressing response, "Withered."

Yes, we are told—daily, weekly and monthly—that activism has atrophied into apathy. (Though, if you can say that twelve times very quickly there's hope for you yet.) The revolution-watchers have always reminded me of the old China-watchers who stood outside the border observing the handwriting on the wall. But this group doesn't interpret posters. They comment on something called fashion in one quarter and clothing in another.

In the late sixties it seemed that every human act was a heavy political symbol. You couldn't eat a head of lettuce, or lie on a redwood chaise longue or open a door for a woman without your politics showing.

You certainly couldn't get dressed in the morning.

The length and location of your hair (on chin or head or legs), the decision to wear a bra, the choice between a dashiki and a suit, all said more about you than those "Hello, I'm Susie from Accounting" buttons they pass out at conventions. You couldn't get into a women's liberation meeting in a skirt (let alone a tie) or into a student radical meeting with a crew cut, or into a black power session with processed hair.

The generation of the late sixties was raised on television and was adept at using visual symbols. They chose to wear their politics on their sleeves. They literally "looked" different to those in the mainstream who watched them on the six o'clock news. The young self-defined radicals separated from Middle America and identified each other as compatriots by these symbols.

But there was a secondary "radical" idea: the idea of getting back to roots, to what was "natural," escaping the confines of Merry Widows and hair-straighteners. Of course, all that was pre-apathy, we are told. This month *Esquire*, in a cynical piece, labels the co-opted and the cop-outs of the black movement. Diana Ross gets it for wearing designer jumpsuits instead of dashikis and the authors lament that black fashion is now more American than Afro. This is the same argument heard about feminists in dresses and the counterculture in closed-toe shoes.

As one watcher commented, "The only commitment they're wearing on their sleeve these days is to Calvin Klein."

But the changing of the garb doesn't necessarily mean the rebirth of fifties politics, any more than the success of Diane von Furstenberg symbolizes (as *Time* raved) the return of rugged American individualism. (The only thing that's truly American about it is the notion of mass-produced individualism.)

There are alternatives to the apathy theory. As the watchers seem to have ignored, those "radical" styles have been adopted by the moderate mainstream. You can't tell the counter from the culture by the cut of their imported French jeans.

African beads are seen at all the best suburban parties and bralessness has made millionaires out of the "natural" bra manufacturers. For that matter, dashikis (some made in Taiwan) have become multiracial attire.

On the other hand, the "committed" may have outgrown the need for symbolic dressing. The importance of total group identification is lessened whenever people grow more secure in a new identity, and, therefore, less self-conscious. You don't have to put on tough clothes if you're feeling strong, and if you have pride in your heritage you don't have to wear it on your back every day of your life.

There never was anything inherently "natural" about African dress, blue jeans or work boots. The hairdo that was natural for some, required hours of curling and combing for others. The bralessness that was comfortable for some, made life miserable for large-breasted tennis players. As for the politics, it was distressing to discover that the tribal jewelry you were wearing belonged to the mortal enemies of your great-great-grandparents, or that the painter's pants you wore to symbolize "solidarity" were made by cheap, exploited foreign labor.

So it went. Fashions changed and sometimes for the simple refreshing sake of change. Instead of being clothed in apathy, the seventies just may be more sensibly suited. Clothes, in the final analysis, are a way to cover and (gasp) decorate bodies, not ideas.

APRIL 1976

THE PERILS OF POUNDS

It occurred to me about two years ago that eating had become the last bona fide sin left in America. That was the year an imaginative sex therapist came out with a book on dieting which contained the memorable line: "Reach for your Mate instead of your Plate."

As someone who had grown up in an era when people were told to sublimate their sexual urges in platters of linguine, I realized that something big was happening. We were actually being told to sublimate our eating urges in sex.

You see, sex was now "healthy" and "normal," while eating was "evil" and "perverted." The same people who read *The Joy of Sex* in public would only eat Reese's Peanut Butter Cups in the closet. The people who were happy after intercourse were guilty after the dessert course.

By now we must all be aware that obesity is the one Imm-Oral State of the seventies. Our Sodom and Gomorrah is one in which puffy people sit around washing down cheesecake with quarts of eggnog.

I have heard the same people who talk about alcoholism as a "disease" and crime as a "social disorder" ("I'm depraved on account of I'm deprived") speak of fat as unforgivable. They may express all kinds of sympathy for an amphetamine junkie, but someone who has gained 10 pounds is accused of "letting herself go." Someone who has a new tube around the middle is guilty of having "no will power."

We judge our figure flaws as character flaws. We are so convinced about the Perils of Pounds, that when a lemon meringue pie is set before our eyes, we label it Temptation. And when we scrape up the fudge sauce which overrunneth its cup, one of us is sure to say, "Isn't this positively sinful?"

Well, with all this unorganized sin around, is it any wonder that religion entered the picture?

At Oral Roberts University, for example, fundamentalists are so sure that leanness is next to godliness, that they cast out of the covenant (and the school) anyone who couldn't get rid of excessive body fat. Half-a-dozen former students are bringing suit. At the very least they should rule that the university's first name constitutes false advertising.

There are several other groups trying to persuade fat people to repent of their sins. They all seem convinced that the weight on our bodies may keep our souls from soaring, and they preach How to Find God and Lose Weight. (When you see that title in *Reader's Digest*, remember that you read it here first.)

Among these get-thin evangelists is Frances Hunter, who has written a book called *God's Answer to Fat*. No one knows exactly what Fat asked God, but apparently His answer was, "Cut calories!"

Another book, by Joan Cavanaugh, is called *More of Jesus and Less of Me*. Ms. Cavanaugh's nonfattening truths read like this: "I can't imagine Jesus coming out of the supermarket with twelve bags of chips, one for each apostle." The lady is tough to argue with.

In Minneapolis this week a group called Overeaters Victorious, Inc., is forming a statewide network of revivalist diet workshops under the motto "He must increase, but I must decrease" (John 3:30).

The Calorie Conscience Movement has all kinds of ramifications for religion. You can kiss the church cake sale good-bye. Passing the plate is going to have a very different connotation. The notion that the devil lies within is still OK, but he's hiding in all those fat cells, and the work of a good preacher is to starve him out.

All in all, Sinners of America, it appears that the current stairway to heaven is lined with celery sticks. Everyone wants to be Born Again . . . three sizes smaller.

DECEMBER 1977

■ BLAME THE VICTIM

There is a sign I pass every day on the way to work which says in bold letters: Health Thyself. The sign is "A Friendly Message" from the Blue Cross/Blue Shield people, who have, I know, a vested interest in its meaning.

But the very tone of it, the sort of Eleventh Commandment, Thus Spake Blue Cross/Blue Shield attitude of it, sitting there above the highway, has slowly rubbed raw a small layer of my consciousness. I have begun to wonder whether the Self-Health movement—of which this sign is more symbol than substance—isn't another variation on our national theme song: Blame the Victim. How many measures, how many beats, how many half-notes is it from the order to Health Thyself to the attitude that blames the ill for their illness?

The titles on the bookshelf of my favorite store are a chorus stuck in this monotone: *Stay Out of the Hospital* instructs one; *The Anti-Cancer Diet* offers another; *You Can Stop* (smoking) cheerleads a third. They tell readers How To design their faces, control their migraines, lose weight, bear children without pain and psych themselves out of everything from back pain to heart disease.

Perhaps the most typical of them is one which touts *Preventing Cancer: What You Can Do to Cut Your Risks by Up to 50 Percent.* And another containing *Dr. Frank's No Aging Diet: Eat and Grow Younger.*

Now I am in favor—who is against it?—of proper diet and exercise. I am against—who is in favor of it?—smoking. I assume that a diet high in calories, cholesterol and cognac would eventually do me in. I think that self-consciousness about health, the desire to take responsibility for the shape of our lungs and calf muscles, is positive, and I agree that we are our own best screening system. But there is a risk. A risk that as we focus on the aspects of self-health we begin to look at all illness as self-inflicted and even regard death as a kind of personal folly.

There have been, among my acquaintances, the relatives of my relatives and friends of my friends, three heart attacks within the past year. One man, I was told, was, well, overweight. "He should have known better." Another woman was, her friends insist, a real "Type A." And the third man, I was assured by the most well-meaning of people, brought it on himself. "He was so out of shape."

Similarly, when people hear reports of cancer, how often do they inadvertently say that the victim should have stayed out of the sun, or off the pill, or away from nitrates?

Now maybe they are right and maybe they are wrong, but I fear that there are many who seek to know the cause of a disease not to cure it, but to judge its victims.

It is reassuring to hear that we can cut the risks of cancer by 50 percent. It is lovely to think that we can eat in special ways and grow younger. In a world of amorphous fears, where carcinogens are the new demons, it is very human to try to analyze illness in order to separate ourselves from it, to assure ourselves that we can be immune. There is a natural tendency to try to buy insurance packages—not of Blue Crosses and Blue Shields, but of diets and regimens and cautions.

But there is also something malignant about some of the extremists who make a public virtue of their health. It is the sort of self-righteousness that inspired a letter writer to suggest to me recently that we eliminate lung cancer research, because "smokers do it to themselves."

There is a judgmental attitude toward ill-health germinating in parts of the country and in parts of our minds that can be spread cruelly. It implies that those who do not "Health Thyself" are not only courting their own disasters, but are owed very little in the way of sympathy. It implies that illness is, at root, a punishment for foolishness.

This feeds into the hope, born of fear, that if we keep ourselves in shape and watch out, we can not only postpone death but prevent it. The notion that death is, in essence, suicide, and something we can avoid, is the most profound illusion of all.

MAY 1978

MEET MR. INDISPENSABLE

At first it didn't sound like a very radical idea. In fact, the President was suggesting a little moderation. In a memo and then a meeting, Carter said that he didn't want his people to work so hard that they jettisoned their families.

"I'm concerned about the family lives of all of you," he wrote. "I want you to spend an adequate amount of time with your husbands/ wives and children . . . you will be more valuable to me and the country with rest and a stable home life."

That was all. But with this plea, he declared a war on workaholism, and that alone was enough to make the average office addict tremble and hug his memo pad closer to his chest.

Carter pulled the rationale right out from under the work habits of thousands of compulsive Americans. For decades the "hard-driving American male" usually had been assuring his wife that he *had* to work in order to get ahead (wherever that might be), and now here was the boss telling his workers to turn out the lights and go home. How, he wondered, would he support his habit now?

Before we all pin on our "I Quit Early" buttons, we should pause for a moment of sympathy. Pity the workaholic, the guy with the sandwich on his desk who looks harassed and is always telling you how hard he works. He believes that he is utterly indispensable to the organization.

Truth is, the organization is utterly indispensable to him. He's hooked.

He began as a young man by actually studying during study hall. On his first job, he learned to play the waiting game, staying longer and later than the Other Guy. Over the years he burned enough midnight oil to melt Greater Buffalo. He was always fond of his family, treating them with what he liked to think of as benign neglect. The "less is more" theory was applied to his children with a consistency broken only by fifteen minutes of play—"Hey, guys, let's throw the ball around"—before he had to go back to work.

After two decades or more of this, the fellow has become a hardcore case, a dutiful soul who can't walk without a destination and who regards leisure as wasted time. His hours are filled like blank spaces on the appointment calendar.

In extremis, the workaholic can't have fun for more than forty-five consecutive minutes without suffering withdrawal symptoms—withdrawing into his briefcase. He can't relax until he's done everything that needs to be done—in short, he can no longer relax.

The terminal workaholic has a Dictaphone in the car, a professional journal in the bathroom magazine rack, and extra briefcases hidden in the liquor cabinet. He is most comfortable behind a desk or in front of a committee.

The only regret he has is that his wife isn't more understanding. But, he has always told himself, so it goes; he has *Important Work* to do. No two ways about it.

Now along comes the guy from Georgia who says that there are two ways about it. Who actually sides with his wife. Who recommends something that sounds suspiciously nutritional: The Well-Balanced Life.

To the workaholic that sounds more like Cold Turkey. The idea of time "off" is enough to give him the DTs. He shudders at the prospect of staring a weekend in the face or looking into the abyss of an evening. The boss has told him to go home, but how will he get his fix?

The truth is that we can't simply declare war on workaholism without funding a string of detoxification centers. We cannot simply cut the average addict off.

He needs a physical therapist to teach him how to do something else with his hands. He needs fellow addicts to call when he feels a strange compulsion to sign a letter, or make one more phone call. He needs friends to pull him away from his desk on bad nights, and groups to convince him that there is a kind of input and output that doesn't fit in a wire basket.

It won't be easy. But if the President is genuinely committed to the struggle, it's possible to devise a program that will free hundreds of sufferers. With the monkey off their back, they may discover that even fun can be fun. If you don't work too hard at it.

FEBRUARY 1977

▇▇▇▇▇▇▇TIME IS FOR SAVORING

A few months ago, when a preening French official descended from his Concorde into Washington, he bragged to Tip O'Neill that he saved four, count 'em, four hours traveling supersonically.

At that point the Speaker turned and asked him, benignly, what he had done with the four hours he'd saved. The official, as the story goes, was taken aback, right aback into silence. This exchange stuck in my mind, and not because I'm snooping into the Frenchman's activities. I'm not that sort of reporter.

But it occurred to me that O'Neill's response was a nice healthy challenge to the time-saving obsession of our lives. I guess the Concorde is as good a place to begin as any.

It has taken the accumulated wisdom of centuries to build this plane, and what have we got? For one thing, a noisier airplane which uses more fuel to carry fewer people in less comfort from one continent to the other at greater expense. We call this peculiar achievement "progress" for only one reason: It does all this absurd stuff in a shorter amount of time than a conventional plane.

Saving time, it seems, has a primacy that's too rarely examined. From the Concorde to the microwave oven to the Speed Reading class, we value saving time more than the way we spend it and more than the values we may sacrifice to it. At times we behave like the efficiency expert in *Pajama Game* whose rationalization for his life was simple: "For a time-study man to waste time / is a crime."

We tell ourselves that we are all busy people. Our lives are geared to the school bells and alarm clocks and factory whistles outside of our control. But on the whole, the time-saving devices—both mechanical and personal—that are supposed to help us save time, don't. They merely allow us to do more in the same number of minutes, leaving us with full schedules and the need to find more ways to save time.

With the aid of the plane, the official and the businessman can turn a two-day trip into a one-day trip. But they are usually faced with two one-day trips. The people who learn to Speed Read don't spend less time reading; they just read more in the same time.

The machines that make it possible for us to do things that we could never do before—like cook a roast in a half hour—also make it more likely that we will do things we never would have done before. Like cook that roast.

These things don't save time, any more than the assembly line saves the worker time.

There is actually no way to bank our minutes away. The best we can do, with the most sophisticated machinery products, is to re-distribute those minutes. And, like the French official, we don't always do a good job of that. We have even become so addicted to saving time that we forget to differentiate between the things we like to do (dining with our families, for example) and the things we hate to do (cleaning the oven). We efficiently shorten them all.

At the end of a busy day, families often get dinner "down to a science": the science of convenience foods, mixes, and fifteen-minute "gourmet" recipes. In some houses, dinner goes from the refrigerator to the dishwasher in less than an hour. Then, having saved all these minutes, rather than spending them with each other, we drop them like quarters in a television slot machine.

Either we spend more and more energy processing ourselves through our days, doing more and more in the same amount of time, or we throw away our "free time" like Daddy Warbucks.

It's not that I want to go back to ox carts, let alone wooden washtubs, but it seems to me that we ought to make some personal judgments about the machines that are pushed on us in the name of the clock. We have to ask: Is it really going to save time? *My* time? Is it going to cut down unpleasant time, or pleasant time? And, as the Speaker would say, what am I going to do with the time I save?

Ultimately, time is all you have and the idea isn't to save it but to savor it. Like the man on the record, James Taylor, says, "The secret o' life is enjoying the passage of time."

OCTOBER 1977

PART TWO
PEOPLE

NORMAN ROCKWELL:
AN ARTISTIC LINK TO OUR PAST

Now he's gone, the tall skinny man with a shock of white hair who always looked like a Norman Rockwell portrait as he bicycled across the small-town set of Stockbridge, Massachusetts.

Now, for a few days his fans and detractors alike suddenly feel a kind of nostalgia . . . for his nostalgia.

There were, of course, critics who called him the Lawrence Welk of the art world, insisting that bubbles floated off the ends of his brushes and that his work was sticky with sweetness. There were others who adored him, saying that he was the artist among con artists. But now they can both be heard calling him an artistic link to our past, a visual historian.

Norman Rockwell was a craftsman, an artist who insisted upon being called an illustrator, and a gentle, sophisticated man. But no, not a historian. His folksy vision of this country was no more accurate than the bleak world of Edward Hopper. His magazine work was no more a total reflection of our society than the photographs of Walker Evans.

Rockwell wasn't a man of many words, but these few were significant: "Maybe as I grew up and found the world wasn't the perfectly pleasant place I had thought it to be, I unconsciously decided that if it wasn't an ideal world, it should be and so painted only the ideal aspects of it—pictures in which there were no slatterns or self-centered mothers, in which to the contrary, there were only Foxy Grandpas who played baseball with the kids and boys fishing from logs and got-up circuses in the backyard."

He knew that he didn't portray America. He portrayed Americana.

I suppose that every society carries in its soul some collective longings, some common spiritual values. We invest these back into our history and then hold them aloft as a standard of comparison for the present. For most of his eighty-two years, through 360 magazine covers, that was what Rockwell recorded: our ideals and our common myths.

As a chronicler, he was born at a perfect time in a perfect place: in New York City, a few years before the end of the nineteenth century. He grew up into the world of hustle and boosters and made it in the competitive and high-pressure business of magazine illustrators. Like many of us, he must have looked back with some longing on the century of Simpler Times and Smaller Towns. So, he made a click, a link with others, sharing with them some vast and powerful yearning for a way of life which he defined as American.

Rockwell painted our American religion—The Four Freedoms —and our real heroes—the common people. He then went on to engrave images of our strongest ideas—not those of equality or even justice—but those of everyday decency.

In the world of Americana, his boys were all Tom Sawyers, his doctors made housecalls and his dogs were puppies. But his subjects were usually the old or the young—as if even he had trouble finding a place for the real, midlife American in his scheme.

He spent his worklife reaching back to make connections. His illustrations in the 1920s often carried the feeling of the 1900s. His paintings of the 1930s have more of the patina of a Teddy than a Franklin Roosevelt. In wartime he carefully drew our peaceful nature and even in his self-consciously relevant work of the 1960s, Rockwell pushed the buttons of the past.

It was as a hard-working artist, a businessman, a husband of three wives that he portrayed the imagined ease of everyday life. His subjects had foibles rather than problems. They lived through a comedy of manners rather than human tragedies. So, it wasn't a mirror he held up to society, but the hungering eye of a man of his time. A man who filled his canvases with what many of us felt was missing.

In the 1960s, after President Johnson rejected a portrait of himself by John Hurd, Rockwell went to paint him. "Hurd, of course, had painted him as he was," Rockwell said later, "while I had done him as he would like to think he is."

Well, consciously or not, he painted America as we would like to think it was. As we would like to think it is at root. His legacy is an interior landscape . . . of our very best side.

NOVEMBER 1978

■ PAT NIXON: PERFECT PAT, PLASTIC PAT

She was the perfect wife, the picture-book wife, self-effacing, loyal, the Outstanding Homemaker of the Year in 1953, the Mother of the Year in 1955, the Nation's Ideal Housewife in 1957.

For years she made her own slipcovers and curtains and clothes, and when her husband was Vice-President she spent some of the "few evenings I had to myself" taking his suits out of the closet and pressing them.

She was brought up to be dutiful and she was. She was brought up to work hard and she did. She was told that "you make your bed and you lie in it," and she did, even if she lay in it alone.

She held her chin up (in public) and never spilled her tea (in public) and never criticized her husband (in public) and she wore a good Republican cloth coat. She never complained. Once she campaigned with three cracked ribs and once with a swollen ankle, and she kept it a secret. She said that she was never cold and never bored by her husband's speeches and, "If I have a headache, no one knows it."

The most outrageous thing she ever did was to smoke a cigarette in public in 1973 with her son-in-law, David Eisenhower. The most typical thing she did was to memorize Robert's Rules of Order before she would preside over the Senate Ladies Group.

She tried to be perfect, and in later years, many called her plastic Perfect Pat, Political Pat, Plastic Pat, she said, "You can adjust to anything if you want to."

Now, as we pick the scab off Watergate again, poring over the revelations in Woodward and Bernstein's *The Final Days*, we hear about a Pat who spent the last days of the Nixon years in a separate bedroom with a separate bottle, while her husband confided his feelings to the portraits on the walls and the tape recorder down the hall. We glimpse them together in the deadly silence of their dinnertime.

We see the tragic figure of a woman who prized self-control above all things faced once again with the lack of any real control over her own life. We see her as Richard Nixon's ultimate victim and again she becomes a symbolic reference point for us in a time of changing definitions about what a wife-woman is and does and owes.

Thelma Ryan grew up in a time when self-denial was a virtue, and self-fulfillment was a vice called selfishness. People didn't talk much about masochism. She believed in will power and never called it repression. She may believe in it yet.

Like so many women of her age and place, she gambled everything on marriage—on the marital draw—and she stood by her man. She hated politics, but she went on the roller-coaster ride of her husband's career with every hair in place. She used her enormous strength to hang on with white knuckles and a tight smile.

She was the "helpmate," the "better half," the woman behind the man, the partner with no voice in the decisions, the woman who knew her place. "Once he makes his decision," she said, "I'm a good sport and will do all I can to help him." She told a reporter that if she wrote a book she'd call it, "I Also Ran."

Once, we now learn, she thought of leaving her husband. But she was then an unemployed mother of two teenaged daughters, and in 1962 there were fewer choices. In any case, she was a good girl, a good sport. Later, people noticed that whenever they left a public scene Pat and Dick dropped arms and moved perceptibly away from each other.

In 1968 she told Gloria Steinem angrily, "I've never had time to think about things like . . . who I want to be or whom I admired, or to have ideas. I never had time to dream about being anyone else. I've never had it easy . . . I'm not like you . . . all those people who had it easy."

Years later a White House reporter said to her, "You've had a good life," and she paused and answered, "I just don't tell all." Now, more of that "all" is being told. There are no Pat Nixon tapes. No Pat Nixon cover-ups. She is a victim and hers is a horror story, a female tragedy that touches even those of us familiar with stories of women's lives of passive desperation.

Perfect Pat, Plastic Pat. There is a scene, not in *The Final Days,* that will haunt us: the vision of these two, husband and wife for forty years, alone now, in a fourteen-room house in San Clemente—a home with no exit.

APRIL 1976

MARTHA MITCHELL:
HERE'S TO THE CRAZY LADIES

A Crazy Lady died last Monday, or so we're told. The obituary described her as a woman who "once refused to bow to Queen Elizabeth, asked a newspaper to 'crucify' a senator, and hit a reporter on the head." Yes, a genuine Crazy Lady died last Monday and here's to her.

Here's to all the Crazy Ladies who ever wanted to be Somebody and settled for being Outrageous. May they rest in peace. Here's to all the Crazy Ladies who were patted on the head while they were harmless pets and were ruthlessly punished when they became serious. Yes, here's to Martha Mitchell.

She wasn't always one of them, you understand. She was once a girl from Pine Bluff, Arkansas, who wore her first evening gown at nine years old and learned that "it was always good to be dumb and blond. You didn't want to get anywhere because then you'd have to compete with the boys. If you knew more than the boys, that was terrible."

So she learned a trick—how to be the center of attention without competing—and she wrote it in her school yearbook: "I love its gentle warble / I love its gentle flow / I love to wind my tongue up / I love to let it go."

Here's to the Crazy Ladies, here's to them all, who wanted to be individuals and settled for being eccentric.

As the Attorney General's wife she became "the Mouth that Roared." She was cute, a feisty little thing in stiletto heels and frowzy dresses and a southern drawl with matching dimples. She was a bit dizzy to be sure, but cute.

And so the President said, "Give 'em hell, Martha." And so her husband said, "She's a little sweetheart. I love her so much. She gets a little upset about politics but she loves me and I love her and that's what counts."

So . . . as I said, here's to all the Crazy Ladies with husbands who think they look cute when they get mad, with husbands who think they are adorable when they have strong opinions, the wives who are indulged and loved—"my wife, I think I'll keep her"—as long as they don't demand to be taken seriously.

Martha Mitchell was one of the loud wives of important men

who wanted to be both independent and safe, and who compromised by being adorably rebellious. She gave us a double message—"Hey, look at me, I'm exceptional," but, "Don't take me seriously, I'm just a dizzy blond."

As she put it, "Well, I try to be dumb."

As a Cabinet wife she felt intolerably ignored. "It's just ridiculous. Because I'm the wife of the Attorney General, I have no right to express my opinions."

But within a year after her first phone call, 76 percent of the population knew who she was. "They all love me, isn't it wonderful?" she said. And like all Crazy Ladies—the Zelda Fitzgeralds, the Elizabeth Rays, the Women under the Influence who dance on tabletops and get a bit tipsy and grab the spotlight—she confused being loved with being famous, and being notorious with being her own person. Here's to all the Crazy Ladies who never see the thin ice.

Martha Mitchell told the "wrong truth." Suddenly she wasn't cute. Suddenly she lost what *Time* called a "certain wacky charm."

She said, "If my husband knew anything about the Watergate break-in, Mr. Nixon also knew about it. I think he should say goodbye." She became the kind of a Crazy Lady who yells into telephones in the middle of the night that "Something's Wrong!" Here's to them.

Her husband didn't pat her on the head anymore. "Martha's late-night calls have been good fun and games. However, this is a serious issue," he said, and called her unstable. After a while he left and took their daughter with him.

When she came out from behind her wackiness, then they tried to call her mad. "They threw me on my bed and stuck a needle in my behind. They're afraid of my honesty. . . . There is absolutely nothing wrong with me except that I am mentally tortured from the torture I've been through. Why did people call me crazy? Because they were trying to shut Martha Mitchell up and they didn't know how to do it."

Well, she was right and here's to her. Here's to them all, all the Crazy Ladies who finally, after a lifetime, refused to stay in their places. Here's to all the frivolous, flaky ladies who dropped the mask of the lovable fool.

Here's to the one who changed too late to save herself. May she rest in peace.

JUNE 1976

■ LYNDON JOHNSON:
A FASCINATION WITH POWER

Now it's Johnson's turn. With the print still wet on the new Nixon book, with the memory of Judith Exner still imprinted over our images of Kennedy, the middle child of the Vietnam Presidents steps into the ring for a psychological profile.

The first bits and pieces of Doris Kearns's long-awaited book on LBJ, excerpted in next month's *McCall's*, show him as a man whose need for dominance was manipulated into its presidential form while he was still a child. "From the boy's fear of being tested," writes Harvard professor Kearns, "came the man's determination that he would be the one to give the tests." And there is more to come.

In the past year we have dug into the lives of our great men, sniffing out the prized truffles, the little secrets of their psyches, the linchpins of their personal histories. Was one compulsively promiscuous? Was one crudely chauvinistic? Was one priggish and celibate? Was one seeking love through domination? Was another seeking to expurgate old terrors or guilts? Was one questing for paternal approval, another for maternal approval? We want to know. We search through their lives in a way that would have been unthinkable a decade ago.

Not that we haven't always been fascinated with the biographies of powerful people. We have. But the emphasis has shifted from admiration to morbid fascination, from analysis to psychoanalysis, from biography to psychobiography, from Roosevelt and Eisenhower to Johnson and Nixon.

Our preoccupation, it seems, is no longer with the people, but with the nature of power. As our gut feelings about power have changed, so have our attitudes about those who are its vehicles and its executors.

We no longer study the lives of great men, but the psychoses of power seekers. We want to find out what went wrong. Where did they get this psychic weakness that we call the love of power? We free-associate that word to others like "force," "control," "dominance." Our mind leaps to the catastrophes of Watergate and Vietnam and everywhere we hear the ring of Lord Acton's maxim: "Power tends to corrupt; and absolute power corrupts absolutely."

The war, the resignation. The sense of waste, the feeling of closure, and the fear of the future that replaces our old hopefulness all have changed our perspective on leadership. To the children of the best and the brightest, power is seen as evil, crippling with unhealthy manifestations in the bedroom and the boardroom. "Power is a weapon. You pick it up and it goes off, it has a life of its own," a young Vietnam veteran wrote.

The idea of "proving one's masculinity," a rite of passage in so many cultures (and a permanent crisis in LBJ's life, according to Kearns), is disparaged and mocked by a young generation of men and women. Semantically and philosophically we confuse the "power over" with the "power to." We confuse the power that is dominating and hostile with the power that is creative and sustaining. We confuse the misuses of power with the nature of it.

Power, in and of itself, is a fuel. It is all potential, with the moral value of a lump of coal. It is simply neutral. The best of our leaders, we hope, will seek it as a tool for service, the worst will continue to seek it as shoulder pads to wear on their egos.

It will remain enormously difficult to tell them apart. In some, the ego and desire to serve may be welded on the same power trip. The best indication of a safety valve on their power drive may be that internal system of checks and balances that we call a sense of humor and perspective. But that neutral lump of coal has fueled many disasters in the last years, and power has gotten a bad name for itself.

For now, we remain skeptical, reluctant to take on any more myths that will be debunked. We may vote for a leader, but we refuse to trust one. We listen to the candidates for the presidency through a filter of suspicion woven out of Vietnam and Watergate—the silent partners of this campaign—and out of Kennedy, Johnson and Nixon. We suspect them simply because they seek power. We ask each other, "Well, let's see, who among them seems to be the least dangerous?"

APRIL 1976

HUBERT HUMPHREY: A "FULL" MAN

I suppose we are always rewriting history, making, destroying, and reconstructing reputations along the way. We often deal with our largest public figures the way we deal with our parents, going from illusion to disillusion, to finally, perhaps, some sort of perspective.

So I shouldn't be surprised at the toasts being written to Hubert Horatio Humphrey—words as elegant as his name. Humphrey is, to all of us who've been around awhile, unique.

He's a man who possesses the sort of tenacity born of optimism, rather than bitterness. His career is in many ways unparalleled, and he's been a figure on the landscape of our national lives, full of richness, for three decades.

The tributes being written now, in his sickness, tip their hats —as Emily Dickenson might have said—to him, with fondness. Yet it strikes me as odd that the current reviews of his life inevitably skim over four years. They excise 1964 to 1968 as if it were a wart.

The toastmasters are, I am sure, being kind. But their kindness is the sort that diminishes the man rather than accepts him.

I am, myself, of the in-between generation. I remember both his civil rights record and the night of August 28, 1968, when he sat in his room twenty-five floors above the Chicago streets. I remember both how he stood up to Joe McCarthy and collapsed beside Lyndon Johnson.

I voted for him that fall after that summer of 1968 (don't blame me, I'm from Massachusetts), but with a sense of his complexity and frailty. I believe that he is a good man who made a bad mistake. The odds are in his favor, as is my own simple affection.

But I wonder, as so many other times, why we rush to a narrow judgment. Why do we need to build a perfect case—for or against— each other and our leaders? We seem to prefer our characters to be stick, or at least stock.

We built John F. Kennedy into King Arthur and now see his part rewritten into Casanova. Roosevelt, Eisenhower, Kissinger, the best and the brightest, are all lit up from one angle or the other. The continual rewriting of the character of Jimmy Carter goes on even now, with each new version being offered as the true portrait.

Yet there is no Definitive Person. Each of us contains a wide variety of possibilities and attitudes. We have the potential for a range of responses—from the charitable to the harsh, from the obsequious to the overbearing, from the "good" to the "bad"—to be tapped by the events of our lives. It's not that we are slaves to circumstance, but rather that our complexity interacts with events in different ways.

Humphrey has always been a man of ebullience and courage. Yet he was also, for a time, cowed by that most intimidating of men, Lyndon Johnson. He is a man of kindness and morality, but there was also ambition. He is an exultant speaker, a verbal hugger—but he doesn't always know when to let go.

I think that, peculiarly, Humphrey's strongest point is his perspective on himself. He—more than the rest of us, perhaps—can accept all that he is and was, even the warts, and go on. He once said about the Vietnam war: "I'd rather be remembered for being wrong than for being a hypocrite."

It seems to me more kind to paint the whole picture of anyone than to draw him one-dimensionally. The need for heroes isn't all that great. The need for a sense of wholeness is. Humphrey, of all men, is full. It doesn't suit his style to edit his past. It doesn't really do him justice.

Years ago, I heard him close a marathon speech to a somnolent after-dinner crowd with a final self-mocking line: "Muriel tells me that I don't have to be interminable in order to be immortal."

He doesn't have to be perfect, either.

NOVEMBER 1977

JACQUELINE ONASSIS: TRIPPING ON HER PAST

No, I am not going to stay up nights worrying about Jackie.

She is not your average unemployed worker, I'll grant you that. For her there will be no embarrassing encounters at the credit office, no humiliation at the bank, no midnight terrors about putting food on the table. She can survive without a paycheck.

Still, I was struck by the announcement of her resignation from Viking Books last week—struck by the way in which her life is still inexorably ruled by a marriage that has been over longer than it lasted.

She began life as a Bouvier and she later became an Onassis. But she was Jack Kennedy's wife for ten years—a fourteen-year lifetime ago—and it seems she will be judged as his widow forever, locked into our National Family Soap Opera.

When the latest of the Kennedy exploitation books, *Shall We Tell the President?* was bought by her employer it could hardly have been a shock. The story about the planned assassination of Ted Kennedy in 1983 is as predictable as it is appalling. If there's a national fear to sell, someone will sell it. If there's a mass emotional button to push, someone will push it.

"She has a feeling of resignation that people will go on using this black material," said Viking publisher Thomas Guinzburg to *Boston Globe* reporter Bob Lenzner, and it had a ring of truth.

Jackie had stayed as far from politics as possible. Her editing work had been on books as noncontroversial as Russian antique arts. But there was no way for her to be isolated from the family business.

After fourteen years of articles and books, after fourteen years of being "sold" by former housekeepers and friends, after Ron Galella, after Mark Lane, after Judith Exner, she must have developed some immunity to trash. After all, the Kennedy family story is like a rigged slot machine. Someone will keep pulling the handle as long as the coins keep falling in their lap. To survive, this in-law had to stop caring, and to lower her threshold of outrage.

In her resignation letter, Jackie wrote: "Last spring, when told of the book, I tried to separate my lives as a Viking employee and a Kennedy family member."

Should she have protested? Should William Randolph Hearst have protested the coverage of his daughter, Patty, in the *San Francisco Examiner?* Her obligation, even her right to protest, seems a bit fuzzy.

After all, she had tried to object to the publication of books before—as in the Manchester affair—and had been accused of trying to suppress them. This time, she was criticized for not trying to suppress one. She had no more ultimate responsibility for the publication of this ghastly little book than the average reporter does for another story in his or her paper.

It was only when this conflict of interest became a public collision that Jackie had to resign. She was called to account in print. Sadly, but almost inevitably, she was unable to separate the Viking employee and the Kennedy family member.

Now, I agree that $26 million softens the blow of unemployment. But even if you inherit $26 million on Tuesday, there is still the business of what you do on Wednesday. And Thursday. And next year.

Jackie isn't a sympathetic character in this national soap opera anymore. She would have had to remain a professional widow to be that. Preferably, an impoverished widow. But it seems to me that she had finally tried to make a life rather than marry one. And she tripped on her past.

Today she is a single, forty-eight-year-old woman, whose children only come home for vacations, who wakes up in the morning with no place she has to go. Her limitations are as impressive as her freedoms.

For the most exceptional set of reasons, she still faces the most universal problem: What do you do with the rest of your life?

OCTOBER 1977

GERALD FORD:
AGAIN WITHOUT A TITLE

It didn't matter that there were ten official weeks of transition. In the end, it felt rather sudden. Within thirty minutes, one man was sworn in to work at the White House and another was let out to play at the Bing Crosby Pro-Am Tournament. Within thirty minutes, the Fords' double bed was moved out of the East Wing and the Carters' sewing machine was moved in.

With the click of the digital clock, the President was gone. Long Live the President.

Now the Carters will have to learn the idiosyncracies of the White House showers and the feeling of power. Now the Carters will be on center stage with the cameras clicking when one signs a law and another enters school.

But there's a Ford in our future too, and I'm not talking about 1980. There's a Ford "future" in our future.

If it's interesting to watch what a man does with power, it's intriguing to see what he'll do with less of it. For the first time in twenty-nine years Gerald Ford will be without a title. He's about to discover what we may all discover if we live long enough—exactly who we are without our job classification, whether it's that of President, full-time mother, stockbroker or lieutenant.

He may even help us think about how much of our own egos depend on the things we may eventually lose, and help us ask ourselves what happens next. Who would Walter Cronkite be without CBS? Bob Dylan without his poetry? What would a doctor do without patients, a minister without a congregation? What is exciting and terrifying about a suddenly unscheduled future?

Lillian Hellman once wrote that "loss, change, an altered life is only a danger when you become devoted to disaster." Ford seems an unlikely devotee. I doubt that he will turn into a brooding disappointed man, recounting mistakes made and precincts lost.

But he is in a crisis, not an orderly transition, and a crisis is a time of heightened feelings and extreme vulnerability. Right now he is both freed from constraints and cut adrift from old expectations. He can choose, as psychologist Abraham Maslow once put it, "between the delights and pleasures of safety or growth."

From the moment he and Betty were helicoptered away from the capital—no doubt chuckling at the weather report they'd left behind for Jimmy—he began to confront these choices. Sooner or later —after Bing Crosby's tournament, after the Vince Lombardi dinner —he'll have to make them.

Will he be the Grand Old Man of the Grand Old Party, or run himself into a Harold Stassen? Will he discover a penchant for teaching, or use his pension for sun-worshiping? Will he grow sideburns or roses? Will he be able to move on, or will he rerun? Will he be able to write his own game plan?

In a sense, Ford will have to resolve his crisis by building again from his own base—his own ego—the person he is without the title.

And since this is the year in which the midlife crisis is in vogue, his passage will be one that holds as much personal meaning as that of the Georgians in Georgetown.

After decades of duties and biannual elections, the demands of constituents and growing children, there is now virtually nothing he "has" to do. That's as scary a liberation as there is. The liberation of an uncharted future.

Maybe he can learn about that from William Sloane Coffin, the man who gave up his tenured ministry at Yale, where Ford will be lecturing next year. Coffin wrote in his resignation letter: "I'm delighted that the future is unsure. That's the way it should be. Growth demands a willingness to relinquish one's proficiencies. So I want to become more vulnerable, or as the old Pietist phrase goes, 'to let go and let God.' "

JANUARY 1977

BELLA ABZUG: SHE'S HOT, AND THE TIMES ARE COOL

In a way, the biggest shock was the picture of her without a hat. It was like seeing a photograph of Moshe Dayan without a patch over his eye.

Bella. Battling Bella. The lady who needed no last name had lost her third campaign in eighteen months and she was sitting in the picture bareheaded, astonishingly diminished. She'd lost this campaign for Congress by one percentage point and lost it the hard way, because of her "personality."

Nobody doubted that she was smart. Everybody knew that she worked hard. But the airwaves—whether they emanated from radio and television or from mouth to ear—were full of one word: "abrasive."

"She was such a stereotype of herself, she couldn't get away from it," said a long-time supporter, Andrew Stein, the New York City councilman. "It's like Carroll O'Connor wanting to play someone other than Archie Bunker, but he can't."

Battling Bella, the woman whose last words after this defeat were "I thank you not to write my obituary," had moved into the past tense last week in everybody's conversation. But in a sense, they weren't so much writing obituaries for her as for "personality" politics itself.

Maybe a 1 percent defeat isn't a message, or a trend, or something to build into a State of the Union address. But I'm as sure as Stein that she lost in 1978 for the same reason she won in 1971. For the same "personality."

After all, there were no shockers about Bella in this campaign against Bill Green. No one was surprised to discover that she is a fighter. Bella Abzug anglicized the word *chutzpah*.

When she was mad, the lady was very, very mad, and for years reporters had portrayed her as they saw her. She was a woman who could take on Vietnam and Nixon. She could also stiff your questions, bristle at a contradiction, shriek at a staff member and intimidate the opposition. Then, in the next breath, or on the next street corner, she would turn around and, remembering the name and age of your kid or mother, ask about them with genuine concern.

Bella Abzug was irritating and endearing, intimidating and energizing, insensitive and hypersensitive. But, full.

Typically, she was considered a feminist by the politicians and a politician by the feminists. She was both, so, of course, she also fought both. She battled the rigidity of Congress and the chaos of women's movement politics.

But at all times she could change the dynamic of a room by walking into it.

Now, however, Small is beautiful and she is Big. The times are low-key and she is high-decibel. The gray people are winning and she is Technicolor. Bill Green is laid-back and Bella rages and cries.

In her own town, John Lindsay is in exile and Ed Koch is in office. In my blizzard-socked city last week, the high-voltage mayor, Kevin White, was on a kamikaze course, while the low-profile governor, Mike Dukakis, could have been elected king.

In the women's movement, too, it's a housewife from Pittsburgh like Ellie Smeal who runs the National Organization for Women, and not Betty Friedan.

Bella lost because she's hot and the times are cool and (never mind that it's a cliché) Jerry Brown can "relate to that." We've decided that personality polarizes, and charisma alienates. We think we're looking for peacemakers. Or is it just for peace and quiet?

Sometimes I wonder what happens next, when all the decibels are lowered and all the leaders are muted into shades of gray and all the controversy is gentled into fireside chatting.

Will we call the peace "boredom" and call the rest period "inertia"?

You can bet on it. The odds are that we'll turn around and ask each other: What ever happened to the pushers, to the movers and the shakers? What ever happened to people who got mad and yelled when they saw things going wrong? What ever happened to the lady who cared? You remember, the Lady with the Hat.

FEBRUARY 1978

MARGARET TRUDEAU:
A LOVE STORY OF THE SEVENTIES

She is like a girl let out of boarding school. There goes Margaret, the *Rolling Stone* photo-groupie. There she goes, describing her bottom to *People* as "cute." There she goes, telling the world that she's turned on by wearing garters and never shows her nipples at state functions. It's all rather embarrassing, this business of having an identity crisis in public.

There are few of us whose twenties would stand up to public scrutiny much better than Margaret Trudeau's, few who would be able to bear rereading the ten most foolish things we did or said at twenty-eight. Just imagine having them all filed away in a newspaper library somewhere waiting for your obituary.

But there is so much delayed adolescence bubbling over in Margaret Trudeau, so much of the "late-bloomer" in the former flower child, that it's rather hard to watch without sadness. It feels as if we've been there before. Another woman off to New York, giddily in search of herself. Another matter of bad timing. Another marriage on the brink of renaissance or disaster. It is in some ways a classic modern romance.

Eight years ago a girl of twenty met a prime minister of forty-nine on the island of Tahiti. They shared a passion for William Blake, the poet who once wrote, "Love to faults is always blind / Always is to joy inclin'd."

Two years later, the bachelor politician was ready to settle down, and the twenty-two-year-old was ready to begin. And so they were married. They were supposed to live in the static country of Happily Ever After. By the time she was twenty-six and he was fifty-five, they had three children, all under three years old. He was still Prime Minister and she was overshadowed, a premature First Lady.

In 1974 she was hospitalized for what they called mental stress. She called it a conflict. "I prepared myself for my marriage to Pierre Trudeau, but not for my marriage to the Prime Minister." The question she took to the hospital was "whether I should just be a mother and wife or whether I should reach out a bit and try to do something on a more professional level."

She chose to try for "more" and avoid the straitjacket.

It was almost predictable. Rather pat. You could explain it all in a sentence or two. Pierre Trudeau had married a time bomb. Margaret Trudeau should have found herself before she'd found herself with a husband and three children. Surely we should all be wise and reasonable with well-planned lives. But 20-20 hindsight isn't a very useful kind of vision.

Since 1974 the Trudeaus have tried, under great pressure, to manage the most difficult kind of change: change without loss. The years since are marked by her attempts to grow up without going away, and his attempts to support an independence that would stop short of divorce. It all happened in the public eye. Her tiniest rebellions—the T-shirt in Cuba, the singing in Mexico—made page one.

She was criticized for ordering a silver car-of-state instead of a black one, criticized for exposing her calves at the White House, criticized for wishing her husband were not Prime Minister. Even her debut as a photojournalist in Canada was mysteriously canceled.

Now they are going to try something else—commuting. Three or four days of work in New York, two or three of family life in Ottawa. Where other couples might have quit or split, the Trudeaus are still trying alternatives.

"The only line he draws is that I don't humiliate him," she says. He says: "If I lost a couple of votes, I'm sorry, but I have no intention of fencing her in."

This "fling" may be an interlude, or a prelude to divorce, or a way of avoiding it. She may become an *enfant terrible* with a "cute bottom," or a grown-up. He may lose her or his job. But for now, they're attempting what so many other more private couples are: to manage the crisis of bad timing, the problems of separate growing pains, the different needs of partners who want to stay married. As a love story of the seventies, it will do.

MARCH 1977

ALEXANDER SOLZHENITSYN: NEITHER AN INGRATE NOR A PROPHET

He sat on the covered stage, a large, solemn, bearded, Dostoevsky-like figure in the oppressive humidity of Harvard Yard.

As he was introduced, it began to rain, the sort of downpour that promised to drench the black-robed graduates and postgraduates, their parents and the alumni, without clearing the air at all. There, facing a rising tide of black umbrellas, Alexander Solzhenitsyn read his speech in Russian while a woman translator spoke over his words in her own heavily accented English.

Together, in this strange, disconcerting duet, they criticized the West and the United States for materialism, legalism, a shallow and powerful press, and—more than anything else—a vital loss of will. And he left the people gathered there with a heavy sense of disappointment.

That dank scene was the background for a week's worth of criticism. Since then, the words of Russia's exiled writer have been repeated and excerpted and talked about at extraordinary length.

Some of us, in a fit of self-flagellation, have simply taken up his message that "the Western system in its present state of spiritual exhaustion does not look attractive." There are always people who accept eagerly from a foreign podium what they might reject from the Sunday pulpit.

Others have been annoyed that the man who wrote about Soviet labor camps had the nerve to be critical of the "free world." They thought he should be so grateful to have free speech that he would exercise it only favorably.

So now our "favorite exile" has been called everything from an ingrate to a prophet to a con man. But most of us had simply, I think, expected more from the man we had thought of as a humanist with a world view, a timeless, stateless philosophy.

On that muggy commencement afternoon, he shattered that illusion.

The author of *The Gulag Archipelago*, of *The First Circle* and *The Cancer Ward*, spoke as an exile rather than an immigrant, a scourge rather than a reporter, a better historian of Russian society than chronicler of America.

Solzhenitsyn made hits on the weaknesses of the West. This is a society in which materialism has bred not happiness but the desire for more things, in which what is legal is often more important than what is right, in which the press is often hasty and superficial.

But when he most fervently criticized America for not embarking on a moral crusade against communism abroad, for not adhering to a spiritual set of values above all others, he sounded like a man of the Russian forties and fifties—a man of the labor camps, confused and out of context in the American seventies.

Solzhenitsyn spent most of his adult life as a victim of persecution that was as arbitrary as it was terrible. He survived the prison camps by unshakable commitment, and heroic moral stubbornness. He survived his years of harassment—years during which he endangered not only himself but his friends—through a powerful belief in his mission as the Witness and Messenger of Evil.

Through his own necessity of seeing the world as right and wrong, black and white, he now scorns our uncertain grays. He calls our sense of complexity, weakness. To this man, anti-communism is a holy crusade to which he has dedicated his life. Anything less, he says, is capitulation.

Solzhenitsyn didn't live here through the Cold War of the fifties and the rebellions of the sixties. He sees now a country that has, in his terms, lost its courage, rather than one which is, in our terms, in search of moderation. He sees us as flaccid, rather than cautious.

Only someone who had never lived in the United States through the Vietnam war could describe, as he did, the "short-sighted politicians who signed the hasty Vietnam capitulation."

His words seeped in, through the mistiness of the afternoon and conversations all week. He stimulated at least a wave of national introspection about our values.

But I was personally left with a sense of irony. Here was, after all, a man who has spent three years in relative seclusion in Vermont, speaking and reading mostly Russian, embroiled in his work on Russian life, coming down to Harvard to comment on America.

He was neither an ingrate nor a prophet that Commencement day. But he sounded like an out-of-town journalist who comes in with his own preconceptions and neglects to do his legwork, his homework. As a reporter, he was afflicted with the precise disease he attributed to the American press: He looked at America in the seventies with "hastiness and superficiality." And then withdrew to Vermont.

JUNE 1978

PART THREE

WOMEN

A BODY BLOW
TO WOMEN

My grandmother used to say that "one man should have one baby." I never figured out if that was a wish or a curse, but I'd like to modify it anyway. I think that the "one man" should be poor and pregnant and not wanting to be, and I think that his name should be Justice Lewis Powell.

It was Powell who added intellectual insult to the body-blow injury the Supreme Court dealt women on Monday. He was the one who wrote the majority opinion that the states don't have to pay for nontherapeutic abortions of women on Medicaid. He was the one who bent logic into a pretzel to explain that this 1977 decision "signals no retreat" from the Supreme Court's 1973 decision.

It would be delicious—maliciously delicious, I admit—to have him pregnant, perhaps even barefoot and pregnant, while I was appointed to explain back to him the wonderful consistency of his interpretation of the Constitution.

To begin with, perhaps I would remind him (as I passed him a slightly salted wafer to appease his morning sickness) that the Supreme Court in 1973 said that he could choose an early abortion freely. Indeed, it said that the state had no right to interfere with his privacy in determining whether or not he wanted to carry his pregnancy to term. It was a matter to be determined between him and his physician.

He might then explain to me that he had chosen to have an abortion. Perhaps he had already borne several children. Perhaps he was trying to get off of welfare. Perhaps he had contracted the German measles. Perhaps he was too young or too old, or his wife had just deserted him, leaving him to support the children. Well, rich or poor (remember, this is a democracy), whatever he decided was his own private business.

But, he might protest, where can I get this abortion? You see, he might have read in the paper that under the 1977 ruling public facilities don't have to perform abortions. The public hospital nearest his home might well be among the 80 percent which don't offer this procedure.

I would reassure him that this fact in no way interferes with, let alone "signals a retreat" from, his 1973 right to choose abortion. Why, he can still go state-shopping or clinic-shopping or hospital-shopping. I might suggest that he hurry a bit, though, so he can have this abortion in his first trimester.

Now, understandably, Justice Powell might look worried and start contemplating whether his robe could double as a maternity dress. The issue of money would probably come up since, in my fantasy, he isn't exactly rolling in chips. In fact, he is among the poor.

After he goes shopping, he has to make sure that Medicaid will pay for the procedure. He knows that Medicaid paid for 300,000 abortions last year. He knows that Medicaid will pay to deliver a baby. But he heard that, under the new ruling, the states don't have to use these funds to pay for elective abortions anymore.

Well, not to worry. I will calm him down with the thought that most states haven't yet banned Medicaid funding for abortions. Of course, there again, perhaps the fellow had better hurry. The amendment, which the Senate Appropriations Committee approved this week, may eliminate the use of any federal money for most abortions in every state.

Then he could only have an abortion if his life were in danger, or if he had multiple sclerosis, renal disease, an ectopic pregnancy, or been raped, or conceived this child through incest. You see, to be consistent—and consistency is very important in the law—the Supreme Court would probably have to uphold a federal ban, the way it upheld the state ban in Connecticut.

But, I would quickly repeat, this would not be a retreat from the Court's 1973 position. You see, I would explain slowly, because he is poor and pregnant and having an anxiety attack, this decision is simply a matter of public policy. It's not that the six justices had opinions on the subject of abortion. It's just that they don't like the idea of using the Constitution to boss the states. They think the law should be made by the legislatures, not the courts. So it was nothing against him personally.

Why, he is just as free as ever since 1973 to decide whether or not to have a child. He is just as free as any member of the middle class. He can still pay privately for an abortion in a private clinic or a private hospital with a private doctor, anywhere he can find one and any way he can get to one.

At that point, despite my best efforts, he might be a touch frustrated. What good does it do him to have the right to abortion if he has no way to pay for it and no hospital that will perform it for him? He might start blubbering about discrimination against the poor. He might even throw himself upon the mercy of the Court, wailing, "You don't understand. I don't have the money to travel. I can't afford to pay for an abortion."

At that unseemly conduct, I would simply have to turn away. My logic, after all, would be intact. I would say judicially: "I can't help you. You see, that's a very private matter."

JUNE 1977

THE POOR
"COMPROMISED" AGAIN

They tell us that Congress is deadlocked on the issue of Medicaid abortions. One immovable force, the House, has met another irresistible object, the Senate.

In a sense, this impasse is a mini-version of what's happened in the country at large. There is no "conference" committee compromise possible any longer between those who are for or against the choice of abortion. Opinions have solidified into granite and minds have closed shut.

By now, the Friends of the Embryo have squared off against the Friends of the Woman with an unwanted pregnancy. Lines have been drawn between those who come down in favor of the quality of life of the woman, and those who come down in favor of the potential life of the embryo.

By now, each group has its own stock of horror pictures. In one album are the photos of women who've died in back-alley abortions. In another are the photos of fetuses cast away in hospital rooms.

By now, pro-abortion people consider the antis rigidly inhuman —"No exceptions? No extenuating circumstances? Never?"—and the antis believe the pros to be inhumanely inconsistent—"How can you say abortion is all right in the first trimester, if you are against it in the third?"

And by now, each is convinced that the other is totally insensitive. The pro-choice people cannot understand how the antis could force a child to bear a child. The antis cannot understand how the pros could allow a human embryo to be vacuumed away.

Like armies in a war of attrition, each is unable to budge the other. Each is sure that the other is not only wrong, but dangerous. We have come to a deadlock.

Abortions in the case of rape are the most symbolic part of that stalemate. The situation rape evokes is a distillation of the entire argument. Rape is the ultimate sexual victimization. If a pregnancy results, there has been no ambivalence, no carelessness, no promiscuity. It has been quite literally forced upon the woman.

In this "pure" situation, the differences between the opposing forces are crystallized. The pro-abortionists look at the woman as the victim, and want to help her. Without having the choice of abortion, they believe, she is an impotent vessel, powerless to control her own life. The anti-abortionists have their sights set differently. They view the embryo as the innocent result. They simply care more for the embryo.

It is seen by both sides as a tragic question of priorities. An unwanted pregnancy, especially one resulting from rape, is a unique human dilemma involving a traumatic conflict of interest within one body. Ultimately, after all the discussion about quickening and trimesters, people take sides: the woman or the fetus.

Yet it seems to me unconscionable for this national moral deadlock to be broken over the backs of the poor. And that's what's happening in Congress right now.

Not only do we see an argument primarily by men over the fate of women, but we see a moral question turned into an economic question.

Abortion is being debated as part of an appropriations bill. Congress isn't overtly in the business of trying to resolve whether abortion is right or wrong. Or even whether they should support it financially. The federal government already supports abortion-on-need through its own insurance plan for employees and families.

What they are arguing is whether they will pay for the poor.

Already they have "conferenced" away the equal payment to the poor for abortion-on-need, and have come to an impasse over the question of pregnancies resulting from rape or incest, or "medical need." It appears that even a narrow definition of "medical need" may be bartered away.

It is ugly to watch us, once again, the most vulnerable, the least well organized, the group with the fewest resources—the poor—are the first to be "compromised."

OCTOBER 1977

ERA:
A SUPPORT SYSTEM

I hate to bring up poor Lydia McGuire. I mean, the woman had enough troubles being married to "Skinflint" McGuire all those years, and my normal inclination would be to let her rest in peace.

But the anti-ERA people won't allow it. You see, next Tuesday, Massachusetts and Colorado are voting on equal rights amendments to their state constitutions. Everyone now maintains that the results of these votes will have a decisive effect on the passage of the federal Equal Rights Amendment (which currently needs ratification in four more states). As is often the case, the more people say the votes are critical, the more critical they become.

Because of this, the anti-ERA folk are doing their end-of-the-campaign fandango. They have again targeted housewives with propaganda designed to convince them that equal rights would mean the end of their right to be supported by husbands in the style to which, say, Phyllis Schlafly is accustomed.

This is the argument they used successfully in New York and New Jersey last year, and almost won with at the Republican National Convention this summer. In Kansas City, a delegate from Alabama, Frances Wideman, summed up the anti-ERA plug to Myra McPherson of the *Washington Post* this way: "My husband is responsible for any bills I assume. He's obligated to get me a fur coat, if he can afford it."

Well, that's where Lydia McGuire comes in. You can see that Mrs. Wideman never heard of the Nebraska housewife, or she would know that she didn't have the right to an indoor toilet, let alone a mink coat.

Mrs. McGuire was the plaintiff some twenty-three years ago in a landmark case on the issue of "suitable maintenance and support money." At the time Mrs. McGuire decided to sue her husband, she was sixty-six and he was eighty. They'd been married thirty-four years.

Charles was what you'd call a man of means, especially for 1953. He had land worth $83,000, over $100,000 in government bonds, and a yearly income of between $8,000 and $9,000. Nevertheless, they lived in a farmhouse without a kitchen sink, or an indoor toilet, or a bath.

The water was drawn from the well, and Mrs. McGuire got money for clothes and groceries from the sale of her chickens' eggs.

She didn't protest this until she became too ill to tend the chickens. Then she found herself totally dependent on a husband whose purse strings had rigor mortis. He gave her no allowance. The last time he'd bought her any clothes was 1949, when he'd paid for a coat. It was not mink.

Finally, she sued. She took her husband to court for home improvements, $50 a month allowance and credit for her necessities. However, Mrs. McGuire lost.

According to the court, her husband was crummy but he wasn't illegal. "The living standards of a family are a matter of concern to the household and not for the courts to determine. . . . As long as the home is maintained, and the parties are living as husband and wife, it may be said that the husband is legally supporting his wife, and the purpose of the marriage is being carried out."

In other words, a living standard above subsistence is left to the discretion of the wage earner. Ironically, it is only in divorce that a woman can claim a proportion of her husband's income.

Of course, the housewives of America aren't all married to Charlie McGuires—he was still driving a 1927 pickup truck when Lydia took him to court.

But the anti-ERA people are talking about the right to be taken care of, right down to the bills for cleaning the mink. That isn't a right you can lose; it doesn't exist.

The ERA won't eliminate the right to the basics, a roof and food. It will extend that right. It will legalize what already exists in stable families, the mutual responsibility of husbands and wives to support each other as possible and as needed.

The specter of husbands forcing their wives out of their homes is a ludicrous one. The specter of the law rounding them up and out is even more bizarre. Equal rights don't interfere with family decisions —chief among them the decision as to whether a spouse will work in the home or in paid employment. That will remain what it is now, a private decision, negotiated by two people who, with any luck, get along a lot better than Charlie and Lydia McGuire.

OCTOBER 1976

NOW WHO'S HYSTERICAL?

The man from the American Medical Association was pretty direct about it. If a woman had hysteria, then the cure might well be a hysterectomy.

Yes, there was something positively Grecian about the dogged line of reasoning pursued by Dr. James Sammons as he testified before the House Commerce Oversight Subcommittee that's been investigating unnecessary surgery.

The word *hyster* began its unfortunate etymological history as Greek for "uterus." It doesn't take a NOW task force to trace its descent into the English word "hysteria—an uncontrollable outburst of emotion or fear."

With that background, it should not have been surprising to find Dr. Sammons telling the congressional hearing that the AMA supported surgery as a means of cutting out fear. He condoned a hysterectomy for women in states of "acute pregnophobia" (fear of pregnancy) and acute cancer phobia.

In the process, he pointed up one thing: Hysterectomies have become big business. In 1975 more wombs were removed than tonsils —725,000 in all, up a full 25 percent from 1970. At this rate, half of all American women over sixty-five will have had their uteri taken out.

Of course, relatively few of these operations are done for the fearful, but Sammons' casual attitude toward the procedure shows up in the statistics. The hysterectomy rate in the United States is two and a half times that of England and four times that of Sweden.

Of all these procedures, no more than 20 percent are performed for cancer or other life-threatening disorders. A large number, however, are done for sterilization, despite the availability of less drastic and less complicated procedures. At Los Angeles County Hospital, for example, 20 percent were done openly for contraception.

That doesn't count the ones that are done less openly. Dr. Malkah Notman, associate professor at Harvard Medical School, has noted that "there is a group of Catholic women who are in conflict about contraceptives. They come to the doctor with 'symptoms.' If they are 'sick' and 'need' a hysterectomy, then they are off the hook. Everybody, including the doctor, goes along with it."

Their operations become part of the conservative estimate that 15 to 40 percent of all hysterectomies are "questionable." In the attempt to understand how this happens, some blame "consumer demand," and some blame surgeons for being profit-motivated and/or knife-happy.

Yale Medical School's Dr. John Morris testified that some California surgeons now pay $100 a day for malpractice insurance, and added, "That can't help but affect some surgeons' judgment." It is known that the rate of operations is higher among the patients of doctors who are paid on a piece-rate (rather than salaried) basis.

Aside from the money incentive, surgeons in general are prone to work by the motto, "When in doubt, Cut it out." Dr. Notman, who has studied depression in post-hysterectomy patients, says, "There are too many hysterectomies done because they appeal to the surgeon's sense of tidiness. It is the obvious way to get rid of the symptoms."

This attitude combines with another, says Dr. Notman: "It's pretty clear that most surgeons think that the uterus is useless once women are done having babies."

A study by sociologist Diana Scully in Illinois found that many surgical residents develop a "sales pitch" for the operation, which she quoted this way: "Think of the uterus as a cradle. After you've had all your babies, there's no reason to keep the cradle."

Surgeons themselves often maintain that women seek, and even shop, for a hysterectomy. Dr. Kenneth Ryan, chairman of Harvard Medical School's obstetrics and gynecology department—who also testified in Washington—doesn't believe that happens very often. When it does, he says, "we ought to figure out why instead of just going ahead and doing it. In the menopausal years, especially, we need more medical care to avoid the procedure rather than encouraging women to have it."

As for the notion of surgically removing the wombs of the fearful, Ryan was set against it. "The AMA went out on a limb," he said. "I think their position has become untenable."

Indeed, during his testimony the man on the limb had also condoned removing breasts, bunions and assorted limbs under similar acute "mental" symptoms. By the end of the afternoon he was calling the Members of Congress "Doctors." There were those who believed that he sounded a touch hysterical.

MAY 1977

MANUFACTURING SEXUAL MYTHS

Those of us who survived the era of "Nice Girls Don't" and the days of "Any Woman Can," only to find ourselves in the time zone of "Everyone Must," will be happy to hear from Dr. Wardell Pomeroy.

Pomeroy has been monitoring the myths of American sex lives since he first coauthored the Kinsey Report way back in the fifties. In those days the big myth was that women participated in sex by lying quietly and thinking of Queen Victoria. It was an idea whose time had passed, and Pomeroy helped bury it.

Now a therapist in San Francisco, he is still in the business of burying sexual myths, including the new sexual myths of the seventies which have sprung up to replace the old crop.

In an interview in *Human Sexuality*, he notes that the old myth that "women are basically disinterested in sex" has been replaced by the new myth that "women have become so sexually aggressive that men can't keep up with them."

The old idea that love is the only thing that matters has been replaced by the belief that technique is the only thing that matters. Those who once insisted that the only well-adjusted teenager was a chaste teenager now assure us that all teenagers are promiscuous. And the notion that sex should be a serious procreational experience has been replaced by the insistence that sex should be a frivolous recreational event.

This is hardly what Pomeroy considers progress. He suggests that the new myths are as false as the old ones. The only thing that's true is the apparent need for myths. In a time of enormous change, he notes, "we continue to manufacture myths to ward off anxieties."

It seems that we'd rather believe in one giant Anything than in Nothing. We are anxious about going through life without a shopping list of dos and don'ts, shoulds and shouldn'ts. We are still trying to figure out what our neighbors, peers and other "normal" people are thinking and doing in bed.

The new myths are easy—if opposite—oversimplifications. "The major function of myths is to keep people from thinking," says Pomeroy, and they do that quite well. They reshape the most complex issues of sexuality into either-or answers. Women who were passive are aggressive. Sex which was serious should be frivolous. Romantic love is out, vibrators are in.

These statements have all the subtlety of the old multiple-choice examinations which, if you remember, were designed chiefly to make life simpler for the grader. That is, of course, the other function of myths. We grade and judge ourselves by them. They deal with people in categories and have a "chilling effect" on our individuality.

The woman today who reads that "The Woman Today" is sexually aggressive tends to worry about whether she should be. The man who hears that techniques are everything worries about becoming a better technician. The teenager who reads about teenage promiscuity is convinced that his or her "qualms" must be a rare social disease.

The myths we manufacture to eliminate anxiety over change mass-produce anxieties over our own personal performance and private attitudes. They send a fellow like Pomeroy back to the debunking board.

What next? A new crop of myths? Having gone from one extreme to the other, what is in store for us now? The Golden Mean myths?

The truth about our sexuality doesn't even lie between passive and aggressive, romantic and technological. There is no public shopping list of appropriate thoughts for such an intensely personal experience. The only truth is a very private one. The rest is myth, pure myth, new or old.

MARCH 1977

A DESCRIPTION
OF REJECTION

She was brilliant. Everyone involved in the case agreed about that.

She was unattractive. Everyone agreed about that, too.

She was overweight, whiny, argumentative, unkempt—the list goes on—sloppy, hypercritical, unpopular.

The life of Charlotte Horowitz—whose dismissal from a Missouri medical school became a Supreme Court case this week—has become painfully public. A description of rejection.

From all reports, she interacted with the world like a fingernail on a blackboard. She was punished for the crime of being socially unacceptable.

Charlotte Horowitz was older than most of the other students when she was admitted to the University of Missouri–Kansas City Medical School in 1972. She was also brighter, a misfit from New York who won her place despite the admissions officer's report that read, "The candidate's personal appearance is against her. . . ."

By the school's "merit system," she was tops in her medical-school class. As her advisor wrote: "Her past record is the best in the school. Her examination scores are at the very top of the school. She has functioned at a high level and has had no problems with a patient at any time." Yet she was dismissed by the dean on the verge of graduation. The grounds were tardiness, bad grooming and an abrasive personal style.

Of course, the case in front of the Supreme Court won't judge those grounds. It will deal with the issue of due process: whether she was given proper notice and a fair hearing; whether universities and professional schools have to extend certain legal rights to their students.

But the theme of this difficult, emotional story is prejudice. The most deep-rooted way in which we prejudge each other. The sort of discrimination which is universal, almost unrootable. Prejudice toward appearance. Discrimination against what we "see."

The most unattractive children in the classrooms of our youth had their lives and personalities warped by that fact. Their painful experiences of rejection nurtured in them an expectation of rejection. That expectation, like some paranoia, was almost always fulfilled.

CLOSE TO HOME

It is a mystery why some "unattractive people" wear it in their souls and others don't. Why one becomes Barbra Streisand and another a reject. But often, along the way, some people give up trying to be accepted and become defensively nonconforming. They stop letting themselves care. They become "unkempt, argumentative, abrasive." And the list goes on.

Everyone's self-image is formed in some measure by the way they are seen, the way they see themselves being seen. As their image deteriorates, their personality often shatters along with it. At that point, the rest of us smugly avoid them, stamping them "unacceptable," not because of their "looks" but because of their behavior.

It happens all the time.

There is no law that can protect children from this sort of discrimination. We are all, in that sense, the products as well as the survivors of our childhood. But the cumulative, spiraling effect of appearance on personality is worse for women than for men. If Charlotte Horowitz had been a man, surely her brains would have alleviated her physical unattractiveness. As a woman, her unattractiveness was further handicapped by brains.

As Dr. Estelle Ramey, a professor at Georgetown Medical School and former head of the Association for Women in Science, said: "If the bad fairy ends up the last one at your crib, you'll be cursed as a brilliant unattractive woman."

But this case isn't a question of the curse, the birth penalty, the "life isn't fair" sort of discrimination. It's a story of a university so "blinded" that its officials felt they had the right to throw away a life and a mind because it was housed in a body that was "overweight, sloppy, hypercritical."

"What's been lost in all this," says Dr. Ramey, "is the contribution a brilliant human being might have made in a field which needs all the fine minds we have."

You see, Charlotte Horowitz was brilliant. Everyone involved in the case could, at least, see that.

NOVEMBER 1977

SUPERWORKINGMOM
OR SUPERDRUDGE?

There weren't any stunning revelations in the news last week. The Bureau of Labor reported that the wage gap between men and women was on the increase, while a *Newsweek* cover story analyzed the fact that the numbers gap between working men and women was on the decrease.

No, there were no stunning bulletins. The monkey-in-the-middle of all this change was again described as the average employed mother who is not only working more and earning less, but bearing the full load of family care. In short, the only equality she's won after a decade of personal and social upheaval is with the working mothers of Russia.

Many of the back-to-work women are still apologizing for changing the rules of the mating game as they were writ back in 1955. They are doing penance by "doing it all," or "juggling" as the magazines put it so cutely. They read cheerleading articles that say, "You, too, Dora Daring, can manage a home and job, can keep your roots blond, your children squeaky clean and have their permission slips signed on time if only you learn a few organizing tricks!"

But one thing that is apparent is that the younger women of America aren't buying it. Superworkingmom looks more like Superdrudge to them.

A generation ago, young women felt that they had to choose between being a housewife and a career woman. Today's young women often feel their choice is between Superdrudge or not mothering at all. Most of the college women I have talked with look upon motherhood as The End. When you talk about having babies, they stare at you.

The "best and the brightest" women in their twenties not only have a horror of being housewives but a dread of getting on that working-mother treadmill.

Still, they may not be seeing the whole story. Both of the main pieces in the *Newsweek* article ended on the note, "Men may well have to spend more time running the house and raising the children." But that isn't future-think. It's happening right now in the bumper crop of two-parent working families bearing their first child in their thirties.

Many of those men already found out that they would have to

share the kids if they wanted them. These days, there is a new version of the old play, *Lysistrata*. In this one, childbearing-age women—especially those with high aspirations—are simply rejecting pregnancy until they get some assurances of partnership parenting.

For a while, it looked as if this generation would simply choose to be "child-free." But now it appears that they have charted a new trend.

Many of these couples discuss everything short of college tuition for the kids before they conceive them. Because of the hesitations of women, the burden of proof has often been shifted onto the men.

It is often the men in their thirties who are pushed to really "decide" if they want to raise, not just "have" children. One friend quizzed her husband as if she were an Internal Revenue agent: "Will you get up in the middle of the night? Will you stay home half the time when the kids are sick? Who will call for the sitter?"

As her husband recalls, "She was sure that the minute we had a child, she would have two jobs and I would be sitting in the living room waiting for din-din."

But, in fact, these couples have gone into parenting differently and seem to offer the most appealing shared life pattern to emerge slowly out of the morass of guilt and conflict in changing expectations.

They may well be the cutting edge of a massive change in the life cycle. By the thirties, after all, many of us have settled some of the issues of personal confidence and professional competence. Many are ready to make compromises, or simply ready to raise children.

In any case the first-time thirties parents seem better prepared for the pressures and ready to share them. The thing that seems to surprise them is the pleasure. They are enjoying kids, not just crisply coping. No one seems to have warned them about that.

DECEMBER 1976

THE NEW ELITE

I've grown weary of reading about the two-worker family as some sort of New Elite with a Cuisinart for every room and a cruise for every February.

I've even grown weary of hearing some economists exercise their social conscience in public by worrying about whether these couples are responsible for a growing gap between the rich and the poor.

It seems to me that there is a rather subtle and updated version of Blame the Working Wife going on. Long accused of every social ill from juvenile delinquency to male impotence, she is now being held responsible for the class structure of America. And never mind that this same class structure kept her at the bottom lo these two hundred years.

The New Elite is in large part a fantasy created by people who do not know the difference between gross income and net income. They are people who tend to overlook such leveling facts as the graduated income tax and the marriage tax—not to mention child care and inflation.

Few of the working couples I know raise polo ponies. They do not consider college tuition or mortgage payments to be elitist activities. They work for solvency, security and self-esteem (in that order). The motivation to work among husbands and wives is very much the same.

But even those couples who are genuinely and jointly members of the working upper-middle class don't deserve to be singled out for blame. It's true that highly paid people tend to marry each other more often, whether they are government administrators, corporate executives or lawyers. People have, I suppose, usually married along group lines of one sort or another.

But previously women were conveniently irrelevant in terms of the economy. They were democratically unpaid, and equally "worthless" to the family checking account.

Now, however, we are warned by economists like Lester Thurow in publications no less capitalistic than the *Wall Street Journal* that "if males who earn high incomes are married to women who could earn high incomes in a perfectly fair and liberated world, the women's liberation will make the distribution of income more unequal."

It is true that adding a woman's high income to a man's could further solidify the class structure. Yet I find myself suspicious of the undertone of these arguments. It seems to find the working wife guilty of the evils of capitalism when she's just had her first bite of the fruit. I don't think it's a coincidence that the family with two incomes totaling as high as $50,000 is considered a serious problem, while the family with one worker earning $50,000 is considered a success story.

As a whole we seem to value economic incentive, individual achievement, upward mobility and all the rest. We envy and respect (more than we resent) the members of the work-their-way-up class, but on the other hand we have a vision of a nation in which the gap between the rich and the poor shouldn't gape at us.

I'm afraid that the working couple is the latest convenient scapegoat for our ambivalance about our class issues. By blaming working wives in particular, people are free to lament inequality while supporting the idea that an individual (at least the male) can freely rise to riches.

If it sounds complicated and conflicted, it is. After all, we are concerned about the inequality of family incomes, but more uncomfortable with the idea of family income ceilings or a radical redistribution of wealth. We are genuinely worried about jobs, but more likely to criticize two-worker couples than to support full employment.

The so-called New Elite is, I'm afraid, an easy target. It distracts attention from the Old Elite, the real elite, and attracts the anger of those in the worst economic stress.

Still, I have a feeling that the blame-the-working-wife game isn't going to play as well as it has in the past. There are too many working couples and too much family need. Women have finally developed some resistance to the sirens of guilt. They are not about to return home in the name of what John Kenneth Galbraith called "convenient social virtue."

This time the problems of the economic system aren't going to be hidden by manipulating the employment of women, and these working couples may force us all to look long and hard at our own ambivalence. Maybe in that sense they are the New Elite.

OCTOBER 1978

MISPLACED, REPLACED, DISPLACED

They were talking about Mrs. Adams in the Senate this week. They were talking about her and Mrs. Hill in the hearing room of the Sub-committee on Employment, Poverty and Migratory Labor.

Now Mrs. Hill and Mrs. Adams were never the sort of women to be talked about in public. Years ago they made their decisions to have private careers. They had children and raised them; they made homes and acquired all the skills of that job.

If all had gone according to plan, according to their expectations, we might never have heard about them at all.

But, a few years ago, as Senator Birch Bayh explained to the subcommittee, both of these middle-aged women lost their only "employer." Mrs. Hill's husband died, and at fifty-three she was without work experience or income. She had a mortgage to pay and seven years to survive until she was eligible for Social Security.

Mrs. Adams for her part was divorced by her husband after nineteen years of marriage. She was among the minority—some 14 percent—who are awarded any alimony at all. But like half of those women, she was never able to collect it on a regular basis.

In short, these two middle-class, middle-aged women with grown children became part of that vast subgroup which Susan Catania, a state legislator from Illinois, described as the "new poor." They were now in the category known in the Senate bill as "displaced homemakers."

Displaced, replaced or misplaced, there are somewhere between two million and seven million American women who were emigrants forced out of a lifestyle which was destroyed by death or divorce.

Women like Mrs. Adams and Mrs. Hill were perhaps the last generation to go into homemaking as a lifelong career. When they were married twenty and thirty years ago, they believed that they had wed security.

Independence wasn't something they chose. It's something that happened to them, and they called it insecurity. It came into their lives with empty nests and empty pocketbooks; it left them uncovered by social policies, and triply discriminated against in the work field by age and sex and inexperience.

It left them in need of some help. Of course, the expression "displaced homemaker" brings forth a vision of armies of middle-aged women camped on the banks of the Potomac behind barbed wire waiting for the soup line to open. But it is also a term of transition, and the bill which is wending its way slowly through Congress is really a Relocation Act.

It offers, not a soup kitchen, but supports for a difficult time. The funds would set up what Laurie Shield, the head of the Alliance of Displaced Homemakers, likes to think of as "experimental laboratories"—one for each state—where women could be aided through the transition, where they could find legal, emotional and job counseling. They would be recycling stations, to outfit the homemakers with skills to fit the work force and help them find new jobs to fill both the public's needs, and theirs.

Basically it would support middle-aged women through the time zone from desertion to self-sufficiency. And from the expectations of one decade to the realities of another.

In some crucial ways, the Displaced Homemakers bill is a stop-gap measure: stopping the gap between the generations.

Joanne Maxey, a state senator from Nebraska, told the Senate hearing: "We are not going to have the problem ten or fifteen years from now, because today's young women are preparing themselves." She is largely right. The young homemaker now has had some tough role models, and most of them plan their second careers.

But women like Mrs. Adams and Mrs. Hill planned a lifetime of mothering and wifing, caring for others, making a home. They slipped on their commitments and fell into the cracks of society. They were misplaced, replaced, displaced.

And, at the very least they deserve a chance to relocate, with a small buffer zone of caring in return.

SEPTEMBER 1977

EQUAL PAY
FOR EQUAL POWER

This is a story about value judgments. About men's work and women's work. And about how the average woman is worth more to her employer than the numbers that come up on her paycheck.

It begins way back in the days when Equal Pay for Equal Work was a nice, comfortable slogan. Only the worst antediluvian—the sort of person who would make George Bernard Shaw look like a feminist—believed that a man and a woman standing side by side doing the same job should be paid differently.

So the notion was that if women put all of their efforts into integrating jobs and enforcing the Equal Pay Act, all would be right, or at least fairer, in the work world.

But something happened on the way to employment equality. Men and women who did the same work began to get more nearly the same pay. But the gap between the wages of men and the wages of women kept growing, until today women earn less than 60 percent of what men earn.

In this, the year of backlash and Bakkelash, only a small proportion of women do the same work as men. Only a tiny number have integrated—with fanfare and front-page stories—the nontraditional jobs held by men.

For every first woman construction worker there are thousands of secretaries. For every first woman electrician and first left-handed, blue-eyed female bus driver there are hundreds more working on a line with other women like them. In fact, 80 percent of the women in the country work in twenty-five job categories, and these are overwhelmingly "women's jobs."

And so, those who want to improve women's lives by improving their paychecks, those who are looking for equity, have begun shifting their emphasis. They are less ardent about trying to urge women out of the jobs they hold—and often like—and more concerned about getting women's jobs reevaluated according to their "real worth,"

The hottest issue now among the advocates and organizers from Seattle to Chicago to Washington, where the National Commission on Working Women held a conference last week, comes wrapped with a new slogan: Equal Pay for Work of Comparable Worth.

Four years ago in Seattle, the state was paying parking-lot attendants more than secretaries. More recently, in the Midwest, a hospital was sued for paying psychologists more than psychiatric nurses. Today, the U.S. Department of Labor ranks child-care workers on a par with dog-pound attendants. And in factory after factory across the country, men who lift weights, however infrequently, are paid more than women who do delicate handwork.

These facts raise basic questions about our sense of worth. As Ronnie Ratner, of the Wellesley College Center for Research on Women, said in Washington: "We are not only trying to eliminate this wage gap, but to place a different value on the work women do in society."

A variety of groups are trying to assess, catalogue and equate the apples and oranges of the workplace. They are asking: Where was it written that a clerical worker is worth less to a company than a truck driver? Where was it written that manual labor is worth more than mental labor (except, of course, among executives)? Is the "invisible hand" of Adam Smith really an indelible marker on unequal paychecks?

In the marketplace, women's work has been paid poorly because women were doing it. Employers paid them less than men because they would work for less because they couldn't get any more— the class cycle of the poor.

But now, people working on "comparable worth" issues are trying to reevaluate jobs without regard to the sex of the worker, to rank them according to their "worth" and then insist on appropriate pay.

It's a far more difficult task than the first one. The notion of paying people according to any standard other than that of the marketplace is a daring one. We don't pay anyone in society—housewives or clergy—according to what we say they are worth. We pay them "what the market will bear."

If assessing "comparable worth" is hard, getting equal paychecks is going to be even harder. It will take more than the consciousness-raising, more than careful point systems, more even than the litigation and the best wishes of the Equal Employment Opportunity Commission.

It will require increased organization and clout among women workers themselves. If there is one slogan that underlines all the rest it's the simplest one: Equal Pay for Equal Power.

OCTOBER 1978

THROW ANOTHER HERO
ON THE FIRE

One of the appalling by-products of the national conventions has been my own discovery that Walter Cronkite depresses me. Throw another hero on the fire.

It became painfully obvious somewhere between his interviews with Miz Lillian and Mrs. Reagan that the senior statesman of television news, the man who interviews world leaders with more ease than most of us can manage at parent-teacher conferences, simply cannot interview women. His encounter with Miz Lillian was disastrous enough, but faced with Nancy Reagan, of all people, he was literally reduced to giggles.

I had the sense that he was trying to get a handle on how he "should" be talking to her, as if there were some secret way of chatting with "the fair sex" to which, being a mere man, he wasn't privy. First he tried a paternalistic approach and then simply dissolved into a little-boy approach. Apparently, father and son were the only available roles from which he could choose.

I can only imagine what he would have done if faced with Maureen Reagan, the daughter who is to feminism what the wife is to traditionalism.

The truth is that I hesitate to put into print what began as a sigh. Cronkite's obvious discomfort didn't push my moral outrage button. That button has less of a hair-trigger than it used to. In time you learn to pick your fights and scale the relative importance of issues and observations.

On a sexism scale of one to ten, Cronkite is only a four or so. I would label him Not Malevolent but a Bit Confused. He doesn't approach the veiled hostility of a Harry Reasoner or a Roger Mudd or that distraught floor reporter who collapsed just trying to greet Margaret Heckler, "Congresswoman, uh, Congressperson . . . What do you call yourself . . . ?" (How about Representative?)

But . . . Now Back to Walter. The reason that I bring up his sad communications gap is that he is suffering from Ancient and Honorable Immunity. There seems to be a lamentable tendency among many women to simply write off older men as hopelessly, terminally incapable of changing their attitudes and dealing with women just as if they were real people.

Every time one woman says, "But look at Dr. Spock, he changed," another will say, "But look at my Uncle Harry, he'll never change." And there do seem to be more Uncle Harrys in the world.

About three years ago, I went to hear I. F. Stone speak to a gathering of journalists. Stone is something of a media cult figure these days, and I was in my looking-forward-to-admiring-him frame of mind. But after a half-hour speech that included two abysmal "dirty" jokes, and the most extraordinary insensitivity to the fact that some of our best friends are women journalists—zap—throw another hero on the fire.

None of the women journalists there confronted him, even when he assumed one was the wife of a reporter. He too held Ancient, Honorable and Hopeless Immunity. His own daughter, a writer, was finally driven to asking why someone didn't *tell* her father. She'd obviously been trying for some time.

Now Back to Walter. We have grown up with Cronkite—almost the way she grew up with Izzy: he is a kind of father figure, or Uncle Harry figure anyway. Most of us have been taught to be polite to our elders and we tend to avoid confrontation with anyone in our father's generation, let alone our fathers themselves. (Freud, where are you when we need you?)

But actually we are being rude. We have written them off, just the way some people write off the very elderly, talking to them like they have lost their wits and are just passing time until the undertaker comes. We are saying, in effect (and with apologies to Cronkite), "And that's the way it is."

Instead of dealing with the older man in the law firm who calls his junior partner "dearie," instead of trying to change the attitudes of the foreman or the boss, we calculate how many more years there are until he retires. We give up on them. In fact, we "patronize" them.

Now Back to Walter. In the spirit of constructive criticism, in the "memory" of I. F. Stone's daughter, I would like to suggest that Cronkite take two transactional analysts, a tape recorder, half-a-dozen assertive-but-kind female college seniors, three Valiums, and a glass of water into a small room for seventy-two hours.

After that, I'll bet "the way it is" isn't what it used to be.

AUGUST 1976

OF ROLES
AND ROBES

When I was in Denver a year ago, I met a telephone repairer of the female persuasion who told me a very funny story. At least she was laughing.

Several weeks earlier, on a service call, she had rung the doorbell of a customer and been greeted with, "Oh! good, you're the man from the telephone company." Well, she was a bit taken aback by that, but proceeded to fix the phone anyway. During the entire time, the woman of the house referred to her as "he" and finally praised her as a wonderful "man."

The customer was what you might call a hard-core resister. Apparently it was easier to accept a rather deviant male with silicone implants than a woman who could fix telephones. But there you are.

The majority of us are not quite so immune to reality. The facts tend to change our attitudes more often than the other way around.

There are, of course, those who will never, under any circumstances, accept women in unusual roles. But it's safe to say that they are a minority in the telephone directory or, for that matter, in the congregation.

Which brings me to the subject of women priests. The triennial convention of the Episcopal Church is meeting in Minneapolis until September 24. It will decide the issue of women priests—an issue which has been a divisive one among the three-million-member denomination for a dozen years.

Four years ago, after much pressure, women were finally allowed to become deacons of the church. Since then they have been trying to scramble up the final rung to priesthood.

In 1972 the bishops asserted that they were in favor of women priests "in principle," and the following year the lower clergy continued to forbid them in canon law. Since a dramatic moment in 1974, fifteen women have been ordained in ceremonies that were challenged and unrecognized by the official church. In response, the church officials went so far as to refuse a $600 donation to the World Hunger Campaign because it was raised at a service presided over by "outlaw" women priests.

On Wednesday the House of Bishops finally voted to permit

women to be ordained as priests. But this weekend the question will come before the more conservative body, the House of Deputies. This body has based its opposition largely on "tradition," and the idea that the parishes are not ready. In doing so, many have managed to misjudge how the public comes to accept change.

Strong pressure already has built to admit women into "men only" roles and robes. The leaders for change made bold steps by ordaining fifteen women. But the masses generally accept the facts after the fact—whether it's women at West Point or at the altar.

We deal with the *fait accompli* better than with fantasies. In prospect, a *woman priest* is a vague, amorphous threat to tradition. In fact, however, she is a human being with a sincere calling. As a species we are enormously resistant to the idea of change—and remarkably adjustable to its reality.

The horrified alumni of Yale discovered after a few years that the sky did not fall over the female dorms of New Haven. The patrolmen in Washington who were opposed to buddying up with women largely accepted them a year later. The same people who couldn't tolerate the idea of a woman doctor went to Elizabeth Blackwell when they were sick. And West Point marches on.

Many are opposed to women in "men's roles" because they've never seen them, they've never tried them. They regard a woman priest with the suspicion normally directed at raw oysters. The prejudice remains unshakable as long as the experience is unchanged.

The way to effect the change the bishops agreed upon "in principle" four years ago isn't some cop-out, piecemeal compromise, but is to take a stand on that "principle"—to admit women priests, and to let "public acceptance" do what it does best: follow.

SEPTEMBER 1976

■■■■■ INFORMATION, PLEASE

Not long ago, during one of those internal shuffles that give meaning to the expression "itinerant journalism," the desk of one employee of a metropolitan daily newspaper was moved to the front of the room.

This, I assure you, meant nothing in terms of status. There is no status in a newspaper. But it put this woman's desk among seven or eight others within range of something called The Door.

Now newspapers are the closest thing in the work world to community drop-in centers. People wander in and out of them carrying every sort of notion and promotion from wedding announcements to dancing-bear advertisements to proclamations about National Tax-payer Week.

Sometimes they even arrive offering themselves as objects of national fascination. There was, for example, a man who used to lumber into my old office in Detroit every January wearing nothing more than a wet bathing suit and doing a seal imitation.

Sitting near any door in a newspaper office thus has certain built-in liabilities. Streams of people are constantly asking you where they should deposit their dancing bears and life stories. Not to mention their wet bathing suits.

Most people would reasonably assume that if they were sitting among seven co-workers, these fascinating inquiries would be divided into seven equal parts. But they would be wrong if only one of this up-front group was female.

The cruel fact of life, as this woman (who shall remain nameless) discovered in months of people-watching, is this: The average stranger would walk into a room, past the charming music critic (and disco dancer), barely glancing at the well-groomed highbrow of the movie critic, avoiding three reporters and one columnist until his eyes fastened on the only person in the room trying madly to find a solution for world hunger ten minutes before deadline.

It was clear that this person and no other had to be the receptionist because she was of the Female Persuasion.

In this way, many brilliant ideas were interrupted and forever lost to the world—including the solution to world hunger. But something was gained. The woman won a daily sense of camaraderie with every female executive who is asked to get the coffee, every woman ever arbitrarily handed a dictation pad, and every female doctor ever asked when the doctor would be in.

In an effort to prove to herself that she was not paranoid, she even conducted a brief sociological study. First she made certain improvements on her own public barriers. She put a bookcase in front of her desk and piled it with newspapers, sweaters and phone books. This, however, only seemed to give people a place to put their elbows and their dancing bears, while asking for information.

Next, under the tutelage of her neighbor she tried to perfect a technique of rudeness. She discovered that there were people who would rather spend ten minutes waiting for her to look up than to disturb the man reading the paper with his feet on the desk behind her.

The woman didn't want to be hostile about this. It wasn't fair to get angry at the poor fellow carrying a case of yogurt samples when he asked where the food editor was. It wasn't his fault. It came with the blue booties.

Yet she gradually became desperate to finish a sentence with something other than a question mark. She was willing to try anything short of a sex-change operation.

So, one day, in a fit of anxiety, she placed a handwritten warning on top of the massive barrier which read: This Is Not a Reception Desk.

What was the result of this, the ultimate weapon, you ask? Well, the first two souls were intimidated. They walked to the back of the room to find another woman. The third smiled jovially over the top and asked, "Could you please tell me where the reception desk is?"

The woman was, either way, defeated.

Now there is a new rumor floating through the office. They are playing musical desks again and everyone is going to be moved.

This time, she is looking for a back seat with a thoroughly rear view. If she doesn't get it she intends to come to work thoroughly upholstered and doing a nifty imitation of an empty chair.

OCTOBER 1978

THE ISSUE IS US

It took seventy-five years to break the iron will of that miserable old misogynist. It took the solid pressure of women's rights groups on both sides of the Atlantic to change his terms.

But finally, to the accompanying sound of Cecil Rhodes rolling over in his grave, the Rhodes scholarships were opened to female applicants. For the first time, thirteen American women were chosen for places on that inner track of the old boys' network.

Well, now, what do we get for the pressure of three generations of uppity women? We get a pleasant nineteen-year-old beneficiary named Laura Garwin, of Radcliffe College, who doesn't "think of myself as a feminist" and has "never had to come to terms as a minority because I have not been discriminated against." We get a young physics major who says, "I guess there is a problem. I haven't come into contact with it."

And we get depressed. You see, Laura isn't the only one. We have a generation of the best and brightest young women ensconced inside formerly male bastions like Harvard or Yale or Princeton who are suffering from shortsightedness and its accompanying complacency. (And there came a generation that knew not yet discrimination.)

Now, on the whole, you have to forgive them. I mean, after all, we wanted to create a world where they wouldn't be refused admittance to Yale. Laura was only six when they included "women" in the Civil Rights Act of 1964. And she was ineligible to drive the day that hundreds of thousands of American women marched to celebrate the fiftieth anniversary of suffrage. Besides, she is a physicist and not a historian.

But it is scary how many of the elite young women today assume that their entire fortune comes from their merit. "I think I applied for the Rhodes for the same reasons that men apply. I think I was probably nominated for the same reasons," says Laura.

I suppose there is a natural tendency in all of us to believe that we are self-made men and women who got "where we are today" on our brains and bootstraps. Ultimately, we do have to make it independently. But it's too easy to forget: You can't win a scholarship on merit if they reject you on sex, or race, or religion.

Maybe Laura should meet another woman who made the news

this week, Patricia Roberts Harris. She doesn't have that kind of amnesia. No way. Carter's HUD nominee was questioned intently by Senator William Proxmire (D–Wisconsin) about her attitude toward the poor and the minorities. Finally she responded, "Senator, I am one of them. You do not seem to understand who I am. I am a black woman, the daughter of a dining-car worker. I am a black woman who could not buy a house eight years ago in parts of the District of Columbia. . . . If you think I have forgotten that, you are dead wrong."

There are thirty-three years separating Laura Garwin and Pat Harris. But there's something else separating them—the door in the face, the "Do Not Apply" sign, the pain in the gut. The experience of discrimination.

Psychologist Robert Coles once wrote, "In this life, we prepare for moments and events and situations that we never actually know about until they are upon us. We worry about wrongs and think about injustices, then all of a sudden the issue is not whether we agree with what we have heard and read and studied and talked about with friends. Rather, the issue is us."

But do we have to experience discrimination personally to identify with others, to be motivated to make changes? What happens when we don't? Do the stories of discrimination begin to sound like old tales of walking four miles in the snow to school? Do the efforts of one entire generation simply pave the way for the complacency of the next?

I hate to think that we can only maintain our sense of group identity and momentum by holding onto the pain. But it is possible that the women's movement, energized to fight discrimination, can founder again (the way it did after suffrage) on its incomplete successes.

Perhaps the hard-won and welcome piece-by-piece victories—here a Rhodes scholar, there a law or two—can siphon off the energy and the woman-power from those who are allowed to live in a protected environment and allowed to forget.

In that case, let me tuck something into Laura's bag for her trip to England next fall. Some words from Patricia Roberts Harris: "Maybe others can forget what it was like to be excluded from the dining rooms in this very building, Senator, but I shall not."

JANUARY 1977

PART FOUR
PERSONALS

BUYING STOCK
IN OURSELVES

When I was thirteen, I went through what everyone around me referred to as a stage. The symptoms of this stage were very simple. Every night I would lose a fight with my father, who was bigger and brighter, and I would then storm upstairs into my room. At that point, the various members of my family would nod knowingly at each other and say, "Um, well, she's going through a stage."

In the mid-fifties, this stage was called adolescence, or the terrible teens. Anyone forced through biological circumstances beyond their control to share the dinner table with a sufferer hoped that he or she would get over it as quickly as possible.

The idea was that having passed through adolescence one would inevitably become a grown-up. A grown-up was someone calm, self-assured, realistic and steady. A grown-up was someone who had worked through turbulence and personal conflicts to find serenity and wisdom. By twenty-eight at the latest.

The ideas surrounding grown-uphood were like those to do with marriage. You got married and lived happily ever after. There was no mention in the "literature" of dirty dishes, infidelity and jammed Disposalls. Similarly, after one became a grown-up one was. Simply was.

Well, it took me a while, but having just passed the halfway mark of my fourth decade (the number 35 still sticks in my throat, but I'll be all right in a week or two), I am beginning to give up on the idea of ever being one. A grown-up, that is.

It has begun to occur to me that life is a stage I'm going through.

This is not, you understand, a treatise on reincarnation. It is rather an exploration of a shared sense that we have given up the goal of being a grown-up in favor of the process of growing. Grown-uphood was, after all, going to be a rather static place, in which no one was gripped by self-doubt and no one yearned for more. It reminds me now of a Brigadoon inhabited by the lobotomized.

I wonder about the people I used to consider stable, happily-ever-after adults. I figure that either I didn't know them very well, or they must have been just a bit dull. It reminds me of a friend's analysis of her post-divorce dating experiences: "All the men I know are boring or crazy." That was her way of saying that everyone she meets these days is in a state of struggle, or has simply quit.

When I turned thirty, lo these many years ago, I devised a kind of five-year plan. I figured that by thirty-five—if not now, when?—I would have resolved nine out of ten personal problems. It never occurred to me that I would get any more.

I have done roughly as well with my plan as the Russians have done with their agricultural goals. It has taken me five years to give the old conflicts names and origins, and to be able to identify them when they crop up again in new fields. I have fallen bushels short of the maturity I envisioned in the form of Margaret Mead or Eleanor Roosevelt. But, like a good commissar, I have revised my goals and given up the notion of self-perfection for that of self-knowledge.

And why not? We are, after all, the generation that has made psychology into a major growth industry. We've bought stock in ourselves, in self-exploration and change. In any case, my new five-year plan is far more modest.

For one thing I have resolved not to castigate myself for not being a grown-up. Instead of judging my life against, say, Mozart, who at my age was almost dead already, I will think hard about Gauguin, who at my age was still a banker.

If anyone criticizes me, I will simply run away from the table and into my room protesting, "I can't help it. I'm going through a stage."

APRIL 1976

THE SANCTITY
OF BEING ON TIME

I am a member of a small, nearly extinct minority group, a kind of urban lost tribe who insist, in the face of all evidence to the contrary, on the sanctity of being on time.

Which is to say that we On-timers are compulsively, unfashionably prompt, that there are only handfuls of us in any given city and, unfortunately, we never seem to have appointments with each other.

The fact is that being on time has become a social faux pas.

The fact is that as a rule of thumb—or pinkie for that matter —the time that the Late-people set as the Moment of Rendezvous is a code. It is a code meaning at least one-half-hour later. The fact is that us On-timers can't get that through our skulls.

We arrive invariably at the appointed hour at people's houses, which means that we get to talk to their children a lot. Which means that we have seen a lot of hostesses in hair rollers. Which means that we have occasionally eaten all the shrimp cocktail. Which means that we are *rude*.

Let me explain.

We are, for example, invited for dinner at 8:00 at the home of friends who live exactly twenty minutes away. We leave our house at 7:50 so that for once we will be a comfortable ten minutes late. Then even the traffic defeats us. We make all the green lights and arrive at 7:56. We circle the block awhile and then enter at 8:01, to the astonishment of the host and hostess, who are feeding the dog.

She starts rifling through the cookbook trying to figure out what to make. He is thinking about taking a shower. We are sure we have the wrong night.

We end up helping with the hors d'oeuvres and putting the baby to bed and mixing the martinis and are still left with enough time to draw a psychological profile of the couple from the magazines on the coffee table.

As for meeting in restaurants, we On-timers are instantly identifiable. We are the only nonalcoholics loitering in restaurant doorways in December. If not, we can be found killing time in the rest rooms or trying to look like we are not alone at the bar.

Now, we all know that these very same Late-people do not

routinely miss airplanes or the beginnings of movies. But as I told a Late-person recently, "If I were a train I'd be gone."

In regard to meetings, there are two kinds of people. Those who hate to wait and those who hate to make others wait. The sadists and the masochists? I hope not. I prefer to think that, for me at least, this problem is an extension of my newspaper-deadline neurosis. Which in no way explains why I end up waiting for newspaper people.

There was a New York magazine piece once that talked about the power struggle involved in business lunches. It intimated that you could always tell the powerless and the powerful. The Indians were waiting, while the Chiefs floated in a half to a full hour later. If you are an On-timer, you cannot make an entrance.

The Late-people, of course, are always terribly sorry, "but something important came up" (as opposed to us, for instance). Besides, they imply, their minds are always so full of big questions (like The Bomb) that they simply never can manage to keep track of time. As opposed to the On-timers, they suggest, who have pea-brains filled with icky little details like the big hand and the little hand on the clock.

The problem is escalating. If you adjust to the Late-people and accept the fact that they're a half-hour behind the time, they up the ante on you and arrive an hour late. If you tell them a half-hour earlier, they will be an hour late.

Then, too, the weight of history is against the On-timers.

Fewer and fewer of us remain. We have even grown to be surprised when anyone else is on time. We have begun to make certain accommodations, like setting our clocks back or bringing the novel we're working on to the dinner parties.

How late we are to recognize that timeliness is passé, that in fact, our time has passed.

SEPTEMBER 1976

"FORGIVE ME FOR BEING GAUCHE, BUT I'M VOTING"

They tell me that apathy is in this year. Very chic. They tell me the majority of Americans are going to wake up and brush their teeth and go to work and never go near a polling booth. They tell me the in thing to do is to say a curse on both their houses and to stay in my own.

No way. Forgive me for being gauche, but I'm voting. Sue me. I get excited on Election Day. I could no more ignore it than I could ignore New Year's Eve.

I'm one of those hardcore voters, the knee-jerk lever pullers. We're the people who get heartburn if we can't get to a poll on time. Throw an election and we'll be there, rain, snow, sleet, hail, and never mind the "lost causes" and "limited choices." We'll be there.

I'm not sure why I belong to the hardcore voters. In fourteen years I haven't had a chance to vote for a presidential candidate I really wanted. Usually I am voting for the candidate who is "well, at least not as bad as . . ." the other one.

The thing is that voting makes me feel good. Voting reminds me that I'm a grown-up. It makes me feel like a genuine, bona fide, good citizen. Just like it says in the League of Women Voters book.

I suppose that's conditioning. In my house, politics was the business of grown-ups. My sister and I were allowed into the family business slowly, the way other kids are permitted a sip of beer now and then. There was a lot to learn.

How did the grown-ups know that Stevenson had lost when he was still ahead of Eisenhower at nine o'clock? Why did you have to "come out of the city" with a big plurality in order to "counter the western part of the state"?

They didn't call them political campaigns where I grew up. They called them "fights." Elections were half sports events, half war, and we learned the voting patterns of wards and precincts the way other kids learned the batting averages of the Red Sox and the battles of World War II. But each election day seemed to have some rite of passage attached to it.

I learned a lot then. I learned how to "work the polls" when I was ten. I discovered when I was twelve that standing in the cold from 8:00 A.M. to 8:00 P.M. felt good, the way fasting or mountain climbing does—the virtue of enduring, sticking it out. I learned about the crazy camaraderie of poll workers and the way cold unites political opponents over hot cider.

I also learned, when I was thirteen and my dad was running for office, that there are people in the world who would snap, "I wouldn't vote for your father if he were the last man on earth."

On one election day, I drank my first cup of coffee and felt positively decadent. On another, I stayed up all night listening to returns and felt dedicated. On another, I learned that fathers could lose, and feel awful. That, too, became part of growing up.

I still remember voting for the first time when I turned twenty-one. There was a sudden rush, a sense that I had been let into a club. When I went to vote with my parents I was convinced that I was an adult at last.

I still have that flush. I have it when I round the corner to the high-school gym and I'm accosted by the poll workers jockeying into position for a last shot at my vote. *My* vote, for gawdsakes. I have it when the ladies cross my name off the list carefully with their sharpened blue pencil and ruler. When they hand me a slip of paper, I still look at my number and try to figure out if it's a heavy turnout and what that means for my precinct and what that'll mean for the state and—damn the network projections—I like to do it myself.

I have the feeling when I bring my daughter into the polling booth with me. She thinks it's very grown-up.

Today, however lukewarm my opinion is, I'm going to register it. It turns out that the act is important to me. I'm part of the process by which grown-ups make decisions, pull levers, select leaders.

So sue me. I'm an unreconstructed voter.

NOVEMBER 1976

IN PRAISE OF
CHEERFUL EARLY RISERS

It was the one thing that Carter kept quiet about until after the election. Not that he lied to us, you understand, but he didn't exactly go around blabbing about it.

In fact, the first we heard about this deep character flaw was when Rosalynn admitted to Barbara Walters that the only thing that bugged her about Jimmy was the fact that he woke *up*, really *up*.

Then, last week we were stunned to discover that, as President, he would be at his desk by 7:00 A.M. The country gasped in disbelief. Job applications to the new administration dropped off by 82 percent. Across the land, the graffito was telegraphed: Jimmy Carter Wakes Up Early and Cheerful.

Now the vast majority of the people in the country have long regarded Cheerful Early Risers as uncivilized louts who probably slurp when they drink out of finger bowls. In fact, the last socially accepted bigotry is directed at them. So, it took a certain measure of guts for this man, who had battered down the prejudice against Southerners, to come out of the closet and admit that he was a member of a group with a bizarre antisocial disease.

All I can say is, "Good for you, Jimmy." Now perhaps the rest of this oppressed minority group can follow your lead and assert their right to live by their own biorhythms.

With that hope, let me herewith confess: I, too, wake up bright-eyed and bushy-tailed. It isn't my fault. I don't mean to. It is just the way I was brought up.

Throughout my childhood—what did I know of other ways?— my father began the day bellowing, "The British Are Coming!"

Occasionally, he alternated this alarm with the cry, "Everybody, Up, Up, Up for Volleyball!" At our house, breakfast resembled nothing so much as Don McNeill's March Around the Breakfast Table.

It wasn't until I went to college that I discovered that this was aberrant behavior (some might call it child abuse). My freshman roommate did not greet each day eager to fend off the British, but rather as an intensive-care patient whose IV bottle would be shattered by a single sound.

While I scheduled 8:00 A.M. classes (you wouldn't want to waste the whole day, would you?), she majored in math because the courses met at noon. We had a wonderful rapport from 1:15 P.M. to 3:36 P.M.

From then on, I made a series of discoveries. Most people do not consider dawn to be an attractive experience—unless they are still up. Most people are congenitally unable to smile before 9:00—something about the cheek muscles. Most people have Do Not Disturb signs strung across their minds for at least one hour post-bed-partum.

By my mid-twenties, I realized that I would never be popular if I continued to wake people up early with fresh insights, or if I continued to sing while I squeezed orange juice. I would even have to give up my imitation of the effervescent Schweppes man while I brushed my teeth.

It was too risky. Statistically speaking, the Cheerful Early Riser is rejected more completely than a member of any other subculture, save those with boot odor. In some states, "morning cheer" is considered cruel and abusive treatment in divorce court.

So, sad to say, I became closety. I learned to pass. I learned to lie still until 8:30 A.M. If I was caught with open eyes at 6:00 or 7:00, I blamed it on insomnia.

I started to say things like, "Oh, Gawd, I can't think without my coffee." I even (and this I am ashamed of) pretended hostility toward my own kind: "Good grief, isn't *she* a little Susy Sunshine this morning." I would do anything to elude discovery.

Frankly, I was prepared to go through life repressing my true nature, denying my heritage, courting mental illness, just for the sake of being accepted by the normal people who cannot manage a synapse before lunch.

But now Jimmy has taken the lead, come brazenly out of the closet. It occurs to me now that we may even be entering an era of Cheerful Early Riser Chic. Hallelujah. At long last I can say it: The British Are Coming! Everybody Up, Up, Up!

JANUARY 1977

TALL PEOPLE GOT NO REASON

She had just finished listening to Randy Newman's viciously funny song about short people—"Short People Got No Reason to Live"—when it occurred to her that she had never actually been short.

To be more precise about it, the shortest she'd ever been in her entire life was Tall-for-Her-Age, which isn't the same thing at all. In a youth that was lined up by height, she was always at the end. Even for posterity she was locked into the back row of every class picture.

When she was an adolescent, everyone else had busily diverted their inches into diverting places. But she used them all up just to connect the ankle bone to the thigh bone. It wasn't that she was "really tall," explained the best friend (of average height), it was just that she had these long legs. For years she tried to think of herself as a basically average-sized person who had been trapped on stilts. It didn't help.

She finally grew from being Tall for Her Age to being Tall for Any Age. She did this at the worst possible moment, just as she looked around and discovered boys. What she discovered was that they were shorter.

In high school, of course, romance hinged on whether a boy and girl saw eye to eye—not to mention shoulder to shoulder. And so, she spent four years sitting down.

When she absolutely had to stand up—in order to walk, for instance—she learned how to do it with her left hip dropped, her right foot extended, her shoulders hunched and her head tilted to the left. All of this made her look like an abnormal person. But at least she was an abnormal person of normal height.

Now, when she wasn't executing this feat, she did spend a great deal of time with "platonic" friends. Platonic friends were by definition men shorter than she.

In college the yardstick by which her eligibility was measured was still a yardstick. Or, rather, two yardsticks. The men she was "fixed up" with came dribbling into her life off of various and assorted basketball courts, and then went dribbling out again to marry the 5'2" pom-pom girl. To this day, she has an abiding hostility toward the short girls who "used up" the tall boys.

The one time she found her vertical match—at last someone she could look up to from three-inch heels!—he was only interested in a horizontal match. Of course, there were some advantages in being tall. No one ever described her as cute, perky or a ball of fun. But in those days, she wanted to be cute, perky and a ball of fun.

Instead, people used to tell her, "With your height, you can carry it." Sometimes "it" was a trunk. Other times "it" was an extra 20 pounds—10 for each hip. But usually it was something atrocious, like a voluminous maroon mohair cape which made her look like a molting Abominable Snowman.

Tall for her age, she was harder to match with clothes than with mates. In shops, salesladies ended up accusing her of having knees that were in the wrong place. Her wrists were incurable exhibitionists. She was told that it was her fault. Why weren't her parts in the right places?

In her darkest fantasies brought on by shopping trips, she always envisioned Seventh Avenue being run by one cutter who had come straight from a cave in Transylvania for the express purpose of making every dress pattern in America fit his warped mannequin.

But, no matter what Randy Newman said, it wasn't the fault of short people. No, it was the mathematical dictator, the Average Person, who insisted on running the world according to his measurement.

Now, however, she was learning to accept herself, inch by inch. She was still Tall for Her Age, but her (short) mother had always told her, "When you grow up, you'll love being tall."

She probably will.

OCTOBER 1977

AT THE AGE AT WHICH
MOZART WAS DEAD ALREADY

Let others freak out at turning thirty or forty. Let others greet their new decades with $12-an-ounce moisturizing cream and anxiety attacks. Not me. I'm no more mesmerized when the zeroes click into place in my life than when the speedometer turns over a new 10,000-mile mark.

But this odd-numbered birthday is different. This one has been lurking around, waiting to ambush my mind. You see, at the age I'm about to be, Mozart was dead already.

Now why, you ask, would someone whose musical career ended in the college chorus line of *Guys and Dolls* be worrying about Mozart?

Because Mozart has always been a convenient symbolic figure in my life. Someone to make me feel totally inadequate. Someone not to be able to live up to. Someone to make me miserable. Nice healthy things like that. I mean, if you want to feel like a wipe-out, there is always the specter of old Wolfgang inking in the G clefs.

Remember when you were five and thrilled at being able to tie your shoelaces? Mozart was composing minuets. Remember when you were thirty and still hadn't "found yourself"? Mozart had finished *The Marriage of Figaro*. Need I go on?

Of course, Wolfgang isn't the only such handy source of low self-esteem and discontent. In the third grade there was always one kid who was on the gold book when you were on the green. There was one guy in college who had his first play produced on Broadway while you were completing your language requirement.

I had two friends publishing novels in New York the year that I was writing obituaries in Detroit.

I suspect that most of us were geared at a young age to all those grades and annual reports. There wasn't any such thing as an overachiever back then. He was just someone ahead of us. Someone to chase.

Now, however, it strikes me that there may be some advantage in arriving at the age at which Mozart was dead already. You don't have Wolfgang to kick yourself around with anymore. It occurs to you that you are far too old to be precocious, and you'll never be a Young

Achiever. You'll never again be able to write *Don Giovanni* at thirty-one.

Instead of whipping yourself to mush after the goals of others, you begin slowly to reset those goals. All this is called learning to live with yourself.

You stop living for *Who's Who* or the obituary column. You begin to give up the notion of living for the record, for others, or for the fleeting immortality of card catalogues and Chamber of Commerce plaques. As one friend put it: "If I'm not going to be Shakespeare, I might as well enjoy life."

At the age at which Mozart was dead already, you begin to gain what some people call perspective and others call "losing the old drive" and others call mellowness. For a day or so you might be repulsively philosophical. You might ruminate on the fact that the earth will be cold in a billion years or so, that most people's life work is their life, and that there's not a whole lot of point in just making points.

The next trick, I suppose, is to learn to accept your limitations without trapping yourself in them and to find some of the important lines: the line between eternal dissatisfaction and smugness, the line between anxiety and boredom, the line between being driven and being immobilized. The line that we describe as a balanced life.

As for me, I may get there yet. I have at least finally realized one truth that comes with the candles: I'd rather be alive than be Mozart.

APRIL 1977

■■■■■■ GOODMAN'S
VICTORY GARDEN

There are other people in this world who have expensive hobbies. There is the fellow who bought a bottle of Bordeaux wine for $29,000. There are several people who have invested an entire inheritance in a postage stamp. There are even people who collect coats of small furry animals and necklaces of large icy minerals.

I, however, grow vegetables.

Now, vegetable growers are generally regarded as compost-heaping, home-canning, economical folk who feed families of twelve all winter long from one 10-by-10-foot patch of soil.

But I suspect that many of them are really like me, closet *extravagantes* who indulge their land as they would never indulge their children, with a flagrant disregard for budgeting. People who would —indeed, may—go bankrupt for their green beans.

I thought of this last weekend when I "put in my crops"—an absolutely ludicrous description for planting a patch of urban land which, left to itself, would bear only one native product: rocks.

In order to make this garden defy its nature and please my fantasies of Nature, I again lavished it with the most extraordinary amount of cow manure, peat moss, 5-10-5 fertilizer, hearty seedlings and hopeful seeds.

In short, I invested $35.78 in 250 square feet of land, if you do not count the cost of *Crockett's Victory Garden*, a year's subscription to *Horticulture*, gardening tools, tall redwood stakes, metal tomato cages, my own manual labor and, of course, the impending bill from the orthopedic surgeon.

It would have been cheaper to have directly showered the land with quarters and mulched it with shredded dollar bills. It would certainly be cheaper to buy the vegetables.

But I am by now so hopelessly addicted to this plot that if someone told me that spreading beluga caviar over the topsoil would make my cucumbers flourish, I would be on the next plane to the Caspian Sea.

And I would not be alone. There are thousands of us, each tilling God's Little Sixteenth-Acre with fortune and fanaticism.

There is, for example, a man who began his garden by buying a jackhammer. His only earth was hidden under macadam. There is another perfectly sane woman who hires a couple every July to vegetable-sit while she is on vacation. And there are, I am sure, a dozen more who have taken out home improvement loans to furnish their asparagus with beds.

But we have all come to this state for the simplest and most attractive of all reasons: vegetable gardening works. It is relatively reliable and relatively controllable. Relative to the rest of life.

The average parent may, for example, plant an artist or fertilize a ballet dancer and end up with a certified public accountant. We cannot train children along chicken wire to make them grow in the right direction. Tying them to stakes is frowned upon, even in Massachusetts.

Gardening is also much more predictable than governing. If you try to fertilize foreign soil with billions, it may ungratefully sprout a generation of anti-Americans. Pour money into an anti-poverty program and you may have only nurtured another middle-class bureaucratic weed.

In real life, it is increasingly hard to know what is needed, who the enemies are and what the results of our best efforts will be, whether we are working in science or education.

But in the garden, the cast of characters, the outline of the thickening plot, is less complicated. Friends are as obvious as the sun. Enemies are as real as the root borer. The goal is as tangible as a head of cabbage. You don't need a consultant to assess failure and success.

Under those fertile circumstances even the tomato that ends up with a $1 price tag begins to look like a bargain. At least it's one investment you can sink your teeth into.

JUNE 1978

MY ZUCCHINI
ARE STERILE

As a rule I resist sharing the details of my most intimate problems, especially the kinky ones, but we all have to break a rule now and then in the public interest and for the private therapeutic value of confession. Therefore, here goes:

My zucchini are sterile.

That is not a piece of graffito. It is a sad tale of infertility. Let me put it another way: I finally have to admit to lavishing time, money, attention and great expectations on four of the only all-male zucchini plants to exist in the memory of my county Agricultural Extension Service. Even though the nice man there told me not to take it personally, this is a toughy.

False pregnancy upon false pregnancy, a veritable plague is occurring in my garden even as we write. Large yellow fruitless (not to mention vegetableless) blossoms come and go in the Whip Inflation Now strip farm that eats fertilizer and brings in a crop at a rough cost of 25 cents per cherry tomato. This godless tenth-acre has broken the local record for nonproducing squash.

In previous years my crop runneth over. And over. And over. It was the sorcerer's apprentice of vegetables, the one that outdistanced the population growth charts of India. By the end of the summer you would pick it just to stop it from growing.

The major problem was getting rid of them. People who were thrilled with a present of one, started hiding when my daughter would make the rounds with another armful. My daughter took to burying them out of self-defense, convinced that if she ate another zucchini her legs would turn green the way Jerry Rubin's legs turned orange from the carrot-juice therapy.

There was a summer or two during which zucchini surprises lurked in everything from soup to bread to the Cracker Jack box. When she was six, I found my daughter picking distrustfully through peppermint-stick ice cream, asking, "Is there any zucchini in here?"

She was right to be suspicious. I learned to make everything out of zucchini with the possible exception of a lamp.

The Department of Agriculture tells us that one of every two families is growing some kind of produce this year. I am sure that it has become popular because it works. I mean, it's one of the few things that *actually* works. You plant a green-pepper seed and you get a green pepper, which is more than you can say about kids, for instance. I know a lot of people who planted a doctor in Ohio and got a bead-stringer in Ghirardelli Square. A pumpkin wouldn't have done that to them.

Which is why I take the whole zucchini thing as a personal betrayal.

Zucchini are supposed to have boy and girl flowers on each and every plant, which is cozy and guarantees offspring. But I had to hit the seed company that had been infiltrated by Zero Population Growth. I planted in May, nurtured in June, fertilized in July, worried in August and what do I have in September? Nothing, *nada*, only borscht for my trouble.

The neighborhood Pollyanna tells me at least I don't have to worry about woodchucks. The neighborhood humorist asks me if I've thought of a sex-change operation, yuk, yuk, and the neighborhood decorator tells me, well, dear, the plants *look* so lovely.

In desperation I finally called in a specialist from the University of Massachusetts, Robert "Waltham Butternut Squash" Young himself. And what does he say? "Hmm . . . well, it happens every once in a while. Four plants you say . . . My, there ought to be some females. We've never understood why it happens. It's something to do with hormonal imbalance."

Terrific. Me and my WIN garden are defeated. I have only one thing left to say to the zucchini: Take two estrogen and call me in the morning.

SEPTEMBER 1976

NOSTALGIA—
IN SMALL DOSES, PLEASE

I have always been suspicious of nostalgia. It's an emotion indulged in only by people who stand a safe distance from the past. At best it trivializes events, at worst it distorts them all out of proportion.

It is nostalgia that turns the stunning pain of the Depression into the Togetherness of the Waltons. It turns World War II into a Good Ol' Buddy Bootcamp. It turns the pimples and miseries of adolescence into the possibilities and hope of Youth. It even turns the thundering dullness of the fifties into the fun of The Fonz.

I am equally suspicious of instant revivals, of critical retrospectives of the immediate past, because we seem to cannibalize our history, gobbling it up as fast as we live it.

Like television commentators, we keep trying to find the Meaning and Significance of events that are still in process. We sacrifice perspective for the play-by-play, when we should insist on a generation gap between current events and history.

Because of all these prejudices, I have been sitting here braced. This is the tenth anniversary of the Class of '68 and I am sure that we are in for another dose of Sixties Nostalgia and Sixties Criticism.

There will be, of course, another batch of I-Told-You-So articles penned by people who hold an eternal grudge against the sixties, as if the decade were a hostile neighbor.

They are the ones who sniff out the former rebels and bleat loudly whenever they find one mated or rooted. They declare that the sixties revolutionaries are seventies reactionaries because they now live on their own ground rather than underground.

There will also be the Faithful, whose eyes still glaze over with fond memories of the good old days when people sang protest songs on the floor of some college president's office. They remember the camaraderie and forget the pettiness and power-tripping. They remember the excitement and forget the fear.

They insist that the sixties will rise again and that people are just, as Carly Simon sings, "playing possum, keeping a low profile."

Well, I was never really a sixties buff. You could pick a better year than 1968 out of a hat. Through those years, I retained a primal fear of crowds, a linguistic distrust of slogans, a self-consciousness about pickets, and an aversion to people who continually chose excess over reason.

I am equally unhappy with those who gloat over the disillusionment of ideals and seek only vindication from history. They seem to regard the sixties as a miniskirt that revealed only the ugly kneecaps of America. They often think of social concerns as a passing fad, something people will (or should) eventually get over.

But now I find that despite all my reservations, I turn nostalgic about 1968 when faced with the present Class of '78. Perhaps nostalgia was always triggered more by the present than the past, but I would, if I could, merchandise two pieces of memorabilia—a small corner of the sixties market—to the people who were eleven or twelve, ten years ago: energy and moral conviction.

If I could shake the energy of those years loose from the excess and the outrage, I would inject it into the Class of '78 like a dose of vitamins—as a defense, not against apathy, but lethargy.

If I could take the moral conviction and separate it carefully—like an egg yolk—from righteousness and intolerance, I would also feed that as a class dinner to those seniors who don't believe they can make a difference. Who don't even believe there *is* a difference.

I see on campuses a lot of students who, as John Fowles once wrote, "boast of [their] genius for compromise, which is really a refusal to choose." Others congratulate themselves on a realism which is really pessimism.

So, surprisingly, I find myself extracting from the sixties—carefully, with a tweezer—precisely those characteristics which seem lacking in the seventies. If nostalgia is a mental pilgrimage to the past in search of what we miss in the present, I guess I have actually become nostalgic.

JUNE 1978

DEATH IS ALWAYS NEW

The woman was flying home across Megalopolis on one of those planes jammed with VIPs. If it went down, she mused, Congress-members, university presidents and television people would have to compete with each other for space in the obituary columns.

The woman had conquered her worst, white-knuckled fear of flying, but planes were still places where she gave a nod to death, tipped her hat to its possibility. Especially last week. That day.

It had been a week, after all, when death had lost its sense of timing. It had forgotten its place. Ended beginnings. Interrupted middles.

The death of the new pope had seemed somehow as unnatural as the death of passengers on the 727 in San Diego.

She had been struck by the suddenness. In Rome, the beginning and end of Pope John Paul I's papacy had come so close together that they hit each other with the sound of two hands clapping in shock. In San Diego, it had been a matter of inches and the sound of two planes crashing.

But now, she was already surprised by her surprise. She remembered a West African proverb: Death is always new. Is it a conceit that makes us think that death should have a better sense of timing? Or is it a hope?

She thought about how we try to control our fears of both the randomness and inevitability of death. How we build fortresses of ideas, hanging onto safety-strap notions like the Life Cycle, or even Death Preparedness.

Whether we read Shakespeare or Erikson, there is some comfort as well as sadness in the vision of life as a cycle with "guarantees" of seasons and stages. We choose to think that there is some predictable pattern of growth and decline. We look at actuarial tables as if they were personal promises instead of estimates, and feel gypped if someone we love doesn't fill out the timetable.

Perhaps that's why stories of accidents and tales of "premature" deaths—whether of a new pope or of passengers in their prime—fill our newspapers and imaginations. They shock our sense of order and threaten the safety of our plans.

We have forgotten that death is "the great perhaps." We expect it to wait politely until our life cycle, like a novel, is completed.

She wondered sometimes whether the belief in the life cycle wasn't just another one of our bargains with death: Wait until we're ready and we won't mind so much.

She had read lately about people coming to terms with death. Others were advocating courses on death as if it were natural childbirth—something for which everyone could prepare. These people seemed to respond to our profound desire that death not be a shock, but something we can control and something we can accept. Keep in its place.

Yet, how few people there are like Edgar Bergen, who say their goodbyes, round off their lives on stage and then, on cue, leave life. It is, perhaps, as singular a feat as making a career as a ventriloquist on the radio.

She suspected that more people, like John Paul I, die just as they have begun something new—experienced some new possibility, grasped some new and vital insight. And many more, perhaps most of us, die like the people on that 727. En route. In the middle of something, if only the middle of creating and elaborating that unique thing, the self.

Her grandfather used to say that no one wants to live to be 100 until you ask the man who's 99. She thought that almost all of us, in some way, die "prematurely."

Ten thousand precarious feet in the air, somewhere between Washington and Boston, she thought that life is rarely finished. It is, rather, ended. At some point in time, as Edgar Allan Poe once wrote, "The fever called living is conquered at last." And it is always new.

OCTOBER 1978

PART FIVE
RELATIONSHIPS

WOMEN MOURN, MEN REPLACE

It was time for their quarterly checkup, the name they gave to the coast-to-coast talks that had kept their friendship healthy over the past two years.

The two friends regularly went over their charts with each other. They checked off the condition of their vital organs, their kids and jobs, family and mutual friends, and probed their old wounds and fresh scars.

Inevitably, the woman on the East Coast came to the subject of her friend's father. She wanted to know how he was doing since the mother's death last fall. Well, the woman on the West Coast said hesitantly, her father was doing fine. He was, in fact, dating a nice woman and it looked serious.

For a few moments you could hear the pennies clicking through the long-distance line—pennies for one thought or another. They filled in the silence, as people often do when faced with an awkward medical bulletin, with all the right phrases: "As long as he's happy . . . It's good he isn't lonely . . ."

Finally, the woman on the West Coast, who is a poet, said: "It's not that I think it's wrong; it's just that I keep thinking: If it were my mother who was the survivor, she would just about now be getting ready to go to a movie with her sister." There was a pause and she sighed, "Women mourn, men replace."

The woman on the East Coast, who is a journalist, blurted out: "That's a gross generalization." The poet answered: "Yes, but a generalization is generally true."

The poet began to list the cases she had entered into the annals of this syndrome. She had the names and addresses of three ex-husbands who, within the past six months, had gone from one home to another with a speed that would impress the van lines. She knew a dozen men who dealt with women as if they were the essential but interchangeable batteries for their portable life support systems. When one ran down, they went out and got another.

The woman on the East Coast remembered the night last week when she, too, had the same thought. She had been at dinner with a male friend who had just ended a five-year love affair. He had experienced, he told her fervently across the *moo shi* pork, the most horrible two weeks. Now, he would like her to meet his new love, Carolyn.

Women mourn, men replace. A gross generalization. Generally true.

The poet and the journalist wanted to figure out why. The poet suspected that men were more dependent on women. She knew many men who could only keep mold in their refrigerators—who were unable or simply unwilling to take care of themselves. She had an uncle who used to say (this was a family joke) that he'd remarried as soon as he'd run out of clean socks. The poet wondered how often women were just interchangeable need-fillers.

The journalist said stuffily: We are all, to one degree or another, interchangeable. The poet said: Yes, it wasn't that fact that bothered her so much; it was the speed of the exchange. The women she knew went through staged withdrawals, with all sorts of symptoms, and had long resting periods before they felt ready to try again. But not the men.

Well, the journalist was by far the more flat-footed of the two. She took the argument and passed it over to the other hand for a moment. Wasn't it equally possible that "women wallowed, men acted"? Maybe women believed too much in uniqueness. Maybe they romanticized themselves into massive depressions from which they refused to get up until they'd lost 10 pounds.

The poet disagreed. She thought that perhaps men tried to tough it out, while women tried to work it out. Men tended to close the doors behind them, to reject regret, to try to take a shortcut through grief. Women tended to, well, mourn.

To the joy of Ma Bell, the discussion went on and on. The journalist finally got impatient. There was too much in their talk that smacked of the old argument: Women Feel More.

Maybe it wasn't that at all. Maybe women would also take this shortcut if they could. Maybe they would replace, too, if only their fingers didn't freeze at the touch of a telephone dial. If only they were invited for a dinner party because the hostess needed an extra woman.

They both liked that argument.

They didn't believe it for a minute.

In the end, the two diagnosticians ran out of time, money and evidence. They were perhaps jealous of the apparent ease with which some men rebounded and recouped. They were suspicious of it, too. They had trouble deciding whether these men had a healthy reaction or a diseased one. But they knew one thing: they wouldn't want to catch it.

They believed in mourning as a way of paying respect to feelings. They were unable to believe they could find a replacement part that would smooth a rupture. They believed people had to heal themselves.

Well, this was the most expensive checkup they'd ever had. But, as the poet said, unpoetically, "it's cheaper than therapy."

FEBRUARY 1978

RELATIONSHIPS

MATING
BY THE NUMBERS

I have just read about another man who divorced his wife of thirty-odd years in order to marry someone more his own age. In this case, I believe, twenty-two. The May-December marriage bug does seem to be going around these days, with even an occasional April or March thrown in.

Relatively speaking, they make Richard Burton's new mating to a twenty-seven-year-old model seem like a peer pairing.

Am I being nasty? Well, I suspect most women somewhere on the July side of life tend to identify with the leftover, left-out older women—otherwise known as the Ghosts of Christmas Future.

They direct some of the same hostility toward older man–younger woman matings that tall girls previously projected toward the coupling of teeny-weeny cheerleaders and members of the basketball team. It wasn't fair. They were relegating anyone over 5'5" to the wallflower collection and the comforting words of their parents, who assured them that when they grew up (assuming they didn't fling themselves from the balcony of the high-school gym that very evening), they would love being tall.

This was about as helpful as telling the recent December trade-in that she was simply too good, mature, wise and together for old menopausal Marvin. Whether that's true or false, it tends to be depressing. It convinces these women that somehow or other they are overqualified for the relationships market—they are the Ph.D.s at a time when the want ads are full of openings for Charm School graduates.

Masters and Johnson aren't any help either. Their suggestion that, logically, older women should mate with younger men doesn't seem to be catching on. While there are some Mrs. Robinsons around, they don't seem to marry younger males very often. The celebrated age difference between Dinah Shore and Burt Reynolds—may they rest in peace—was fifteen years (August and October, maybe, but not December-May). For every Garson Kanin and Ruth Gordon, you can find ten couples like Justice William O. and Kathleen Douglas.

Those women who have had relationships with younger men don't always seem thrilled with them. As a fifty-four-year-old woman said, "Let me put it this way: He'd never heard of Alger Hiss." Most want to pick someone their own age.

Perhaps the idea of regaining-youth-through-marriage isn't as appealing if that youth was filled with such peak experiences as putting one-year-olds into snowsuits.

Our tendency toward December-May marriages may depend on our attitude toward aging. Some of us would just as soon not, thank you very much. The December husbands are often the sort of older men who tell you to go ahead and punch the old tum-tum and feel how strong their stomach muscles are. They will occasionally challenge their grown sons to arm-wrestling matches.

I have observed some of those men who divorced Wife One, when she got a bit uppity, to marry Wife Two. A decade later, it turns out, Wife Two is also getting a bit uppity. (It does the heart good.) The younger woman who marries someone "old enough to be her father" often finds marriage an equalizing experience. It's hard to think of him as a mentor after watching him walk around in his socks and shorts for a few years.

Having just finished *Passages*, by Gail Sheehy, however, I am feeling more sympathetic to the Decemberites and more convinced about the sense of mating by numbers.

Her book on the adult life cycle offers us the comforting notion that if we truly deal with the crises of life, we should have worked through our problems and be in terrific mental shape in time for the undertaker.

Having survived all the "Switch 30s" and "Catch 40s" that she describes, the idea of going through it all again with a young spouse begins to pale a bit. The fate of the older man may be to have a wife going through a What-am-I-going-to-do-when-I-grow-up crisis while he is preparing for retirement village.

In the end, I will let my uncle (November) have the final word on the subject: "Oh, God, it's not for me. I couldn't hold in my stomach long enough."

AUGUST 1976

A WORLD
OF SURVIVING WOMEN

The woman was seated in a wide semicircle of bridge chairs in the senior citizens' meeting room waiting for the music recital to begin. She was there for her daughter, who had spent three weeks memorizing her piano music and was ready to play in public.

Slowly, the elderly audience walked into the room. There were women helping each other, arm in arm. Women rearranging bridge chairs for each other. Women greeting each other. Women . . . In the group of fifty persons it was easy to count the men as one . . . two . . . three.

Well, of course, she thought. Everyone knew that women outlived men. She tried to wrap herself in the comfortable normalcy of the words "of course." But the truth was that she felt an old reality in a new and stunning way: Middle age was a world ruled by the powerful men, but old age was a world inhabited by its surviving women.

It was as if some mysterious plague was transmitted from one man to the next, passing over their wives and sisters for another seven years. It was considered a matter "of course."

She held this "discovery" out at arm's length and looked at it. How ironical. When the women in the room were born, the life expectancy for them and their husbands, their Charlies and Eddies (may-they-rest-in-peace), was about the same: fifty-four years. They were raised to build their lives around those men they married. But the center didn't hold, and now these elderly women lived alone together.

To this observer, halfway through her own life expectancy, they were suddenly the Ghosts of the Future.

She thought then of her friend and their conversation that day. If a group of archeologists dug into their friendship, they would find thick layers of time and energy, sharing and acceptance. Their friendship had survived earthquakes of mutual disappointment, and volcanic eruptions of anger, and had been rebuilt again with honesty and warmth.

But today, like so many other days, they had spent their telephone time talking about the men in their lives, past and present. They were of an age when women talked more about love than death, and it was, perhaps, their major.

Their sociology was a composite of "he said" and "she said." Their mathematics was a matter of figuring out, "What do I want?" "What can anyone expect?" and how great is the difference between these sums. Their linguistics were in defining trust and commitment. And for business, well, they discussed the advantages and disadvantages of living together versus marriage as if they were discussing condominiums versus houses.

Oh, they also talked about children and parents, work and ideas. But, in truth, they were most fascinated with the subject of men and women. Their relationships with men were subjects to be analyzed. Their relationship with each other was assumed. They were friends. Of course.

But now, in this company, she wondered about their priorities and assumptions.

Well, it was her daughter's turn to play the piano, so she stopped wandering and focused. For a time, the umbilical cord of her own empathy was tied, one nervous stomach to the other. When the girl found her way through the pieces, the women applauded as if it were Carnegie Hall.

But later, after the exchange of pride and pleasure, after the girl was in bed, she went to her shelf to find a story Doris Lessing had written.

This particular tale was about two women whose lives and marriages and families and love affairs had been entwined for decades. Then, in middle age, after the death of one husband, the wife of the other has a clear, almost prophetic vision.

Looking across the familiar room at her friend, she really sees, really knows. "Yes, that is how it would all end, two aging women with their children who would soon have grown up and gone. . . . Their future, hers and Muriel's, was each other. She knew it. But it was neurotic to think like this and she must try to suppress it."

JUNE 1978

RELATIONSHIPS   133

THE EXPRESSION GAP

They had begun talking about literature and ended up talking about men. That in itself wasn't unusual. The women often began talking about energy, or artichokes, or the Middle East, and ended up talking about men. They were, after all, old friends.

This time they were discussing *The Women's Room*. The novel by Marilyn French had appealed to them as a saga, a kind of *War and Peace*—without the peace—which ranged over the past twenty years of women's lives.

It followed one woman from postwar suburbia to Cambridge consciousness-raising to the sort of independence that felt like strength on Monday and loneliness on Tuesday. They had all read it, flinching with recognition along the way, exhausted by the trip, the effort of turning all those pages of experience. They had overdosed on truths.

Though an imperfect book, French had shown the emotional texture of women's lives to be indigestibly rich. Her women were like hollandaise sauce, lush, but always on the verge of curdling. But the men in that "room" had less flavor than Ry-Krisp. There was nothing much to them. They were flat and altogether unpalatable.

So, they ended up talking about men, because, as one said, "Aren't there any men in books with redeeming social value?"

The others chuckled. They were all women who were married or otherwise involved and their men were not Ry-Krisp. One was moussaka, another was beef Wellington, the third was, they all agreed, bouillabaisse.

They were, in short, complicated and nourishing men. While they were more likely to share the ingredients of their emotional recipes with women than with each other, they were definitely not Ry-Krisp. They weren't even steak and potatoes.

So the women tried to think of some books for a parallel male reading list. A Men's Room, perhaps. Where were the men writing about their private lives, the interior landscape, the changes in their experiences over the past ten or twenty years?

Joe Heller? The men in his book, *Something Happened*, had less "redeeming social value" than Marilyn French's. They were automatons in the science-fiction world of corporate life. Their batteries were charged by self-hate. They were nothing but dry martinis.

134   CLOSE TO HOME

Norman Mailer's men once had at least the garlicky aroma of sexual rage. Now, as art imitated life, there was nothing left of them but the pathetic cocktail-party pugilism. A cosmic anger had turned comic.

The menu went on. Saul Bellows's men had been chopped in middle age into mince pies of anxiety. John Updike's confused commuters were barely holding themselves together. They were as solid as crème caramel.

These authors were not writing about men's experience today. Philip Roth, the man who could write brilliantly about being a boy in the forties, had never come of this age. His *Professor of Desire* had received tenure without manhood. He was archaic and even his lust was as dry as a soda biscuit.

While the libraries were filled with books about the changes in women's lives—enough for a room of their own—there was little being written for a Men's Room. Oh, there was a touch of guilt now and then, a *mea culpa* or two. There was Avery Corman's new novel about men and children. But there wasn't an "Eric" Jong, or a "Martin" French, or a "Frank" du Plessix Gray.

One of the women said that it was part of the Expression Gap, something that would only be closed in time. Women's lives had produced an emotional life so rich they'd often choked on it, and eagerly written about it. Men had just gotten a permission slip to that part of the deep interior of their lives.

The women thought about that. When they got together, they started out talking about the Middle East or energy or artichokes and ended up talking about their personal lives. When the men they knew got together—even those who were bouillabaisse and moussaka and beef Wellington—they began talking about the Middle East, and ended talking about the Middle East. There was still that difference. You could read all about it.

DECEMBER 1977

TOO-GREAT EXPECTATIONS

I had just finished another one of those articles about the seventies that made me feel guilty for not being depressed.

It said that depression is to the seventies what anxiety was to the sixties and passivity was to the fifties—the Mood of Our Time. It even quietly suggested that anyone who wasn't depressed was probably shallow, insensitive, and maybe even a touch stupid.

With that thought in mind, I called up my friendly neighborhood touchstone on these matters and asked her if she thought that everyone was really all that depressed.

"Not everyone," she yelled in her abrupt fashion into one of those horrible little telephone boxes on her desk. "Just the men."

Well, I started ambling down the list of people I know—this was not a scientific poll, you understand—and it seemed to me that she was more or less right. While the women I know seem energized and even a touch manic, depression is running through the male half of the species like an Andromeda strain.

An outrageous number of men, especially in the over-thirty-five age group, seem to live with a sense that somehow or other they haven't measured up. It doesn't actually matter what they are doing. The general sense of a failed being comes from their internal measuring rod. It has more to do with expectations than achievement.

"All the men I know were raised to be President of the United States, while all the women I know were raised to be their mothers," bellowed my friend into her machine. "If you're a woman doing more than your mother did, you feel successful. If you're a man and you're not President, you feel like a failure."

While that is a bit simplistic, it does seem that a vast number of men were raised by books with nagging titles like *Why Not the Best?* They often spend their adult lives convinced that they are second best. Women, on the other hand, often had such low ceilings on their hopes, that they feel enormously proud if they get out of the basement. It's all, as they say, a matter of relativity.

I have two friends, for example, who are both writers in their late thirties. They have the same number of book titles, the same degree of fame, the same incomes. She thinks that what she has accomplished is terrific. He thinks that what he has done is barely sufficient.

"He compares himself to someone who wins the Pulitzer Prize," she explains. "I always thought that if I could be married, have two children and just have a job, any job—writing obituaries for a small-town weekly—it would be a big thing."

The truth is that she considers herself an overachiever and is, at times, excited about it. He considers himself an underachiever and is, at times, depressed about it.

A teaching couple I know suffer the same syndrome. She is tickled to have tenure, while he flagellates himself regularly for not having written the Definitive Work.

I have the sense that a lot of men were set up for disappointment. So few could "measure up," so many were given the chance to "fall short." It reminds me of a bumper sticker I once saw: Life Is a Failure Opportunity.

I don't think this mass case of depression is part of a sexual seesaw—as women move up in the world, men feel relatively lower— although there may be some of that. Men are still suffering from expectations that were not only too high but too narrow. On the other hand, women at this moment in history have suddenly outreached their childhood. But they have widened their definition of success, rather than transferring it. To the women in this transitional time, success is graded on a point system that counts personal as well as professional values.

Of course, it's possible that women are just a generation or two behind men. It's possible that as girls are raised to go for the top, a few will reach the Senate Chamber and the rest will reach a midlife downer.

But it would be nice if, for once, women were the role models. The alternative is, after all, rather depressing.

SEPTEMBER 1977

LOVE WITHOUT STAYING POWER

I grew up on movies like *Sabrina* and *Gigi* and assorted other fifties flicks that all faded out with a man and woman walking hand in hand into the sunset. So it took me a while to see the handwriting on the wall, or should I say, the new message on the screen.

In fact, it took me until this summer to realize that virtually every love story of the seventies seems to have a built-in terminal disease of one kind or another. It isn't just Erich Segal's problem; it's an epidemic.

I remember when movies used to end at the beginning. There'd be this rousing chorus of "Here Comes the Bride," a meaningful kiss and "The End." There was never the slightest hint that there might be a ring around the collar of their future.

Now they all seem to end with an ending. It's gotten so that what passes for a happy ending is a no-fault divorce.

The only scene in all those *Scenes from a Marriage* that showed Marianne and Johann treating each other like caring adults was the one that came long after their divorce. *The Way We Were* was one of the first movies that showed the way we are—out of "forevers." Barbra Streisand and Robert Redford found out that love didn't conquer all. It didn't even conquer politics.

Since those movies, we've done a slow two-step all the way into the Modern Romance: the love-mating-dismantling scenario by which art is imitating life on a big-screen scale. There aren't any love stories about permanence anymore. There are mostly sugar-coated serials.

The two romance movies of the summer—*New York, New York* and *Annie Hall*—both give you a picture of the state of romance: weak in the nerves, flabby around the pectoral, without any staying power. They are movies about the people who survive romance, rather than romances that survive.

In *New York, New York* Robert De Niro and Liza Minelli play the lovers whose relationship makes Dorothy Thompson and Sinclair Lewis look like a mental-health-poster couple. *Annie Hall*'s romance goes on between Woody Allen and Diane Keaton, whom I think of as the Lame and the Halt entries in an emotional handicap tournament. In both flicks, boy meets girl and they fall in love. So far, so good. At this point the curtain is supposed to fall while the music swells to the tune of "Love Will Keep Us Together." Only they don't play it that way anymore, Sam.

The mismatched romances of the seventies seem as inevitable as the star-kissed ones of the fifties. In the old myth movies, you knew the moment the camera panned from Doris Day to Rock Hudson that they would end up married. In the seventies, when one basket case meets another, you figure it will never work out.

The fact is that the romance in which permanence was the ideal has been replaced by the romance in which impermanence is the central reality. In the Woody Allen flick, he flash-backed to enough disastrous matings to make you throw in the towel, or at least the ticket. But in a sense, these new "real" love stories are about the endurance of the romantic spirit confronted with all those "irreconcilable differences." In the face of all the endings in town, no one seems to close the final curtain. The survival of the romantic impulse may be the victory of hope over experience, but there's something remarkable about it in as hopeless a "realist" as, say, Woody Allen.

For that reason he deserves the last word on the subject. At the end of *Annie Hall*, Allen repeats a joke about the man who tells a psychiatrist that "my brother thinks he's a chicken." "Why don't you commit him?" asks the psychiatrist. And the brother answers, "Because I need the eggs."

Allen sees that as the perfect analogy. Why do the romantic realists keep up this long-running serial of beginnings of endings? Well, that survivor says it's because "we need the eggs."

Here's to the future of eggs.

AUGUST 1977

THE TAPESTRY
OF FRIENDSHIPS

It was, in many ways, a slight movie. Nothing actually happened. There was no big-budget chase scene, no bloody shoot-out. The story ended without any cosmic conclusions.

Yet she found Claudia Weill's film *Girlfriends* gentle and affecting. Slowly, it panned across the tapestry of friendship—showing its fragility, its resiliency, its role as the connecting tissue between the lives of two young women.

When it was over, she thought about the movies she'd seen this year—*Julia, The Turning Point* and now *Girlfriends*. It seemed that the peculiar eye, the social lens of the cinema, had drastically shifted its focus. Suddenly the Male Buddy movies had been replaced by the Female Friendship flicks.

This wasn't just another binge of trendiness, but a kind of *cinéma vérité*. For once the movies were reflecting a shift, not just from men to women but from one definition of friendship to another.

Across millions of miles of celluloid, the ideal of friendship had always been male—a world of sidekicks and "pardners," of Butch Cassidys and Sundance Kids. There had been something almost atavistic about these visions of attachments—as if producers culled their plots from some pop anthropology book on male bonding. Movies portrayed the idea that only men, those direct descendants of hunters and Hemingways, inherited a primal capacity for friendship. In contrast, they portrayed women picking on each other, the way they once picked berries.

Well, that duality must have been mortally wounded in some shootout at the You're OK, I'm OK Corral. Now, on the screen, they were at least aware of the subtle distinction between men and women as buddies and friends.

About 150 years ago, Coleridge had written, "A woman's friendship borders more closely on love than man's. Men affect each other in the reflection of noble or friendly acts, whilst women ask fewer proofs and more signs and expressions of attachment."

Well, she thought, on the whole, men had buddies, while women had friends. Buddies bonded, but friends loved. Buddies faced adversity together, but friends faced each other. There was something palpably different in the way they spent their time. Buddies seemed to "do" things together; friends simply "were" together.

Buddies came linked, like accessories, to one activity or another. People have golf buddies and business buddies, college buddies and club buddies. Men often keep their buddies in these categories, while women keep a special category for friends.

A man once told her that men weren't real buddies until they'd been "through the wars" together—corporate or athletic or military. They had to soldier together, he said. Women, on the other hand, didn't count themselves as friends until they'd shared three loathsome confidences.

Buddies hang tough together; friends hang onto each other.

It probably had something to do with pride. You don't show off to a friend; you show need. Buddies try to keep the worst from each other; friends confess it.

A friend of hers once telephoned her lover, just to find out if he were home. She hung up without a hello when he picked up the phone. Later, wretched with embarrassment, the friend moaned, "Can you believe me? A thirty-five-year-old lawyer, making a chicken call?" Together they laughed and made it better.

Buddies seek approval. But friends seek acceptance.

She knew so many men who had been trained in restraint, afraid of each other's judgment or awkward with each other's affection. She wasn't sure which. Like buddies in the movies, they would die for each other, but never hug each other.

She'd reread *Babbitt* recently, that extraordinary catalogue of male grievances. The only relationship that gave meaning to the claustrophobic life of George Babbitt had been with Paul Riesling. But not once in the tragedy of their lives had one been able to say to the other: You make a difference.

Even now men shocked her at times with their description of friendship. Does this one have a best friend? "Why, of course, we see each other every February." Does that one call his most intimate pal long distance? "Why, certainly, whenever there's a real reason." Do those two old chums ever have dinner together? "You mean alone? Without our wives?"

Yet, things were changing. The ideal of intimacy wasn't this parallel playmate, this teammate, this trenchmate. Not even in Hollywood. In the double standard of friendship, for once the female version was becoming accepted as the general ideal.

After all, a buddy is a fine life-companion. But one's friends, as Santayana once wrote, "are that part of the race with which one can be human."

NOVEMBER 1978

THE JUST-RIGHT WIFE

The upper-middle-class men of Arabia are looking for just the right kind of wife. Arabia's merchant class, reports the Associated Press, finds the women of Libya too backward, and the women of Lebanon too forward, and have therefore gone shopping for brides in Egypt.

Egyptian women are being married off at the rate of thirty a day—an astonishing increase, according to the Egyptian marriage bureau. It doesn't know whether to be pleased or alarmed at the popularity of its women. According to one recent Saudi Arabian groom, the Egyptian women are "just right."

"The Egyptian woman is the happy medium," says Aly Abdul el-Korrary of his bride, Wafaa Ibrahiv (the happy medium herself was not questioned). "She is not too inhibited as they are in conservative Moslem societies, and not too liberal like many Lebanese."

Is this beginning to sound familiar? Well, the upper-middle-class, middle-aged, merchant-professional-class man of America also wants a "happy medium" wife. He is confused. He, too, has a problem and he would like us to be more understanding.

If it is no longer chic for a sheik to marry a veiled woman, it is somehow no longer "modern" for a successful member of the liberal establishment to be married to what he used to call a "housewife" and what he now hears called a "household drudge."

As his father once wanted a wife who had at least started college, now he would like a wife who has a mind, and even a job, of her own. The younger men in his office these days wear their wives' occupations on their sleeves. He thinks he, too, would like a wife—especially for social occasions—whose status would be his status symbol. A lady lawyer would be nice.

These men, you understand, now say (at least in private to younger working women in their office) that they are bored with women who "don't do anything." No matter how much some of them conspired in keeping them at home Back Then, many are now saying, in the best Moslem style, "I divorce thee." They are replacing them with more up-to-date models. A Ph.D. candidate would be nice.

The upper-middle-class, middle-aged man of today wants a wife who won't make him feel guilty. He doesn't want to worry if she's happy. He doesn't want to hear her complain about her dusty American history degree. He doesn't want to know if she's crying at the psychiatrist's office. He most definitely doesn't want to be blamed. He wants her to fulfill herself already! He doesn't mean that maliciously.

On the other hand, Lord knows, he doesn't want a wife who is too forward. The Saudi Arabian merchant believes that the Egyptian woman adapts more easily to his moods and needs. The American merchant also wants a woman who adapts herself to his moods and needs—his need for an independent woman and a traditional wife.

He doesn't want to live with a "household drudge," but it would be nice to have an orderly home and well-scrubbed children. Certainly he wouldn't want a wife who got high on folding socks—he is not a Neanderthal—but it would be nice if she arranged for these things to get done. Without talking about marriage contracts.

He wants a wife who agrees that "marriage is a matter of give and take, not a business deal and 50-50 chores." It would help if she had just enough conflict herself (for not being her mother) to feel more than half the guilt for a full ashtray.

Of course, he sincerely would like her to be involved in her own work and life. But on the other hand, he doesn't want it to siphon away her energy for him. He needs to be taken care of, nurtured. He would like her to enjoy her job, but be ready to move for his, if necessary (after, of course, a long discussion in which he feels awful about asking and she ends up comforting him and packing).

He wants a wife who is a sexually responsive and satisfied woman, and he would even be pleased if she initiated sex with him. Sometimes. Not too often, however, because then he would get anxious.

He is confused, but he does, in all sincerity (status symbols aside), want a happy marriage to a happy wife. A happy medium. He is not sure exactly what he means, but he, too, would like a wife who is "just right."

The difference is that when the upper-middle-class, middle-aged man of Arabia wants this wife he goes out and buys one. His American "brother" can only offer himself as the prize.

JULY 1976

OF TRISCUITS,
BREMNER WAFERS AND DAILYNESS

The guest arrived early and found them bickering about the garbage. The wife wanted the garbage pail emptied before the company came. The husband thought that was ridiculous. It would only be filled up again later.

The husband walked into the living room and began putting the magazines into matching piles on the coffee table. He saw that, once again, his wife had ripped something out of *New Times* before he'd read it.

He snapped at her and then went back into the kitchen to put the Triscuits on the plate with the cheese. She said that Triscuits were tacky and replaced them with Bremner Wafers. He said that Bremner Wafers tasted like paste.

The guest, an old friend, quietly took the ice cubes out of the tray, put them in the ice bucket and listened. It was pre-party tension, of course. They ought to have a pill for it, she thought. Yet, these two had never quarreled quite the same way before they were married. Their battles now carried the sounds of attrition. There was an install-ment-plan sameness to it, a familiar irritation. The irritation of famil-iarity.

They used to argue, but about politics or "commitment" or work. She remembered the night they almost came to blows about slavery. The question was whether or not they would have been like the white slaveholders if they had grown up there and then.

The man said, yes, probably, they would have been that bad. Institutions, he thought, had the effect of molding people. The woman was livid—*no!*—she insisted that people were in control of their lives, not institutions. They had argued about Good Germans and Soviet Dissidents, about South Africa and free will and structures.

Now they argued about garbage bags and Bremner Wafers. It made the guest wonder. Was marriage another institution that formed the relationship, molded the people? Was dailyness a debilitating dis-ease?

The husband poured himself another drink. The wife counted. The guest watched the cataloguing of irritations, and questioned whether the list of little "issues" always grew longer and finally overwhelmed the big issues, even love.

She'd seen it happen before: A wife stacked the records on the stereo. A husband whistled when he was getting dressed. She used his razor blade for her legs. He hogged the bathroom. She always let the gas tank run out. He never remembered the club soda.

She could not watch an otherwise sane person sitting in front of a football game for two whole hours. He could not listen as she spent $4.65 talking long distance to someone who was "just a friend." He poured his coffee, let it sit until it was cold and then threw it away. She put her cigarette out in the dessert plate.

The guest hated to think that marriage always came down to garbage pails and Bremner Wafers. She was single. Aside from the newly divorced who only want to see marital disasters around them (to lower their own sense of failure), most single people want to believe that marriage can be joyful. If only to keep their options open.

But often that joy was strained through the hassle of weekday living. There were all these expectations. Familiarity kept breeding generations of disappointments and annoyances. Marriages often turned into courtroom dramas of unmet responsibilities. She forgot the inspection sticker. He forgot the coffee beans. He left his toenail cuttings on the side of the sink. She left the hairdryer in the only bedroom plug.

The guest poured herself a glass of wine. Finally the rest of the company came. They spread cheese on the Bremner Wafers. The wife went out with the empty cracker plate and filled it up again—this time with Triscuits. The garbage rose to the top of the pail. The husband went outside to empty it.

Over coffee, the husband, expansive and funny, described Philip Roth's new book as the last gasp from a dying culture. His wife, liking him, spread approval across the table, and her bare feet found his, under it. As he poured brandy, she told the story of their disastrous attempt at city farming—the end result was one $15 tomato—and he laughed and put his hands on her hair.

The guest thought: It's okay. Their affection had bobbed back up again through the surface of irritations. They had beaten back the dulling routines once more. The familiar fondness had won over the familiar annoyance.

Tomorrow there would be more Bremner Wafers and garbage pails to conquer. For now, they were okay.

OCTOBER 1977

RELATIONSHIPS

SINKING THE RELATIONSHIP

There was this kid in my grammar school, the kind of kid who only got valentines from those of us whose mothers made us send them to everyone. Even then, he would only get the ones that were 25 cards for 25 cents.

I mean, it was sad. But to tell you the truth, Willie was a real wonk.

Last week I ran into Willie the Wonk at the five and ten. It turns out that since we'd last met, Willie had gotten a Ph.D. and married, and then settled down and gotten divorced. Now, he was, and I quote, "relating to a woman in Providence." Together they were "really into exploring intimate relationships."

Now let me tell you, I covered my mouth lest anything untoward spill out. At that moment I regretted sending him even the crummy valentine that had come on the perforated cardboard saying, "Gee, you're swell."

But, as they say, everything has its sunny side. Meeting Willie finally pushed me into making public my radical Valentine's Day proposal for 1977. Which is, ladies and gentlemen, boys and girls, sons and lovers, to renounce "relationships." In word, though not in deed.

I hereby propose striking out meaningful relationships (gag), intimate relationships (bleh), and working relationships (ugh).

Once upon a time, the only Relation Ship was a boat that carried the family over from the old country. Those were the days when only New Yorkers and battered wives got divorced. The rich may have had relationships, but they called them affairs. The only affairs Willie's forebears attended were the kind where they fought over who would take the centerpiece home.

Now, as I recall, somewhere along in the sixties, international relations became too grim and we all turned to our personal lives. Which we instantly turned equally grim. At that moment, the word "relationship" was born.

A relationship, unlike a love affair, is something which is carefully negotiated to be "self-actualizing" and "growth-oriented" and "nonbinding." It is written along the lines of the model approved by the National Mental Health Association. It is then signed by two consenting adults who are too embarrassed to tell their friends that they've fallen in love.

In truth, one never falls into a relationship. One is too mature, healthy, sensible and dreary for that. Rather, one enters a relationship as if it were a law firm.

"Relationship" is a cool, McLuhan-ish word. After all, one can relate to almost anything—a food processor, a book, even Willie. The word has always sounded more mathematical than poetic. Try as they might, few poets could ever work with: "How do I relate to thee, let me count the ways," or "Come live with me and be my relationship."

It is even harder to write a relationship song: "Relationship is a many-splendored thing." "I relate to you a bushel and a peck."

It just won't sell. The term is too measured, calibrated, passionless. It is hard to send flowers to a relationship.

As for Working Relationships, well, that has always reminded me of a mom-and-pop store of the feelings. Meaningful Relationships make me think of the English professor who had us read *Hamlet* and count the water images. And Intimate Relationship sounds like something you'd only have with a bathing-suit saleslady.

It is time that we bid farewell and jump this particular ship. I hereby take the pledge. Up with love, down with relationships. Even Willie the Wonk deserves better than that.

FEBRUARY 1977

Part Six

Six

Family

FAMILY:
THE ONE SOCIAL GLUE

They are going home for Thanksgiving, traveling through the clogged arteries of airports and highways, bearing bridge chairs and serving plates, Port-a-Cribs and pies. They are going home to rooms that resound with old arguments and interruptions, to piano benches filled with small cousins, to dining-room tables stretched out to the last leaf.

They no longer migrate over the river and through the woods straight into that Norman Rockwell poster: Freedom from Want. No, Thanksgiving isn't just a feast, but a reunion. It's no longer a celebration of food (which is plentiful in America) but of family (which is scarce).

Now families are so dispersed that it's easier to bring in the crops than the cousins. Now it's not so remarkable that we have a turkey to feed the family. It's more remarkable that there's enough family around to warrant a turkey.

For most of the year, we are a nation of individuals, all wrapped in separate cellophane packages like lamb chops in the meat department of a city supermarket. Increasingly we live with decreasing numbers. We create a new category like Single Householder, and fill it to the top of the Census Bureau reports.

For most of the year, we are segregated along generation lines into retirement villages and singles complexes, young married subdivisions and college dormitories, all exclusive clubs whose membership is defined by age.

Even when we don't live in age ghettos, we often think that way. Those who worried about a generation gap in the sixties worry about a generation war in the seventies. They see a community torn by warring rights: the Elderly Rights vs. the Middle-Aged Rights vs. the Children Rights. All competing for a piece of the pie.

This year, the Elderly Rights fought against mandatory retirement while the Younger Rights fought for job openings. The Children Rights worried about the money to keep their schools open, while the Elderly Rights worried about the rising cost of real estate taxes.

The retired generation lobbied for an increase in Social Security payments, while the working generation lobbied for a decrease in Social Security taxes. The elderly wanted health care and the children wanted day care and the middle-aged were tired of taking care. They wanted the right to lead their own lives.

At times it seemed as if the nation had splintered into peer pressure groups, panthers of all ages. People who cried, not "Me First" but, rather, "My Generation First."

But now they have come home for Thanksgiving. Even the Rights are a family who come together, not to fight for their piece of the pie this day, but to share it.

The family—as extended as that dining-room table—may be the one social glue strong enough to withstand the centrifuge of special interests which send us spinning away from each other. There, in the family, the Elderly Rights are also grandparents and the Children Rights are also nieces and nephews. There, the old are our parents and the young are our children. There, we care about each others' lives. There, self-interest includes concern for the future of the next generation. Because they are ours.

Our families are not just the people (if I may massacre Robert Frost) who, "when you have to go there, they have to let you in." They are the people who maintain an unreasonable interest in each other. They are the natural peacemakers in the generation war.

"Home" is the only place in society where we now connect along the ages, like discs along the spine of society. The only place where we remember that we're all related. And that's not a bad idea to go home to.

NOVEMBER 1977

YOU CAN
GO HOME AGAIN

The car was packed to the roof with their luggage, their baby stroller, their diaper bag and all the other goodies sold as optional equipment with each new child. The husband had wrapped his son like a sausage into a swaddling of a snowsuit and put him, too, into the back seat.

The couple was headed home for the holidays. This time I was driving them to the airport, that first way-station on their annual migration. They carried with them the proof of belonging to the family on the other side of the air route: The husband bore his wedding band, the wife her freckles; the boy wore his red hair, which had been officially declared "exactly like" that of his grandfather.

Soon the wife's family would be together, all in the same area code. For once, no one would be directly dialed. For once they would be person to person . . . in person.

The roadway to the airport was already jammed. Day by day it was building to the peak load, the crescendo of traveling horrors, Thanksgiving Eve. That night the most penny-pinching soul damned the torpedoes and full-fared ahead. Home for the holidays.

It was good to be going home, the wife said to her husband as he struggled with the small boy trying to liberate his baby feet from the snuggy. He agreed.

He remembered something from one of the obituaries written last week about Margaret Mead. Being a citizen of the world, she said, meant being at home in many places. Holding his baby, he wondered about that. How many of us actually do feel at home in many places? How many more of us simply feel strange away from home?

The couple had spent their childhoods in other area codes—503 and 312—and in other environments. Each was a transplant, a cutting from a family tree, or at least a family plant. When they were young, everyone had simply expected that they would put down their roots wherever there was "the best opportunity." Now, sometimes, the wife remarked that the most transportable plant—the Wandering Jew— wasn't named for a willing immigrant but for a historic exile.

It wasn't the first time I had driven friends to the planes or trains or buses that took them away to their families. Many of my friends need a holiday to go home; many accept the idea that long distance is the next best thing to being there. And don't think much about what's best.

My family on the other hand, has always been there. Through luck and choice, we share not only an area code but a zip code. Together we own eight bridge chairs, one thirty-cup percolator and a single electric drill. We play musical children and cars. Like some collective, with more enthusiasm than skill we trade: knitting lessons for disco lessons, nursing for gardening, carpentry for listening, day care for storytelling.

We complain to each other and about each other. We have helped each other sometimes and other times wrestled with our inability to help. We have been the keepers of our continuity. The people we can tell the truth about our children.

"Any marriage," W. H. Auden once wrote, "is infinitely more interesting and significant than any romance, however passionate." Well, I was never sure of that. But I have always thought that any family—with its history and its soap-opera intensity—was more interesting than any other collection of people.

So I suppose my own experience has made me question the notion that it is normal to leave home and vaguely suspect to stay. We are regarded as either "strong enough" to make it on our own or "not daring" enough to take the risk.

Our nation was founded by leavers; we are the grandchildren of leavers. We are a people who peculiarly regard self-fulfillment as an independent activity and who look upon our family lives as exercises in self-denial.

If we were playing a national game of word association, how many of us would identify the word "personal" with "growth," and "family" with "obligations"? It seems that we continually jettison our support systems to avoid obligations and lose our context in the pursuit of a "better life."

"Each society," wrote Dr. Mead, "has taken a special emphasis and given it a full and integrated expression at the expense of other potentialities of the human race." We have taken the "I" over the "we"; potential over history.

My passengers were upwardly mobile, with emphasis on the mobile. They had left home for better schools in area code 415 and then for jobs in 202 and 212. Now they lived in 617 and had parents who touch-dialed their grandchildren. They were "at home" only on holidays. And wondered what they had gained and what they had lost.

But today, as the car finally pulled up to the entrance, the couple tumbled out grasping strollers and sausage, carrying with them an air of vacationers. They were people for whom family was not a routine but an occasional pleasure-seeking trip. So they went home excited. And I went home . . . thankful.

NOVEMBER 1978

THE ILLUSION
OF PERMANENCE

The child was being supremely patient—rather as if she were talking to someone who'd been brain damaged. She explained the situation all over again.

She had a friend who lived during the week with her mother and stepfather and half-brother. On some weekends, the stepfather's son visited with them, too, although he really lived with his mother and stepfather. On weekends, this friend went to visit with her father and stepmother, and the two children by her stepmother's first marriage. Of course, sometimes the stepbrothers weren't there because they were visiting their father and his wife and their children.

The child recited this as if it were her school schedule. Nothing unusual. The girl had long ago accepted the idea that, in many families, time is partitioned on a calendar, and children are borrowed and returned on schedule like library books. In her experience, families were often stretched out in long chains of step-parents and half-siblings—chains forged out of broken and rewelded marriage bonds. That was the way things were.

It was the mother who had difficulty coping with all this. She'd grown up with the notion that the biological family was fixed. Permanently. Now, the continual splitting and reforming of "nuclear families" reminded her of movies of bacteria, microscopic social diseases.

It wasn't that the woman couldn't see the handwriting on the divorce agreements. Or on the marriage contracts. She knew any number of people who had a former husband or wife in common. She'd once been to a party where half the guests were intimately connected by a divorce lawyer. But it still sounded so Hollywood to her. It sounded so Richard Burton–Elizabeth Taylor–Eddie Fisher–Debbie Reynolds.

She'd heard recently that the last of the couples from the novel *Couples* had split. The author himself, John Updike, was preparing to remarry Martha Bernhard who was once married to Alex Bernhard who was now married to Joyce Harrington who was once married to Herbert Harrington who was the only butcher the Harvard Class of '51 had produced.

At this marital news, all of her computer lights—which had

been programmed in another decade—flashed, "Disruption! Disintegration! The Breakdown of Society!"

You see, the woman was still uneasy with the redistribution of husbands and wives. She wanted to be able to tell the marriage without a scorecard. She was uncomfortable with the continual resettlement of children as if they were refugees. They all seemed to have mismatched names and addresses.

But, on the whole, the children accepted it. She overheard snatches of conversations that startled her: "Are your parents still married?" "After I get married and divorced . . ." It seemed that for every one of the children whose family was tangibly, irrevocably "destroyed," there was another whose family had been extended, in steps, or step-parents.

Was this worse? Most of her own generation had lived in tight "forever" structures, in some ways unable to cope with change as adults. They were now often terminally inflexible. Would the kids who were growing up with a sense of flux be more flexible? Or would they be unable to cope with permanence?

The woman didn't know. She had a gut feeling that every generation of children is brought up to accept the world in which their parents lived. They are emotionally equipped to fight the last war. But perhaps they are equally unprepared for the unknown: their own adulthood.

Thinking about it gave her a headache, especially since she was listening carefully again. The child continued, slowly, patronizingly. She had another friend who lived with her father and her stepmother who has a child by an ex-husband who is married to a woman who . . . Who probably once believed in permanence.

SEPTEMBER 1977

THE NEW
FAMILY CONTRACT

There has always been a deal, a kind of bargain struck between the generations. Traditionally the social contract between parents and children stated simply, "We'll take care of you while you're young, and you take care of us when we're old."

But now, they say the deal's off. The poll-takers and observers suggest that we're in for a shaky renegotiation of the family business. Daniel Yankelovich described the changes this way: "There's a new unwritten but implied contract that says parents have a right to their lives, but in exchange, children don't owe them anything."

The vision he and others project is of uncaring digits in a family "unit"—disconnected members of what used to be a whole.

In a survey among the 23 million American families with kids under thirteen, Yankelovich noticed a trend among parents away from self-sacrifice to what he calls a "new preoccupation with self-fulfillment." A full 66 percent of the parents agreed that they should have lives of their own despite the demands of children, and almost the same number (67 percent) felt that children have no obligation regardless of what parents have done for them.

The seeming sterility of this picture pushes our Death of the Family Button. We react with nostalgic comparisons to the families of yesteryear. And yet, I wonder. We do have a crisis mentality that sees the moment and not the process. But why should we assume that the dissolution of a binding contract means the end of all strong family ties?

This is a country founded primarily by people who left their families behind. There's always been a tension here between the individual and the family, independence and dependence, as well as between self-sacrifice and self-fulfillment.

The parents of young children—people in their twenties and thirties—wouldn't be motivated to forge a new deal if they'd been satisfied with the old one. Many grew up with a mixture of gratitude, guilt and resentment for the "self-sacrifice" of their own mothers and fathers. Some discovered that even martyrdom exacts a price—including often the expectation that children fulfill the lives of the self-sacrificing parent. Perhaps this was a legacy they didn't want to pass on.

Originally that contract had been based on economics. In the Good Old Days, parents gave birth to cheap labor and old-age security plans. They were never thrilled to become dependent on their children —children who were more often dutiful than delighted about supporting parents—but they had little choice in the matter.

The social policies of the past half-century—from Social Security to pension plans to Medicare—were designed to give them that choice. They supported the self-reliance of the elderly and the economic independence of the generations. But out of these changes evolved a new attitude toward parenting. Kids are no longer an economic necessity. Instead, they are often regarded as an economic liability. Every year someone else seems to put a price tag on them. Last month it was Thomas Espenshade, an economics professor at Florida State University. He pegged the cost of raising a child in a middle-income family at $64,000.

Perhaps the people who look at life as a series of sound economic investments will not choose to become parents. Is that a loss? Does that spell the end of the parent-child relationship?

There are always some who believe only in the strength of the ties that bind them. The family handcuffs—economic necessity, even psychological guilt trips—are dropping away. They leave behind primarily the ties that connect us by choice and with affection. The professor who made that $64,000 estimate also talked with parents about the positive values of raising children. They listed their profits in three categories: happiness, love and companionship; personal development; child-rearing satisfactions.

In a sense, the new contract asks more of family members, not less. It suggests a family held together, not in a spirit of self-sacrifice, but of self-fulfillment; a unit held together by emotional investments, not economic ones.

We have always claimed that love was the glue of the American family. Now we are beginning to test its sticking power.

MAY 1977

THE FAMILY/CAREER PRIORITY PROBLEM

One day last week Ed Koch left his Greenwich Village apartment to take the M-6 bus downtown. About the same time he was being sworn in as mayor of New York City, my friend Carol was turning down a job as a top executive of a New York corporation.

On the surface, these two events seem to be totally unrelated, except for the fact that they took place in the same city. But I don't think they are. You see, Ed Koch is a bachelor, and my friend Carol is married and a parent, and there's a difference.

No, this isn't a story that ends with a one-line complaint from Carol: "If it hadn't been for you, I would have been a star." (Or a mayor, for that matter.) Nor is it a story of discrimination. Her husband didn't put his foot down. Her parents didn't form a circle around her shouting, "*Bad* mother, *bad!*" until she capitulated.

Carol chose. She wanted the promotion so much she could taste it. But the job came with weekends and evenings and traveling attached, and she didn't want to miss that time with her husband and sons. She couldn't do both. Knowing that didn't make it any easier.

Carol isn't the only one I know making these decisions. Another friend refused to move up a rung on the professional ladder because it would have meant uprooting his family and transferring his wife out of a career of her own. A third couple consciously put their careers on the back burner in order to spend time with the family they'd merged out of two previous marriages.

These were not bitter choices, but tough ones. As Carol said, it isn't possible to give overtime at work and decent time at home.

Once it was normal for a man to devote his energy entirely to his work, while his family was taken care of by his wife. Once men led the public lives and women the private lives. Now that gap is closing, and another one is growing between family people and single people. Everywhere it seems that men and women who care the most about their private lives are living them that way, while the single people have become the new upwardly mobile.

In Washington you can see the difference. There, a twenty-eight-year-old bachelor such as White House aide David Rubinstein works more than sixteen hours a day and eats vending-machine meals, while a guy like Representative Lloyd Meeds (D–Washington) decides not to take his family through another congressional election fight, and drops out. There, despite the attempts of the Carters to encourage family time, the government still runs on excess. As one observer puts it, the only way to get the work done is to be single or to have a lousy marriage.

In New York the successful politicians (aside from Koch) now include Carol Bellamy, the single head of the city council, and Andrew Stein, the divorced borough president. The governor is a widower, the lieutenant governor is legally separated.

All around us the prototypical workaholics are single, with Ralph Nader leading the Eastern division, and Jerry Brown bringing up the West. And in the U.S. Senate last year there were enough divorces to justify legal insurance.

I don't think that this is something "movements" or legislation can solve. I am reminded of the moment in the movie *The Turning Point* when Anne Bancroft and Shirley MacLaine realize that they both wanted it all. These two women hadn't chosen in their lives between work and family in the classic sense, but between workaholism and family: between the sort of success that demands single-minded devotion to a goal and the sort of "balanced" life that includes family and work, but precludes overachieving. In the end the star was a bachelor.

The decisions they faced are the rock-bottom ones, the toughies. How do you divide the pie of your life—your own time and energy?

Today, the cast of characters is changing. It isn't only men in high-powered work lives and women at home. But the choices have remained the same. There seems to be an inherent contradiction between the commitment to become number one, the best, the first, and the commitment to a rich family life. A contradiction between family-first people and work-first people.

The irony is that we need decisionmakers who care and understand about children and private lives. And I wonder how we will find them if the room at the top becomes a bachelor pad.

JANUARY 1978

STAY TUNED FOR
THE NEXT GENERATION

A long time ago it occurred to me that soap operas were popular, not because they spiced up the humdrum everyday life of the people, but because they reflected that life. They were realer than real. The Average American Family looks a lot more like *As the World Turns* than like the Brady Bunch.

Family life is the one melodrama in which nearly everyone participates. Will Aunt Sarah ever forgive Cousin Susy? Will Charley's boy stop breaking his mother's heart? Will Lillian stop drinking and Sam stop chasing? And what about Naomi?

This is the stuff that keeps members of a family connected to each other by an intricate shared history and an umbilical cord known as the telephone.

The only thing as grabbing as the drama of one's own family is that of other families. This is true whether they are famous like the Roosevelts, fictional like the Bellamys or "average" like the six American families currently being profiled on television.

The story of the Haywards is such a soap opera. Brooke Hayward's best-seller about her family is appealing even to those who never heard of her father, agent-producer Leland Hayward, and never saw her mother, actress Margaret Sullavan.

Her book, *Haywire*, plays the favorite family game: What went wrong? The author and eldest child tries to unravel mysteries worthy of Procter & Gamble: Why did her parents get divorced? Why did her mother commit suicide? How did her sister die? Why had her brother been in a mental institution? Why did that perfect family pictured on the book jacket shatter so totally?

Above all, she tries to deal with the relationship of parents and children as cause and effect.

There's much that's moving in this family book. Her father is portrayed vividly, a man legendary for his personal energy and for his attachment to the telephone. Her mother is larger-than-life, an actress obsessed with being a mother, one who created a stage setting of her home and a leading role out of a relationship.

Despite the title, this is not the story of a star-kissed family that crashed suddenly. It seems clear, rather, that nothing "went" haywire. It was haywire from the beginning.

Yet there is something unsettling about this family-ography, and I think it is the author. She wrote the book in order to understand. Immersed in her parents' lives was the story of her childhood, the roots of her own life. But I wonder about a forty-two-year-old woman (with three children and two ex-husbands) who is still so obsessed with her parents and childhood.

Although Hayward doesn't judge them harshly as people, she does sentence them as parents. Guilty. Her mother ruled by edicts and withdrawals. Her father was eventually divorced from all of them. Driven by separate demons, Margaret Sullavan and Leland Hayward were exceptional. They were both more, and less, than normal parents. In this book, they are blamed for their children's disasters.

I wonder what their side of the story would be. Would they in turn blame their parents? Would the grandparents then blame the great-grandparents? What is the statute of limitations for guilt? At what point does a woman with a twenty-year-old son own her own life?

I don't want to be harsh. Some of us have childhoods we enjoy; others have childhoods we must recover from. Brooke Hayward is still amazed that she survived. Perhaps she couldn't begin to grow up until she was an orphan.

But she reminds me of too many people, past forty, who still look back over their shoulders, blaming current events on family history, using psychology as an excuse rather than a tool. "Do you want to know about me?" they say. "Let me tell you about my parents."

This is a family book, a story about parents and children. But, sadly, her perspective is exclusively that of the child. What's absent is any sense of Brooke as a parent. We need this to complete the cycle, because the most intriguing part of the family soap opera is the effect of our parents on our parenting, and the way our own childhood is transmitted to our children's childhoods.

To hear about that, unfortunately, we may have to stay tuned to the next generation.

APRIL 1977

THE WRONG SIDE
OF THE GENERATION GAP

Last week, seventy-six-year-old Henry Jumping Bull complained in public about the younger generation. Like every other older generation since his grandpa, Sitting Bull, was knee-high to a buffalo, he lamented the fact that "the kids these days" had lost the old values and were going to hell in various and sundry handbaskets.

Well, I hate to take issue with him, but the fellow does seem to have his sights on the wrong side of the generation gap. While in the sixties middle-aged parents were appalled at the lifestyles of their children, in the seventies midlife children are trying to cope with the changing lifestyles of their parents' generation.

A friend of mine just experienced what could only be called generation shock. Her sixty-year-old widowed mother was coming up from her Florida home for a two-week visit. This in itself presented no more than the usual problems—"if she tells me once more to fork-split the English muffins . . ."—but this time Mother was bringing the New Man in Her Life.

The question before the house was (are you ready?), "Should I put them in one bedroom or two?"

When I suggested that she ask her mother, this thirty-four-year-old woman, who has read the collected works of Carlos Castaneda and meditates with her husband and children twice a day, shrieked, "I can't ask my mother *that!*"

It's all very confusing. A father in our crowd who regularly threatened death and dismemberment to his children if they were out past midnight is now widowed and having a "relationship," mind you, with a fifty-eight-year-old divorcée on Cape Cod. His thirty-eight-year-old son was concerned that he may marry this woman despite the fact that they are not of the same faith. It is now the father who has to suggest to his boy, "Why? Are you afraid we will have conflicts bringing up the children?"

There are all kinds of symptoms of this role reversal going around. There are "children" who find themselves listening to tales of their parents' dates. There are parents who find themselves worrying about whether they should bring their new friends home to meet the children. Not to mention the grandchildren.

Then, of course, there are growing numbers of so-called senior citizens who are living together with more Social Security and less legality. Two widowed and/or retired singles find the cost of marriage very dear in terms of lost pensions or reduced Social Security, and so many don't marry.

This leads to a certain awkwardness around Thanksgiving, etc. About a year ago, Jane Otten of Washington described her difficulty finding a way to talk about the woman her son was living with. "This is my son's uh . . ." Let me tell you, that's nothing compared with introducing your father's "uh."

The worst case of judgment reversal came from the husband of an old roommate of mine who was visiting from Oregon. This man I once described as the only middle-aged junior at Harvard. He was tall, skinny and stuffy at twenty and still is. He informed me that he is not at all sure he will allow (sic) his children to visit with their grandmother and her "uh," because he is not sure he wants them exposed to such, and I quote, "immorality."

And the beat goes on.

It seems to be a lot easier to deal with change among our children than our parents. We have come to expect that "kids will be kids," adolescent revolt and all that. But our parents are supposed to be the safe repositories of tradition against which we—not they—can revolt. They are supposed to go down the road of retirement life baking cookies, puttering in the garden and taking their grandchildren to the zoo.

"Remember when sixty-five was old?" my former roommate asked me in a voice that I can only describe as wistful.

It would be terribly convenient, of course, if our parents would really retire, would lead their lives according to the original life plan, beading Christmas skirts and refinishing rockers, without being touched by death, divorce, disaster, vulnerability, insecurity or, certainly, sexuality. After all, doesn't the generation in the middle have enough trouble with their children?

There are those of us who seem to insist that it is inconsiderate of our parents to still be in a state of change after age fifty-five, or sixty at the latest. Especially when we want them to be our Parents, for heaven's sake, and they keep turning out to be people. The nerve of them.

I simply do not know what is happening to the older generation these days.

AUGUST 1976

PART SEVEN

PARENTS AND CHILDREN

A CELEBRATION
OF THE EMOTIONS

This week, when madness came east in repeated bulletins, like weather reports of a western blizzard, something happened here at home so benign as to seem hardly newsworthy at all. Two of my closest friends had a baby.

The arrival of Julia was a personal, almost selfish pleasure, the kind that comes when another small person joins the cast of characters and enters the circle of those to care about, wonder about and watch.

But there was more than that. Talking with my friend about the specifics—the 9 pounds and 1 ounce, the 21 inches and 12 hours—it occurred to me that this birth was the only thing that had happened this week that made me celebrate the emotions. I felt again some pleasure toward—rather than simply fear and horror of—the irrational side of human nature.

You see, they were the second set of my friends to have a baby within the past month. They belong in fact to a whole category of people who have had their first children in their thirties, thereby creating a slight boom—a pop perhaps—in the birth curb. They are, as Nora Ephron ruefully described herself, "a trend."

This population is of course portrayed as a prototype of the New Planned Parents. We are told that they are the ones who waited, the ones who carefully resolved the restlessness of their youth and the direction of their careers before they had children.

In some crucial way they are regarded as the first generation to make a rational decision to have children in an era when parenting is defined as an option, even a lifestyle. These Planned Parents are the ones who weighed the claims of parenting and nonparenting. They are heralded now as the Parents of the Age of Reason.

Well, as Margaret Mead would have said, "Piffle." Piffle to the human conceit of rational childbearing. Reason may determine the timing of children and the number of children, but I think it has less to do with the decision to have a baby—before or after thirty—than with the decision to fall in love.

After all, reason is only an early warning system and a safety checklist. Rationally these new and older parents had seen more, seen every pitfall and peril of parenting among their friends. At thirty or thirty-seven, they knew the slim margins of error and the wide probability of making an error. If reason is statistical, then to any rational person, the numbers would suggest the difficulty of being better at this job than any other parent, even their own.

Reason advises people to reduce the risks of their life. Reason is cautious in the face of change. Reason cannot really imagine the depths of feeling and connection that come with childbirth, the way in which the palette of human emotions opens up from primary colors to a vast and subtle rainbow. Reason can only think of diapers.

These trendy parents, the Age of Reason people, go now into the family business in a milieu which overestimates the pains and underestimates the pleasures of children. If they were truly rational, even sensible, surely they would have remained childless.

But the fact is that after all the parent tests are taken, after all the pros and cons are calibrated, after all the timers are set, the desire for children is fundamentally and humanly that. A desire. As Nora Ephron explained her maternity, in this peer group, "I wanted to have a baby."

If it is reason that inhibits us, it is desire that impels us, and we are hardly immune to that at thirty or thirty-seven. It's desire that makes us believe that we can do it right and desire that urges us to take the risk.

What is that desire? A biological urge to reproduce? Surely in part. But I think there is also the impulse to share in the most natural of human experiences, to find meaning in the most fundamental of human tasks and to find a connection in the most primal of human relationships.

Let others praise the rational parent. I find it peculiarly reassuring, at least in this tragic week, when Julia was born, to remember that some of our most primitive, deepest instinctual human emotions also give life.

DECEMBER 1978

THE PARENT TEST

As a long-term follower of the famous adage "Starve a Cold and Stuff an Anxiety," I could hardly get through *The Parent Test* without washing down my lemon meringue pie with a quart of eggnog.

It wasn't that I flunked. It was rather that I kept losing points for the characteristics which I considered proof of sanity. I lost one point because I would never, under any condition, drive a school bus, and another point because I couldn't live comfortably on half my income. I lost more points because I wouldn't want to have children like my friends' children.

It was all enough to turn me away from ever being a mother, if I weren't one already. But that was, I suspect, the point.

The Parent Test, for those of you who are watching your weight (take my advice and abstain), purports to test your aptitude for parenting before you get locked into the family business. I'm sure that it will be devoured by the very people who are so uptight about the Decision—to have or not to have—that they would gobble any guide placed before them.

But this is really a test of Why Not to Be a Parent. It should have been subtitled "201 Ways to Feed Your Fantasies of Failure."

The coauthor of this book is Ellen Peck, whose previous interest in children was limited to teen-age acne commercials and a book called *The Baby Trap*. A founding figure in the Non-Parents organization, she has long written about parenting as a trail of delights that extends all the way from diapers to pimples.

To be fair, this time she and her coauthor, William Granzig, labored hard to offset any impression of an anti-parenting bias.

To be fair, they failed.

They are, for openers, a decade behind the times. They actually introduce their effort with the belief that "anyone growing up in this society has, prior to reading this book, received predominantly warm, romantic impressions of parenthood and children."

If that were on her quiz, I would have answered, "False." The decisionmaking couples of today couldn't find a "warm, romantic impression of parenthood and children" on a Gerber food label.

In the fifties, people came down with diabetes from the sugar-coated version of motherhood. But in the seventies, couples can barely unpurse their lips long enough to say "baby." They've been oversold on the hassles of parenting. They've OD'd on the horror stories. *Carrie* is their image of childhood and Sisyphus is their role model for parenting. They are suffering, not from romanticism, but from terminal conflict.

I know a dozen couples who can't decide whether to have children. They can't even decide how to decide. They want a rational, actuarial kind of life-plan, and this test feeds right into their anxiety. The search is on to unearth the "right reason" to have children and to find out who are the "right people" to have them.

Peck and Granzig are pretty good at finding out the "wrong reasons," of course: "Broadly speaking there are four major categories of motives for parenthood—egotistic, compensatory, comforting and affectionate—and the odds are the first three of these four categories will cause you trouble." They had me absolutely convinced that any poverty-stricken, child-hating nomad is unfit.

But they are lousy at explaining why anyone—other than a child psychologist–school-bus driver who plays entire games of Monopoly with five-year-olds and enjoys being abused by teenagers—would ever want to give birth.

The problem is that they, and the borderline couples I know, are talking about children in general. In the abstract. But we don't have them in the abstract. We have specific people we call our own.

The best-prepared, the most hyper-planned of us, still find that parenting is twenty years of on-the-job training. The pleasure of being a parent isn't reasonable or objective. It doesn't lend itself to grades. At the risk of sounding "warm," not to mention "romantic," it is the extraordinary experience of having short people who hang around awhile, who change you as they change, who push and prod and aggravate and thrill you and make life fuller. Who are, more than anything else, irrationally special to you.

Parenting demands a risk and not a scoreboard. As far as I'm concerned, you can pass the celery sticks. This was my final exam.

MARCH 1978

PARENTS AS PEOPLE
(WITH CHILDREN)

I once owned a record with a song on it that began simply, "Parents are people, people with children . . ." If I can find it again, I'll send it right along to John Silber, the president of Boston University, for his collection.

You see, it was Silber who told the parents of 3,000 incoming freshmen last week that they'd better not go back to being people just yet. The man said in no uncertain terms: "Every one of our students deserves a parent who is not going through an identity crisis. It is time that America faces up to the implications of having too many people aged forty and aged fifty asking questions that they should have answered when they were seventeen to twenty-five, namely, 'Who am I and what ought I to do?' "

No, the president wasn't going to let them off the hook just yet. "When you send your youngsters to the university, I hope that you will at least pass a four-year moratorium on that question . . . and stick with whatever it is you are doing until your son or daughter graduates."

His message to the parents of 400,000 college freshmen in America is a succinct one: Four More Years.

Now, don't misunderstand me. In the best of all possible worlds, I would assign two totally fulfilled, completed and contented adults to each child. It would be, as they say, swell. Not only do I think that every student deserves a parent who "isn't going through an identity crisis," but I also think that every parent deserves a student who isn't going through an identity crisis.

However, life being what it is, we are stuck with each other. The notion of telling parents to hang in there on the old straight-and-narrow for the sake of children who are now pushing twenty, or twenty-two, is just a touch strange.

Silber seems to think that an identity crisis is something you should have—if at all—before you are twenty-five. Once you've had it, you never have to worry about getting it again—sort of like the measles. You are supposed to find out once and for all "who you are" and "what you ought to do"—and then go out and do it and be it until, presumably, you drop dead.

If you forget to have your identity crisis at the proper time, however, you're out of luck. It's just like the time you missed long division because you were out sick.

In real life, the problem with parents-who-are-people is that they (gasp!) change. Now this is a situation which, admittedly, their children would often like to arrest. But it's inevitable for all but the dreariest, most self-satisfied of grown-ups who go through life in a plastic capsule, protected from the infections of the world around them.

They would also have to be protected from children because, ironically, it's children who are the most powerful catalysts of change in their parents' lives. They arrive with a crisis—"Who am I—a me or a mommy?"—and they leave us with one—"What do I do with the rest of my life?" (Indeed, if Silber would like to prevent midlife crises, perhaps he should send the kids home—with their $3,850 in tuition, if you please.)

By the end of our time as parents, most of us are ready to move on. Adolescence becomes an endurance contest and the most devoted parents—the sort who never miss a 6:00 A.M. hockey practice—are hanging on for dear life as their children casually say things like, "You're not going out looking like that, are you, Dad?"

At that point, the parents who have spent the last several years "postponing" don't see an empty nest ahead, but a full life. Suddenly they can drive their own car, work their own hours, make love with the bedroom door open, listen to their own music. They can change houses or roles, they can eat in peace or silence or both. They have gobs of time—including the time for an identity crisis.

The only people who avoid risk, who never face a crisis or two, are those who stop changing. They postpone their own lives—four more years here, four more years there—until they don't have them. They are the parents who never were, and never become, their own people.

And, by the way, you know who's the first to criticize the sacrificial parent? The first to pull away? You guessed it. The children.

SEPTEMBER 1977

THE MAKING OF
A FATHER

When he lived with them, he had been a visiting father. The sort who has his children brought in on a tray at cocktail hour and collected before dinner is served. The sort who prefers his children to come shiny-clean, cheerful and in small doses.

He had sniffed at them as if they were corks from a new wine bottle. At the scent of crankiness or illness, they had been promptly sent back to the kitchen, and to the mother who had been held more or less responsible for such a lapse in the quality of the wine cellar.

It's true. He'd always wanted them Handi-wiped and Band-aided, 98.6 degrees and in full repair. He'd been a bit like the Moluccan terrorists who'd panicked after one night of epidemic in the stomachs of their hostages—terrorists unable to deal with flu, who had sent the schoolchildren home, to their mothers.

But things were different now. He was no longer a live-in visiting father. He had signed on the dotted line of a very formal agreement, full of clauses and subclauses, one of which read: "The father shall have reasonable visitation rights."

But now that he was officially, legally, the visiting (or visited) father, something remarkable happened. He had made his first full connections with the small people in his life. In a peculiar way he knew this was his first Father's Day.

In the last ten months he had become a father, not just a designated name on a birth certificate. He discovered that this transition wasn't unique with him, but he wasn't entirely sure why it happened to so many divorced fathers.

When first apart, he thought he would be a recycled bachelor with mustache and medallion. But somehow he'd felt rather silly. He saw too many men who'd turned in 10 pounds and all their good sense for a mirror over their bed and a high-rise studio apartment full of "swingles."

So instead, at thirty-five years of age, he chose paternity. Ten years earlier he had been more or less drafted. This time he really chose it. Out of loneliness and guilt at first, and out of pleasure at last, the visited father finally established a rapport with his children. He spent more time with them in ten months than he had in ten years.

They were with him through Wednesdays, weekends and vacations, through the flu and sunburn and carsickness and various attempts at fratricide.

Alone with his children, he took intensive on-the-job training. The mother who had been designated the expert by all of them wasn't around for consultations. He had to cram. Indeed, the father developed a repertory of attitudes on subjects like these: Should his daughter have dessert if she refused to eat the vegetables? What was the appropriate punishment for a ten-year-old boy who spread honey all over the cat? Would another Egg McMuffin have serious repercussions on their genes?

He became the kind of parent who knew how to braid hair and limit junk food and tuck in tired bodies—and yell. He learned what his children liked to eat, what they hated to wash, and where they were likely to have left the other sneaker. He learned that even when they'd seen each other at their worst, they liked each other.

Alone with his children, he'd found them to be remarkably interesting. That was an odd word to use, but there it was: interesting. It was his son who explained to him quite clearly why there was no such thing as nothing, "because then nothing has to be something." It was his daughter who pointed out the absurdity of the sign on the corner that read: Go Children Slow. "That doesn't make sense. It should read: 'Go Slow, Children.' "

The visiting father who had never had time for his children *made* time. Period. He met both teachers. He had seen one child play "Kanga" and the other play hockey.

Sometimes he was jealous. Of men who had custody of their children. Of live-in fathers. He wondered why he had waited so long.

But at least he had learned. When he *couldn't* take them for granted, he discovered that you can't take them for granted. What he had with his children was what they created. They had made him, at last, a father.

JUNE 1977

THE BELATED FATHER

There is a small clipping, no more than 2 square inches, that has been in my file marked "Fathers" since last fall. It's a simple story about a judge in western Massachusetts who, when confronted with a fifteen-year-old kid in trouble, made an unusual judgment. He sentenced the father to thirty days of dinner at home.

There are some other things in the folder. One is a letter to an advice column from a woman whose husband has never kissed their baby son because he said, "I feel funny kissing a guy." Behind that letter is a statistic: "Ten percent of the children in this country live in fatherless homes."

There is also a quote from a novel about the children of the sixties, written by Stephen Koch. It says, "Who among those fiery sons, with their vague and blasted eyes, really connected with his father; who even knew, let alone admired what the father did in that invisible city of his? Fatherhood meant delivering, or not delivering, checks. It meant not being around, or being unwelcome when around. It meant either shouting or that soul-crushing silence most deeply installed in the soul of any red-blooded American boy: Dad mute behind his newspaper."

I wish there were something else in the file folder, some story; some role model you could applaud.

There are so many young fathers who don't want to be like their own dads. They feel awkward when they find themselves alone with their fathers today. They flip through their own mental files on the subject. There is Father Knows Best and Fathers Knows Nothing, Father as Pal, and Father as Trans-parent. There is even an occasional full-time father—who trips in all the pitfalls of full-time mothers.

None of these will do. They don't fit. They don't feel right. So these sons are trying to devise their own role models, to be their own first generation. They are becoming—what shall we call them?—working fathers.

Margaret Mead has written that "human fatherhood is a social invention." Maybe so. But they are re-inventing it. They want to be involved in the full range of their children's lives, to know which days the kids have to wear sneakers for gym and which kid would starve before he'd eat cauliflower.

They are learning to deal with kids when they are crying or

174

dirty or hungry. As one father said, "When I was a kid, my father would play ball with me, but the minute I hurt my knee, we'd both call for my mother. I don't want to divide my kids like that."

He wants the kind of relationship that is only woven in the intimacy of daily, time-consuming routines during which you "learn" what they call intuition—the second sense that tells you one kid is worried and another is sad, and the difference between a cry that is tired and one that is hungry or hurt. These fathers don't want to be Sunday events.

On the other hand, they have new guilts. They feel guilty if they miss the school play and guilty if they are tired or out of town. They can't push it down justifying their absence with the need to Make It, or with the notion that children are women's work.

They wonder: "Can I be a successful worker and a successful father?" Their bosses are usually men of their father's generation whose offices are geared to full-time mothers and absent fathers. If they refuse overtime will they get ahead? What if they can't travel their way to a better job?

At the office they suddenly find themselves wondering, Did the babysitter show? I wonder if that bully in the playground is bothering Bobby again? Finally they wonder whether they have enough energy left over from work and fathering for their own lives and plans and marriages.

And when they describe all this, all this that is so new to them, they notice their wives quietly smiling. These fathers, you see, are becoming—well, how should we put it? Like us.

JUNE 1976

THE RIGHTS
OF UNWED FATHERS

The image of the unwed father was always a seedy one. He was the man who skipped town one step ahead of the shotgun. He left behind him a woman "in trouble," and a child who grew up as a swear-word.

The only paternity cases ever heard about when I was growing up were the kind that proved who was the father and forced him to 'fess up and pay up. We were far more concerned then with pressing responsibilities on unwed fathers than with ensuring their rights.

But, gradually, things have changed. In 1950, only 3.9 percent of the children in this country were born out of wedlock. In 1975, 14.2 percent were. Most of their fathers still remain anonymous and tragically disconnected. But there are a number of men, and a body of law, gradually developing around the new kind of paternity issue—the rights of the unwed father.

Last week, the U.S. Supreme Court heard the latest and potentially most important of these cases, *Caban v. Mohammed*. They heard the arguments for and against a father who is challenging a New York statute. It says that an unwed mother can agree to the adoption of her children without the consent of the father.

The case touches on many sensitive legal and emotional points. Should the rights of an unwed father be different from those of a married, or formerly married, father? Should they be different from the rights of an unwed mother? How carefully can we balance the interests of the children and the interests of the adult?

The story behind this litigation is as tangled as many other human relationships. The parents lived together from 1968 to 1973 and together had two children, who bear the father's name. After their separation, the mother married, but the father maintained a strong presence in his children's lives. At one time or another, he had extensive visitation rights or full custody. He always had a major decision-making role.

But about three years ago, the mother and the stepfather petitioned to adopt the children. Adoption would have ended all the legal rights of the natural father, including even his right to visit his children. At that point he fought—fought the mother and the state, declaring that the law was unconstitutional because it violated his rights to due process and equal protection of the law. Now, when the Supreme Court hands down its decision, it will fill in a major gray area of new law on fathers' rights.

Historically, men like Abdiel Caban had no rights to their illegitimate children. Then, six years ago, in *Stanley v. Illinois*, the Supreme Court struck down a law which had made illegitimate children the wards of the state upon the death of their mother—even if their father was alive and living with them. For the first time, the Court acknowledged the status of an unwed father and kept a family intact.

But this year, they ruled against the rights of another unwed father in a Georgia case, *Quilloin v. Walcott*. They said that this man —who had maintained virtually no contact with his children—could not suddenly come upon the scene to veto the adoption by a new stepfather.

Both of these cases—decided for and against unwed fathers— hinged neatly on the best interests of the children. As Paul Kurtz, of the University of Georgia Law School, says, "The overriding consideration is the best interest of the child." But he says that in *Caban v. Mohammed* the question is whether "the best interest of the children is 'best enough' to outweigh the rights of the father."

A lower court had ruled that the two children would fare better in the world if they had the same name as their mother and stepfather and were no longer illegitimate. But is the difficulty of bearing a different name or even the stigma of illegitimacy greater today than the risk of losing contact with a parent? Is it so great that it outweighs the man's right to be a father?

Surely an unwed father shouldn't have an absolute right of veto over adoption. That would create havoc. It seems to me appropriate that, at this time, his rights should be calibrated in terms of his commitment. There's a vast difference between the father who has lived with his children and the one who has deserted them. Perhaps the rights of both mothers and fathers have to be "deserved."

But in this case, the psychological effects of the adoption on the children are not crystal-clear, and the father has a powerful desire to remain a parent. It seems both unfair and discriminatory to allow an unwed mother the unchecked right to dispense her children—and even to sever their ties with their father.

One of the major issues of this society, after all, is how to restore, maintain or strengthen the relationships between men and their children—in or out of marriage. We can't seek or demand responsibility from fathers while denying them appropriate rights. They, too, need this legal security as insurance for their emotional investment.

NOVEMBER 1978

MOTHER
IN THE MIDDLE

She was thinking about Mother's Day. Although she was definitely not a member of the Hallmark, Candygram, Long-distance-is-the-next-best-thing-to-being-there generation, holidays did have an effect on her. They made her do some reassessing, and Mother's Day was no exception.

You see, she was a mother. To be more specific, she was the daughter of one mother and the mother of one daughter. Which made her a Middle American Woman, the one standing between the generations. She was the one who transmitted the past to the future in a million silly ways. From the moment of maternity she discovered a well of little phrases from her childhood just waiting to pop up: "Good night, sleep tight" . . . "Upsy-Daisy" . . . "Don't do that, your face will freeze" . . . "I'm going to count until ten . . . one, two, three. . . ."

But it wasn't just phrases she translated from one generation to the next. It was more than that. She carried the memories and values of her childhood into the experiences of mothering.

Like so many of her peers in the ranks of Middle American Woman, she was a working mother, and the daughter of a Traditional Mother. That Traditional Mother—who surely was thought of as a Modern Mother when she was young—hadn't been frustrated or chafing or carping or smothering. Her rhythms and interests had fit the pace of her life. She had the patience to teach a four-year-old how to tie shoelaces and the time to teach a five-year-old how to read. She had been a full-time nourisher.

The Working Mother was different. From the time she was in her twenties, the traitorous thought ran through her mind with the power of a mantra: "If a mother devotes her life to raising a daughter who becomes a mother who devotes her life to raising a daughter . . . what makes her different from a hamster? What is the meaning of her life?"

Many things—including the death of her father—made her believe that full-time nourishing was a terrifying, risky business. She was one of the women that psychologist Abraham Maslow wrote about: "It is best to consider the discontented woman as . . . simply wanting *more*."

For her, *more* was work. The daughter of the Traditional Mother was a Working Mother. It fit her own rhythms and interests. But, as most working mothers in the middle discover, she hadn't eliminated the conflicts in her life, she had exchanged one set for another.

Sometimes she was sure she had the best of both worlds and sometimes she thought she had the hardest. Double the pressure, double the fun. Sometimes she was sure that she wasn't doing enough. Other times she was sure that her demands on herself were unreasonable. She wondered if eventually mothers would learn to feel less guilt, or if fathers would learn to feel more guilt.

In any case, woman in the middle discovered that her job in no way lessened her investment in her child. She thought sometimes about what Lillian Hellman said: "Most women want everything. They want leadership, they want to be darlings. They want to be Marilyn Monroe and they want to be Madame de Maintenon. At the same time, they want to be President." She'd forgotten something: They also want to be perfect mothers.

This Working Mother tended to compare herself as a mother to her own. She was so much less patient. She was so much busier. She didn't make brownies or costumes. She didn't let her daughter stay home with Monday-itis. She wasn't always there when something hurt. Her best efforts to make attractive, nutritious dinners, with parsley and philosophy, degenerated sometimes into peanut butter and grunts.

She worried: Is a half-time mother half a mother?

But when she felt caught in an elaborate cultural change game —"Mommie in the Middle"—there were two people who helped.

There was, on one side, the Traditional Mother grown into a wildly prejudiced grandmother who insisted that "you must be doing something right" since the grandchild was so clearly, incontrovertibly and unarguably magnificent.

On the other side, there was the daughter who didn't have any other mother to compare her with; who played "going to work" naturally as a part of playing house; who was loving and wonderful company and assumed—of all things—that when she grew up, she'd be just like her mother.

On the whole, when the mother in the middle—the middle of generations, the middle of social change—finished her assessment, she decided that she was in a pretty good place.

MAY 1977

YOUR BETTER
BASIC SUPERMOTHER

I have now been through two generations of Mother's Days, which is odd, considering that my daughter is only eight. But it seems like we've passed through time zones in our notions of mothering and especially in our tyrannies of supermothering.

The Supermother, for those of you who haven't met her, is that Perfect Person against whom we compare ourselves in order to fully experience failure, not to mention self-loathing, and a complex labeled inferiority. She is the lady we carry around in our heads just for the guilt of it.

Now the Supermother who was reigning when I first got into the family business was your better basic, devoted, selfless Total Mother whose children never had runny noses because she was right behind them, wiping. Her children were the ones in the school lunchroom with sandwiches cut in the shapes of turkeys at Thanksgiving and bunnies at Easter.

She was the one who made Halloween costumes out of potato sacks and decorated dinner with parsley, and once—following the instructions in a woman's magazine—made a bookcase out of used popsicle sticks. She was relentlessly cheerful and was actually known to have initiated and completed an entire game of Monopoly with two six-year-olds. She loved car games.

Even on Mother's Day, she was delighted to clean up the kitchen after those helpless urchins—daddy and the kiddies—had made her breakfast in bed. Weren't they cute, after all?

Now, personally, I was never able to get my radish flowers to blossom even in cold water. And the place mats I made from a magazine pattern ended up costing $4.65 apiece (they were also excruciatingly ugly). Furthermore—bad person that I am—when I am carpooling children on a July day in my unair-conditioned car, my strongest desire is not to lead a wholesome chorus of "Ninety-nine Bottles of Beer on the Wall." I am more likely to be fantasizing about an impenetrable soundproof plastic chauffeur's barrier around my seat.

So, you can see why I was delighted to watch the demise of the Supermother. She had to go. At a time when nearly half the mothers in the country were also employed outside the home, the Supermother wasn't going to get the right amount of worship time.

But the problem is that Supermother I has reappeared as Supermother II, a new, revised, updated model—from traditional to transitional. She is now "Supermom at Home and on the Job."

The All-Around Supermom rises, dresses in her chic pants suit, oversees breakfast and the search for the sneakers and then goes off to her glamorous high-paying job at an advertising agency, where she seeks Personal Fulfillment and the kids' college tuition. She has, of course, previously found a Mary Poppins figure to take care of the kids after school. Mary Poppins loves them as if they were her own, works for a mere pittance and is utterly reliable.

Supermom II comes home from work at 5:30, just as fresh as a daisy, and then spends a truly creative hour with the children. After all, it's not the quantity of the time, but the quality. She catches up on their day, soothes their disputes and helps with their homework while creating something imaginative in her Cuisinart (with her left hand tied behind her back). Her children never eat at McDonald's.

After dinner—during which she teaches them about the checks and balances of our system of government—she bathes and reads to them, and puts the clothes in the dryer. She then turns to her husband and eagerly suggests that they explore some vaguely kinky sexual fantasy.

The transitional Supermother does not ask for help, by the way, because she has "chosen to work" and therefore, she reasons, it's her problem. Besides, she can do it all. Up, up and away . . . As for me, I wish her the best of luck and I truly hope she has paid up her health insurance.

Supermom II, you see, is still overcompensating like mad for not being Supermom I. She probably is anxious because she doesn't put raisin faces in the kids' oatmeal. She is making up for her guilt trip to the office.

But the time has come—why not, it's Mother's Day, isn't it?— to jettison all the accumulated Kryptonite, and dump the Supermothers of today and yesterday overboard.

No Supermothers need apply.

MAY 1976

A MONTH
WITHOUT TIMETABLES

This time at least she didn't embarrass her daughter, a child who had acquired a sense of dignity in her ninth summer which she wanted to see displayed, like the flag, in public places.

This time she didn't double-check her daughter's store of stationery, money, zip codes, telephone numbers, timetables. She restrained herself from running down the checklists of her own anxieties —Things to Be Careful Of, Things to Remember—as if she could wrap up her child for a month in a life preserver.

This time she simply turned her daughter over to the temporary custody of a stewardess who knew her only as the unaccompanied minor in seat 9-D, and said goodbye.

They were vacationing away from each other again this August, vacating the joint territory of their home, the field on which they played out their lives together. While they were apart, some of the worn patches down the middle would have time to grow in and be green by the fall season.

As she walked back, past the security guard and the baggage counter, the woman ran down her own mental list for August. A month without timetables. A month without Having to Go Home. A month when she could let go of all the minor details that collected like carpet fuzz in the corners of her brain—lunch money, permission slips, appointments, missing books and socks. A free month.

Before she even finished this list, she began to contradict it. A month without having to go home is a month without a reason to go home. Time without pressure and schedules is time without form and rhythm.

For a minute she struggled to figure out which was her "real" feeling—free or rootless?—and then gave up. The "real" feeling was, as always, locked in ambivalence.

That was the thing about having kids. You decide to have a baby and end up with a range of feelings that run from the rapturous to the murderous with four thousand stops in between. One minute you wish they had boarding school for two-year-olds and the next minute you dread the idea that they ever grow up and go away.

Before you have children, you only deal with a corner-store

stock of emotions. Afterward you discover an inventory that would rival the supermarket, and half of them are in competition with the other half.

The set of feelings she was dealing with today—having left her unaccompanied minor on the plane—were those of dependence and independence, distance and closeness. She realized that this was probably the middle summer of their time together. Half time. Nine years down. Nine to go. Nine years had passed since the first shock of dependency and nine more would pass before the final shock of separation.

These were the years when you try to work out the difference between protecting kids and smothering them, between fostering independence and displaying indifference.

The experts say (at one time, she'd been a child-psychology book junkie and read them all) that parents should make kids feel secure, but not babied. They say to help them feel independent but not neglected. They say to be there for them and to let them go.

They say that parents should be dependable to their children, without becoming dependent on their children. They say parents should lead their own lives, without neglecting their kids. They say that everyone is supposed to play the accordion of closeness and separateness in such a way that they all remain whole and yet caring, complete in themselves and yet attached to each other.

But they don't say how. Sometimes she wonders how many psychologists can dance on the head of a parent.

Well, she didn't really know anyone who managed to live that sort of balanced life every day. Mostly the parents and children she knew careened away from each other and then collided together. The only happy medium was the one the mathematicians could make by averaging out their extremes. Their ambivalence.

Maybe this August she would take leave. It was her half time, too. She would be both free and rootless now. In the fall she would begin the second half. Nine more years? Only nine years? "Both," she answered—striking ambivalence off of her summer list.

AUGUST 1977

NINE-YEAR OLDS, MEET MONET

She was on what the school called a "field trip," as if the fourth graders were anthropologists and the Museum of Fine Arts were a foreign land.

It was, in some ways, a meeting of different cultures. The nine-year-old chatter splintered in huge marble hallways built to echo nineteenth-century discussions of Art. The blue jeans and T-shirts jarred with the gilt frames holding priceless paintings.

The class had gone to meet one of the woman's favorite people —Claude Monet—and so, she had gone along. Not to introduce them, you understand, but to accompany them.

There she was struck, not by the contrasting cultures, but by the contrasting values of one culture. The children had been taken en masse to meet an individualist. They had come, clutching worksheets in one hand and best friends in the other—the channel markers of the social system—to see the work of a man who rebelled against his own artistic system.

Watching them giggling together and sharing answers she thought again: They are becoming socialized, for better and for worse.

The worksheets and friends were, in one way or another, the constraints of society on the ego. How they performed on paper and with each other would inevitably be marked down on the up-to-date report card under the headings "Learning Skills" and "Social Skills." Yet the paintings on the wall were the work of the disciplined but essentially "unsocialized" ego of the artist who believed in the primary value of self-expression.

If, like Monet, they skipped school to go to the sea, or drew cartoons of their teacher, they would be labeled "social problems." If they had the nerve to believe that their own rebellious notions were better than the collected wisdom of the École des Beaux-Arts, they too would be considered antisocial egotists.

The nine-year-olds, scattered around the rooms full of luscious landscapes, were, on the whole, good kids. You didn't have to remind them to keep their hands off. They had been almost civilized out of the real Me-Decade, the first years of life. Totally selfish at one, outrageously self-centered at two, by now the cutting edges of their egos had rubbed off against each other and the adults. They raised their hands and waited their turns and followed directions. They had learned the art of survival—cooperation, and orderliness, laced with hypocrisy and covered with suppression.

They were becoming socialized. For better and for worse.

She thought of all the conflicting feelings and messages that went into this process. Be yourself but get along with others. Be popular but don't follow the crowd. Write an imaginative story within these margins and in this time. Paint . . . by numbers.

They say that societies get the children they want. The imaginative three-year-old becomes the reasonable ten-year-old. The nursery-school child who asks, "How do they get the people inside the television set?" becomes the middle-school child who reads the ingredients on the cereal box. The two-year-old exhibitionist becomes the twelve-year-old conformist who won't wear the wrong kind of blue jeans.

As kids grow up, they are less exhausting and less imaginative, less selfish and less creative. They are easier to live with. Their egos come under control. They become socialized, for better and for worse.

We train selfishness out of them. Yet, ironically, some who resist, like the artists, may end up giving the most to others. The product of the most egotistical self-expression may become a generous gift available on the museum wall or the library shelf.

The fourth graders finished their hour with Monet. They were impressed with Impressionism and would, for a while, remember the man they'd met. They left, with their worksheets in one hand and their best friends in the other, still chattering. They passed, in reasonable order, through the doorway and down the massive staircase.

Very few of them had read or understood the words printed on the wall of the exhibit. They were copied from a letter Monet had written to a friend: "Don't you agree that on one's own with nature, one does better? Me, I'm sure of it. . . . What I'm going to do here will at least have the merit of not resembling anyone else, or so I think, because it will be simply the expression of what I myself have felt."

JANUARY 1978

REMEMBER THE 35-CENT SCHOOL LUNCH?

It has begun to occur to me that school is a bargain. It isn't simply because it keeps kids off the streets; it also manages to keep them away from the refrigerator for six or more hours a day, five days a week. This astonishing figure is approximately five and a half hours longer than any of the rest of us can keep them away, with or without locks, guard dogs and threats of physical violence.

This thought has overwhelmed me in the past week, during which pantries all over America have begun to resemble the defoliation pictures of the Ho Chi Minh trail.

Remember the 35-cent school lunch? Well, 35 cents is what it costs to warm up their teeth for the main event. Most of us have by now discovered that our children eat at roughly the minimum wage, $2.35 an hour. That means they are gaining on us.

My own daughter is eight years old and weighs 50 pounds. These pounds are cleverly spread over her rib cage in such a way as to utterly conceal the fact that she can eat James Beard under the table. Since school closed I have considered eliminating the middleman altogether and feeding her quarters as if she were a slot machine. I want to see if I can make her eyes come up double oranges.

She and her pals—whom I have dubbed the Galloping Gourmands—make army ants look as if they are on a religious fast. Our neighborhood has been renamed "The Moveable Feast" because on any given day you can see them grazing from house to house.

The first day after school closed, a neighbor came home to discover that 4 pounds of fruit, a watermelon, two jumbo cans of water-packed tuna, a loaf of bread and two half-gallons of milk were missing. At first they were afraid that the compost heap had eaten them, but the only thing they found there was a rotting rind. At that point they noticed their two sons hovering over a cherry-tomato plant in the garden, waiting for it to ripen.

They then tried to institute a closed-door policy. For three days the sign on the refrigerator read: "Open for business 7–8 A.M., 12–1:30 P.M. and 6–7:30 P.M." But they gave up when the boys began to look at them with the fondness Oliver Twist reserved for the manager of his orphanage.

Still, they are lucky. Their children have not yet reached their teens. It is a well-known fact that any teenaged boy consumes 10,000 calories just growing. If he rouses himself for more strenuous activity, such as brushing his teeth, his calorie count goes right off the chart. For this reason he tends to cruise the refrigerator continually. He will eat anything that does not eat him first, and he treats family food as if it were all-you-can-eat night at Howard Johnson's.

A teenaged girl, on the other hand, is always dieting. At no time will she allow anything more caloric or less expensive than a Cranshaw melon to pass her lips. Except, of course, when she is devouring teenaged stew (french fries with ketchup) with her friends and on her allowance.

But it is the college kids, home blessedly for the summer in order to store up for the winter, who are referred to affectionately as "The Plague." These youngsters insist that they haven't had a thing to eat since September and they attempt to prove it. Their parents, who were previously feeling pangs of empty nest syndromes, suddenly understand why Mother Robin pushes out the young.

These young profess total independence, and some measure of scorn, for anyone not currently into Kierkegaard. But they feel comfortable waiting for Rock Cornish hens to be dropped into their open beaks. When they are not waiting, they are defrosting things—like the small filet mignon you were saving for your fiftieth wedding anniversary in 1993.

They will eat it as a snack and leave you a list of things to buy, like mung beans and organic honeycomb. They will not use the money they are earning because they are saving it for school—to which we hope they will return, leaving the scorched earth behind.

It's not, heaven forfend, that we begrudge our little children food. Home after all is where the cornucopia is; and food is love, they say. But there is no way to keep up with them. They empty faster than we can fill. Besides, a disloyal thought has begun to creep over our nurturing instincts: Have you ever tried to love a locust?

JUNE 1976

VIOLENCE
IN THE CLASSROOM

Last week the Supreme Court upheld child abuse. Oh, they didn't call
it that. The newspapers labeled it "spanking." The justices wrote in
measured tones about "corporal punishment."

But five members of the court—the Nixon Four Plus One—
determined that kids are not protected by the Constitution from being
beaten in public school.

The court wasn't just talking about a slap on the wrist or a
swipe at the butt. In *Ingraham v. Wright,* they'd heard the story of a
severe beating of two boys in Dade County, Florida. One was struck
more than twenty times with a 2-foot-long paddle and had bruises that
kept him out of school for eleven days. The other was hit hard enough
to lose the full use of his arm for a week. No one disputed the facts.

Still, the justices ruled that the teacher hadn't violated the
rights of the students. You see, they said, the kids didn't have any
rights. Under the Eighth Amendment, criminals in prison and soldiers
in boot camp are protected against "punishment." Kids in school yards
aren't.

Justice Byron White, dissenting, wrote incredulously, "If it is
constitutionally impermissible to cut off someone's ear for the commission of murder, it must be unconstitutional to cut off a child's ear for
being late to class."

But the majority disagreed. As their decision now stands, in
most of the United States a teacher may willfully turn around and slug
a student, without any warning, without a hearing, without due process, without the consent of a parent. Only two states, Massachusetts
and New Jersey, and a handful of cities protect children from this
physical violence. Twenty, like North Carolina, have laws allowing
"reasonable force to . . . correct pupils and maintain order." In the
rest, a teacher who hits a child is safer from prosecution than a parent.
Certainly safer than a parent who hits the teacher back.

This decision gives a green light to the cane and the rod, the
paddle and the fist. And to the violence that hides behind the cool
judicial words—corporal punishment. It maintains the position of the
teacher as sole judge and jury in the classroom. It allows even those

few who maintain a reign of terror, to feel secure and "right" in their position.

"Spare the rod and spoil the child. Whip them into shape. Teach them a lesson." These expressions reflect centuries of law-and-order child-raising. Too many, not unlike the Supreme Court, confuse discipline with violence.

In a Gallup poll five years ago, three out of five Americans said they believed in corporal punishment. In 1975, two out of three teachers in a National Education Association study favored "paddling." Only the American Psychological Association stands unalterably opposed.

There is perhaps still a general belief that the teacher who strikes a child is behaving as a fair-minded dispenser of judicial sentences; or at least as a beleaguered defender of civilization in a blackboard jungle, holding the line against the Lords of the Flies.

But, in fact, physical abuse occurs most often in elementary and junior high schools, when children are still too small to fight back. It occurs more often against minorities, and slow learners and the emotionally troubled.

Teachers, like parents, are apparently most likely to hit and spank and paddle when they are angry, frustrated, overworked—and not worried about retaliation. Occasionally, they hit out of sadism.

The legacy of physical punishment as a technique of child-raising dies hard in this country. It took more than a century to protect children from the most sadistic parent. It may take as long for the state legislatures to do what the Supreme Court has refused—to offer protection of the underaged people in school.

It is bizarre, though, at a moment when we are obsessed with violence—violence on television, violence in the streets—that we continue to allow adults to teach it in the classroom by the most potent method of all: example.

APRIL 1977

■ IT'S TIME
TO TURN OFF TELEVISION

It was a mind-boggler. Right in the middle of the *Newsweek* cover story on children and television, Dr. Benjamin Spock spoke.

And what advice did the seventy-three-year-old author of *Raising Children in a Difficult Time* give? Well, he said that he had recently brought his stepdaughter and granddaughter to New York, but never even got them to the Bronx Zoo. "I couldn't get them away from the goddam TV set," he reported. "It made me sick."

Terrific. Thanks for the help, but may I ask, Dr. Spock: Why didn't you turn off the TV? All the talk about children and television finally comes down to this question. Why don't more parents simply take the dial in their own hands and move it 90 degrees counterclockwise when their kids have had an overdose?

For the past several years, our attitude toward the tube has sounded suspiciously like a running commentary on a deteriorating marriage. The qualities that once seemed so endearing are grating now. The problems we once minimized are now unbearable. The old "idiosyncracies" stick out as major flaws. Television—once a pleasant divertissement—now seems like a habit we can't break and a presence we'd like to be rid of.

The fact is that this marriage is beyond minor repair. Though our attention has been focused for the past several years on improving the appalling programming and advertising aimed at kids, the truth is harsher. Even if every program were educational and every advertisement bore the seal of approval of the American Dental Association, we would still have a critical problem. It's not just the programs but the act of watching television hour after hour after hour that's destructive.

But the majority of parents neither monitor the shows their kids are viewing nor limit the number of hours. The average preschooler is tuned in for 23.5 hours a week. The average teenager has watched 15,000 hours.

Parents let their kids stay hooked for the same reason they let them get hooked: to keep the peace. It was television that pacified the baby, television that often ended arguments between sisters and brothers, television that kept them "out of trouble." In the process of pacifying the kids, many parents pacified themselves right out of the habit of being in charge. They've "kept the peace" not by resolving arguments but by letting them dissolve in front of the screen.

In the passive spirit, they have given up the kids' brain time along with some grown-up responsibility and a lot of family time together. Now, when those same parents make a lunge for the knob, they're greeted with full-scale resistance from the kids. To keep the peace they have to give in to the "peace machine."

At some point or other, parents have tuned out their own feelings. They see some fifteen-year-old sitting slack-jawed in front of the set and block out their first reactions. Instead of dealing with the kids, they "deal" with their guilt. After a while they convince themselves that the "little ones" are peaceful when, in fact, they are comatose.

TV addiction is often hereditary. Anyone whose own prime-time commitments have been pledged to the networks is going to have a tough time locking the kids out or forcing them to cut back. But we are, after all, "Raising Parents in a Difficult Time." It's the grown-ups who have to do it. When they find themselves or their family watching TV—not watching a special program, but mindlessly "watching TV" —it's time to turn it off.

It's up to them, after all, to disturb the peace and to finally break the dullest and deadliest of treaties.

FEBRUARY 1977

TOYS, PSEUDO-BIOLOGY AND THE PURSUIT OF PROFITS

It's easy to understand why we get uptight at the idea of scientists toying around with biology when we see what the toy manufacturers have done with it.

After spending as much money on research as the National Institutes of Health, and hiring the combined imaginations of Mary Wollstonecraft Shelley and Gray's *Anatomy*, the toy people keep coming up with products that make a clone look like an attractive alternative.

The latest announcement out of Mattel-It's-Swell land is that "It's a Boy!" To be precise, it's a few hundred thousand boys. The boy doll is cleverly named Baby Brother and is, the advertising insists, "built exactly the way little boys come into this world."

But the "anatomically correct" (more about that later) doll is just the latest entrant in what has become toyland's fictions of Facts of Life Series.

Baby Brother is a direct descendant of Barbie and Ken, but not that way. Barbie and Ken were not "anatomically correct." Barbie was G-rated, with nary a button for her belly, and Ken had what Ernest Hemingway once called "an emasculating war wound." Considering these handicaps, they produced quite a brood.

The Sons of Ken are a tribe known as Male Action figures, marketed to boys who are never to think of them, God forbid, as dolls. They are so uptight about their masculinity that they have names like Torpedo Fist, The Whip and Warpath—you get the idea—and are geared to such All-American, all-boy pastimes as war and total annihilation.

At the same time, a variety of baby-girl dolls were born like Athena from the head of Zeus—or the head of the toy corporation—who possess an increasing number of "biological functions" which stop just short of Midol.

There is an appalling little creature called Baby Alive who teaches millions of preschoolers the notion that an intestinal tract is a straight plastic tube from the mouth to the diaper. And there is Growing Up Skipper, a dear little ten-year-old who goes through adolescence—with nary a pimple nor a temper tantrum—when you grab her left arm and turn it 360 degrees.

When she was "born," I predicted that the doll market would expand in the direction of Menopausal Mary—press the button and see her get hot flashes—or Dieting Dorothy—watch her hip line grow and shrink as you lift her hand to her mouth. Which just proves how limited my vision was.

Instead, the doll manufacturers—armed with market research —merged the male "action figures," the "biological functions" and the growing idea that it just might be all right for William to want a doll. With fear and trembling and long discussions on his "anatomical correctness," they made Baby Brother.

Which, by the way, they promptly marketed for little girls. The first ads pointed out that he was "bouncing brother" to all the other dolls in "our little girl's family." Only in *Ms.* magazine was it promoted this month as a doll for your "child." (Is it possible that *Family Circle* subscribers have boys and girls while *Ms.* subscribers have children?)

In any case, I have had a sneak preview of Baby Brother, because in this business of investigative reporting we are sent to many, many places and to scrutinize much questionable activity. I come away still convinced that a sock doll and a bit of imagination are better and cheaper than all of this toying around. Dolls are supposed to be props for the young imagination, not amateur entrants into Madame Tussaud's Wax Museum.

But more to the point. Whenever the toy people fiddle around with biology their products end up more confusing than ever before. "It's a boy?" Well, it's a bump, anyway. If he is Baby Brother, who, pray, is Baby Sister and is that supposed to be "anatomically correct"?

When Growing Up Skipper was first marketed, a Mattel spokesman told me dead-pan that the doll had "opened up a very healthy family dialogue about the whole growing-up process." No doubt. Parents couldn't let their kids run around thinking that if they twisted their arm around they'd hit puberty faster. One can only shiver at the thought of "Growing Up Brother."

Right now Baby Brother is to a baby brother what Baby Alive is to a baby alive—pseudo-biology in pursuit of profits. The toy manufacturers have decided, alas, that anatomy is their marketing destiny. Let's just hope they keep their hands off DNA.

AUGUST 1976

ADULTS AND KIDS:
A RELATIONSHIP GONE AWRY. I.

Item One: The schools may not open in Cleveland next fall because the adults voted down school financing. Item Two: In Riverside County, California, it is now legal to ban children from cities. Item Three: In movie houses all over America this week, another monster-child of the adult fantasy, *Damien*, is busily murdering the grown-ups around him. Item Four: In St. Louis, the Board of Education has just gone back to basics: the rattan switch.

These are four of the recent bulletins from the front lines. They are, in different ways, warnings that something has gone wrong in the most basic relationship of any society: the relationship between the community of adults and children, between the present and the future.

Adults have slowly turned inward, defensive. In places they are now voting for themselves, separating themselves, even "arming" themselves, against children. They are the human signposts of the erosion, bit by bit, of a wider sense of responsibility and connection between generations.

Once upon a time—a real time—children were regarded as the inevitable, natural condition of life. They were also an economic necessity for families—free labor for the present, insurance for the future. In that same time, communities were smaller and more stable, and kids were looked upon as the grown-ups of the future. There was a wider, more immediate sense of the investment an entire community had in the people its children became.

Now, increasingly, parenthood is regarded as a personal, individual decision—even a "lifestyle," whatever that may be—made apart from community interests. Kids are listed not as economic assets, but economic obligations. Each year someone tallies up the cost of raising them as if they were sides of Angus beef. And each year someone also tallies up their cost to the town or the city and wonders if they are worth it. Recently, in many places, the voters have said no.

It is no coincidence that in Cleveland people cut taxes against schools, or that the first thing lost in the wake of Proposition 13 is summer school in Los Angeles. It is not a coincidence that the voters would like most to slash Aid to Families with Dependent Children.

There is a growing belief that each family should be on its own:

a feeling that kids should be cared for totally by Those Who Choose to Have Them, and kept out of the way of the rest of the Child-free World.

The transience of our society makes it easier for people to dismiss the issues of the young and easier to vote selfishly along generation lines. Adults rarely think about schools or playgrounds or no-children housing until they have babies. They forget about these things when their babies are grown and gone.

It might be hard for an elderly couple, however pinched by real estate taxes, to vote against the new school or day-care center their own grandchild needed. But their grandchildren usually live far away.

The breakup of families (which we call mobility); the fact that parenthood is seen as a personal decision; the economic independence of generations of family members—all of these things make it easier for people to choose to lower their taxes rather than raise someone else's children. They make it easier to put up legal barriers rather than welcome mats.

It is all part of the process of separation, the centrifuge of generations and community. Increasingly, under its influence, grown-ups treat kids as if they were someone else's puppies. They are to be admired when they're cute and well-behaved, abhorred when they're messy or needful or expensive, and always kept off the grass of adult territory.

But when the comfortable, caring connections break down between generations, the old, fearful image recurs. Now the child is seen as a monster, a little devil capable of murder. And the adult becomes a ruler—with a rattan in his hand. The reemergence of this hostile relationship is the second half of this story.

JUNE 1978

ADULTS AND KIDS:
A RELATIONSHIP GONE AWRY. II.

There is a moment in *Damien* when the thirteen-year-old is told by his teacher that he is the devil. He goes into his room, where he discovers the mark of Cain on his head and, horrified, races down to the water crying out, "Why me?"

This one scene raises the movie out of the category of pseudo-religious trash and makes it an allegory of child psychology. It is, after all, a turning point when the child accepts the adult knowledge of his evil and becomes evil. A turning point when the adult projection becomes an adolescent reality.

This image of the child-as-monster—whether in *Damien, Carrie, The Exorcist,* or *Rosemary's Baby*—is as old as swaddling, child sacrifice and original sin. But it's no coincidence that the theme re-emerges now, just when the caring connections of adults and children seem so frayed and when their relationship is often one of hostility and fear.

The history of childhood is, in itself, an ugly one in which the abuse of children was actually an "improvement" over centuries of infanticide.

Until recently, battering was a normal method of child-raising, whether the child was a pauper or a prince, like Louis XIII. Even the "best people" battered. Milton beat his nephews for "instruction." Beethoven beat his students for mistakes. Sometimes he even bit them. There is one record, only a century old, that carries the proud arithmetic of a German schoolmaster who counted 911,527 strokes with a stick, 124,000 lashes with the whip, and 1,115,800 boxes on the ear.

Today, at least, when we hear about some horrendous child abuse—whether it is the million cases in the country, or two recent tragic cases in Massachusetts—our stomachs churn at the details. But when we ask why, we have to listen to psychiatrists like Dr. Richard Galdston of Children's Hospital, when he says this: "The term *monster* is the word most frequently used to describe the abused child."

What happens, then, when a whole society—one which had barely begun to support the notion that children have the right to space, health, education, adult help—starts to think of them again as monsters?

Today's children, disdained as socially useless and regarded as the personal problems of their own parents, are considered expensive and intrusive. Monstrously expensive. Monstrously intrusive.

Adults in California cut child services. Adults in Cleveland put the schools in jeopardy. But worst of all, adults, from the justices of the Supreme Court to the members of the St. Louis Board of Education, publicly sanction child abuse.

Of course, those who sit now, debating the size and flexibility of the latest piece of school equipment, the rattan switch, see themselves as well-meaning instructors, even peacekeepers, even defenders of civilization. They point out that 70,000 teachers are battered each year by students. They hold clippings about the seventeen-year-old in Washington who murdered her mother. They tell true stories about the elderly who live in terror of youth gangs.

But they forget who taught these children the lessons of fear and hostility. They forget that the rattan is used almost always on young children, and teachers are battered almost always by older children. They forget that even Damien didn't want to be a devil. Some even use the "monstrousness" of children as proof that kids "deserve" nothing more than abuse and neglect.

There are, of course, adults and parents who lavish enormous, even excessive, concern on children. They support an industry of advisors, consultants and authors. But they exist in a community context which, after a brief and hopeful time, seems to be turning back against children.

Today, there are fewer adults with a responsible, sensitive commitment to children and, therefore, to the future. Having confused permissiveness with neglect, and authority with abuse, the generations now splinter into hostile camps. The adults often try to protect themselves with zoning laws, barbed wire and rattans.

They threaten us with a retreat to the darkest age of society: to a history of childhood which is too monstrous ever to be repeated.

JUNE 1978

THAT TACKY OLD THING CALLED HOPE

The sophomore had come home for the holidays dressed in Cynicism Chic. He appeared rather stylish, like a photograph for a college mood piece. On his campus, expectations were being worn quite low, like hip huggers.

Before he had unpacked, he told his parents that he had finally, and irrevocably, become a Realist. He was ready to bear the harshest winter truths. Nothing, he said, ever really changes. Individuals can't actually make a difference. Hope is naive, he concluded, wrapping his cynicism snugly around him.

The sophomore had always been a listmaker, and so now he itemized the reasons for his "realism." Politicians are interchangeable digits paralyzed by the systems they "lead." Today's cures turn into tomorrow's problems. Ban one chemical and ten more spring up, with their own carcinogens. War is inevitable and pollution irreversible. Oh, the events in the Middle East had temporarily jarred his disbeliefs, but they too had bogged down a bit. In any case, he would not abandon his abandonment of hope for Sadat.

The boy had brought home a friend. They spent a great deal of time in his room, meditating. In view of the situation, they said, they were "working on detachment." They wanted to clear away the rubbish that cluttered their minds so that they could see things clearly. They talked as much about "removal" as two sanitary commissioners. But their notion of rubbish was the idea that things could get better, that they could change.

Of course, the sophomore shook up his parents. "The Shakes" are an occupational hazard for parents of the college-aged. Their children bring home philosophies and opinions the way they once brought home woodworking and clay handprints. They brought home atheism to one generation of parents and mysticism to another. They grew left wings and right wings at the most inconvenient times. They memorized copies of Chairman Mao and Carlos Castaneda and recited Henry Miller over dinner with grandma.

This year, along with their laundry and ravenous appetites, they had brought home cynicism and a side dish of Zen.

In truth, this boy's parents were very vulnerable to his new style. They were also victims of a disappointment gap which had grown between their expectations and reality. They were hardly the harpies of hope.

Ten years ago, so many parents had found it hard to argue in favor of The War, or in favor of the status quo. Now these two found it hard to argue against cynicism. The son had challenged his parents, not by taking the opposite view, but by taking the extreme of their own view.

The parents knew that change was difficult. The sophomore said it was impossible. The parents knew all about the possibilities of failure. The sophomore said it was inevitable. The boy spent all week diving for the bottom line . . . and working on detachment.

But something curious happened to the parents between Christmas and New Year's. They found themselves saying things they hadn't even remembered that they believed. Cynicism can be an excuse for inaction, the father said. Detachment is a cop-out, the mother said. If you don't believe in change, you have a ready-made excuse for giving up, they both said. Things can change. Slowly. People can make a difference. Somewhat. It's important to try, they said, and believed.

The father rummaged through some of his old stuff one night and found a book he'd once brought home on vacation. It was written by a philosopher of detachment, Albert Camus, who'd still never really lost his belief in people. Feeling a bit silly, he read it at the dinner table: "If we listen attentively, we shall hear amid the uproar of empires and nations, the faint fluttering of wings, the gentle stirring of life and hope. Some say this hope lies in a nation, others in a man. I believe, rather, that it is awakened, revived, nourished by millions of solitary individuals whose deeds and words every day negate frontiers and the crudest implications of history."

The father didn't, of course, change the son's mind. He and his friend went back to school on New Year's Day with clean laundry on their backs and a new supply of protein in their bodies.

But the parents thought that they had, in a curious way, once again gained something from the interaction with their sons. They had come to the borders of their own despair, observed their bottom line, and argued themselves back, part way.

Cynicism was chic, yes, but these two, at least, would start the new year with some of that tacky old thing called hope.

JANUARY 1978

A HALFWAY HOUSE

For many years I was certain that Thanksgiving was a plot devised by the Turkey Population Growth lobby. But, more recently, I have decided that it is truly brought to us by the American Family Psychoanalytic Association, in order to study midlife-crisis parents and their identity-crisis children.

For those of you unfamiliar with the middle-class American Life Cycle patterns, every September, at enormous expense, a large segment of the population send their children off to Institutions of Higher Adolescence, known as universities. These institutions are charged with the responsiblity of managing the transition of America's youth into adulthood.

Ideally, they are to produce totally delightful twenty-two-year-old graduates who are independent but caring, articulate but agreeable, and fully appreciative of their parents' wonderfulness. In short, "the children we would have regretted not having when we were older." These institutions, like all modern rehabilitative centers, allow the wards out on furloughs at carefully managed intervals known as holidays.

During each of these furloughs—of which Thanksgiving is the first—the issue is to discover how the new lessons fit into the old setting. Not to mention vice versa.

The kiddies come home with a mixed agenda. They want to be taken care of on the one hand, and prove their independence on the other. They drop their laundry in the utility room and their opinions in the dining room.

They are hurt if their parents have forgotten to stock up on their special brand of low-calorie soda, and horrified if these same parents expect them to eat their favorite roast, since they "don't touch meat anymore." They want to be treated like visitors who get clean sheets, while conveniently forgetting that visitors ask before they use the car.

Their parents meanwhile have their own adjustments to make. You see, those who were prepared for an attack of the empty-nest syndrome in September are aghast at the symptoms of a full-nest syndrome in November.

In the past six weeks they have discovered what it's like to have sex when you don't have to outwait your teenage children—"Not now, *they* are still awake"—and what it's like to have dinner-time conversation instead of arbitration. After years of "running a household," they are learning to live together. Now, vaguely distressed at having a household of children, they have reams of guilt—"Does this mean I don't miss my children? Does this mean I don't love them?"—which leads them into overdosing their young with nurturing and role-playing.

The separate issues of parents and children meet across the groaning board known as Thanksgiving Dinner. Next to this encounter of generations, the University of Texas football field is as calm as a chessboard.

There is, for example, one daughter who has come home with a definitive analysis of her parents' relationship—"sexist"—and now wants to institute a plan for changing it: "Mother, you carve the turkey." Then, there is the son who is taking an American history course on the sixties and informs his father that "Jack Kennedy was a fascist" (an opinion his father calculates costs $465, not including books).

To add to the family fun, there is a son who has decided that it is time for him to be honest and direct with grandma, so that "she will know where I'm coming from," which is generally an X-rated dictionary. And, finally, there is daughter's Mystery Guest, whom she introduces to eighty-three-year-old Aunt Jane as "my lover," in case anyone had not noticed.

Mother, in turn, tells her daughter (in front of the lover) to brush her hair. Father reminds his son to "Kiss your Aunt Polly hello," and in glorious unison they tell their twenty-year-old to "Finish your peas or no dessert."

Dinner thus ends in a draw, and the turkey ends in a curry. Or a fricassee. Or a salad. Everyone is momentarily aghast at the speed with which they fell into their old roles, but the beat goes on.

The holiday home is a halfway house between childhood and adulthood, between parenthood and friendship, and it's difficult to work out these transitions in a 108-hour furlough. But this is just a beginning. If Thanksgiving can be handled without a major bloodletting, give thanks for that. Remember, there are only thirty recovery days until Christmas.

NOVEMBER 1976

JUDGING THE PARENTS GUILTY

I don't know what "psychological malparenting" is, I don't have a three-part working definition of it, and so I don't know whether or not Tom Hansen was a victim of it.

But I do know that the twenty-four-year-old from Boulder, Colorado, is suing his parents for this sort of malpractice, as if they'd been doctors all those years and he'd been an anesthetized patient. As if they had willfully bungled the case.

He's suing them on the assumption that every parent is a board-certified expert on childhood, and that their errors were the "intentional infliction of emotional distress."

Hansen, a kid living on Social Security and a little bit more, a kid who's been in and out of mental hospitals, wants his parents to pay for lousing up his life. He tallies the damages at $350,000.

As a legal case, Hansen's suit doesn't have a prayer. The courts avoid getting into family business unless it's absolutely crucial, and they're not about to try to decide the issue of whether Hansen's father subjected him to hard labor back in 1968 when he sent him into the yard to dig weeds.

But the case has grabbed our attention in the past month, and not just because it sets a legal precedent. We're fascinated because this grown-up child has done in public what so many others do in private: He's proclaimed his parents guilty for his own life.

Hansen told a reporter that he filed suit as an alternative to killing his own father. He chose, instead, character assassination.

But how different is he, really, from the others we've known who, at twenty-four or fifty, still eloquently trace their present problems to the traumatic incidents they've filed away in their own mental legal briefs against mom and dad? How different is he from those who point a private finger at father's neglect and mother's smothering, at misunderstanding and . . . malparenting? Isn't it a favorite indoor game of the times?

From Philip Roth on, there are lists of those who analyze their childhoods, not to understand them but to wallow in them, not to change their present lives but to rationalize them. They wrap themselves in difficult memories like comfortable excuses. They declare themselves as "innocent as children" of their own actions, free of responsibilities for adulthood. They confess, saying, "My parents did it."

No one denies that kids are shaped—warped or well-formed—in part by their parents. No one denies that some are subject to everything from murderous abuse to arbitrary authority to the unrelenting pressure to achieve. But it is also true that kids live in a wider world, and that they respond to the same events, the same families, the same world, in unique and sometimes unpredictable ways.

The Hansen family story appears to be a tale of expectations upset, anger unchecked, an adolescence in the late sixties that was as traumatic for the parents as for the child. If Tom Hansen can sue his parents, then he could sue his peers, his teachers, his town, perhaps even the times in which he lived. Surely he could sue his grandparents and their parents, because parenting is a legacy from one generation to the next.

But it seems to me that there must be a statute of limitations on blame. At some point a child has to own his own life, or find himself hooked forever to an umbilical cord that also determines the future.

After all, the creepiest part of the Hansen story isn't the man-child's vengeance toward his past, but how committed he is to it. As his mother said: "This is his sole reason for existence, talking about all the things his father did to him."

Pathetically, he has finally found an occupation: to be the living proof of his parents' failure. Now, if his life improves, his case diminishes. If he is ever happy, he lets his parents off the hook.

Like how many others, his life is a monument to his parents. Even as a self-proclaimed failure, in this destructive way, Hansen can succeed in one goal: to remain Exhibit A in his own malparenting suit.

JUNE 1978

PART EIGHT

FOIBLES

A FAILURE OF FAITH
IN MAN-MADE THINGS

There are those who have faith in man-made things and those who do not.

I do not.

I do not have faith in elevators. I do not have faith in planes, subways, bridges or tunnels.

I do use them. Of which fact I am very proud.

I have, for example, a friend who chose his dentist because the dentist's office was on the first floor. I know a journalist who became a national expert on trains because he can't bear flying. I have another friend who sold his island house after living there only weeks because he had dizzy spells on the bridge. (The alternative route—a tunnel—was completely out of the question.)

I don't think these people are neurotic. Rather, it's a question of degree. How many of the rest of us travel on, over and through man-made things comforted only by our private *escape* plans?

That's the dividing point. People who have faith in man-made things do not have *escape* plans. I do.

I have an escape plan for the elevator. I will escape Certain Death if the elevator drops twenty floors suddenly—which I fully expect—because I will be jumping up and down. I read once that if you jump up and down while the elevator is crashing you have a 50 percent chance of being up while it's down and softening the impact.

Don't tell me if it's not true.

I have an escape plan for the final subway stall. If somewhere between stops, the transit line dies and there are four hundred of us squeezed into one car so tightly that no one can move an arm to break a window, I will escape. I will be at my usual post, nose in the door, gasping the one thin stream of air as it comes through a crack.

On the whole, I am more philosophical about airplanes. I look quite relaxed: seated, belted (no, I never take off my seatbelt, not even between here and Paris) and reading a paper before take-off. I repeat ten times, "Well, it's out of my hands now." But look closer. I am in the last row, because I remember from a Jimmy Stewart movie, *The Phoenix*, that you've got the best chance of surviving near the tail. I will *escape*. If I weren't so concerned about looking cool, I would ride on the plane's rear lavatory floor.

As for bridges, I remember the Galloping Gertie. Other bridges look sturdy enough, but there is only one railing between me and the water. When I drive over them, I roll up my window, because if my car plunges into the water—it is possible, it really is—there will be an air bubble in it. I will be able to breathe until I collect myself and then execute a perfect *escape* like the ones you see on television.

Don't tell me if it isn't true.

My greatest phobia is about tunnels—maybe because my escape plans stink. Every time I go through a tunnel, I expect the Ultimate Leak. And I haven't figured any way out against the rising water except (1) drive for it or (2) run for it.

I do try to control myself. After all, I have driven through two thousand tunnels without even using the windshield wipers. But I am prepared for the worst.

I don't know how tunnels are built, or bridges, or elevators, or airplanes. I don't know how or why they work. So why should I believe they're safe? How do I know they won't break with me on, in, over or under them?

My escape plans are nothing more than an attempt at control. I know that I don't want to be dependent on the metal of a bridge, or the concrete of a tunnel. In truth, I don't really want to depend on man-made things at all. I hate being that far from Control Central. A severe failure of faith.

I suppose I would make one lousy astronaut.

MAY 1977

▉▉▉ NO WORKING PERSON
MUST EVER NEED ANYTHING SERVICED

It was her fault, of course. The Working Mother's fault. She was the one who had bought a yellow rug. I mean, a *yellow* rug. She should have known better.

You see, her living room was never one of those "Please Do Not Touch" exhibits open only to visitors. In fact, the floor of the room was where the dogs napped and the kids did gymnastics.

So, naturally, it got dirty and there she was looking down at two-canine-sized spots and an overall tone of lime-grime. She knew then that she had willfully violated a cardinal rule of American life: No Working Person Must Ever Need Anything Serviced. Or Repaired, Delivered, Picked Up or Otherwise Touched at Home.

She'd had a similar problem back in 1974. It was the last time the Working Mother had bought anything she couldn't carry home in her string bag. It was a refrigerator.

She's bought the frost-free, two-door wonder in one of those highway stores that stay open late to accommodate working families. It was only after her credit card had transported the sale irretrievably into some vast computer thousands of miles away that she asked about delivery. It turned out that there was absolutely no coincidence between the times they delivered and the times she was at home.

If it hadn't been for her mother, the woman's relationship with the refrigerator would have been limited to visiting hours.

Basically then, if the Working Mother was stuck with this lime-grime, double-dog-spotted rug, it was her own fault and she deserved not an iota of sympathy. I mean, the Working Mother had read John Kenneth Galbraith's economic analysis of the subject, hadn't she? She knew that the entire service industry was geared to the myth that every house had its housewife and that this housewife's patriotic duty was to be thrilled at the idea of hanging around scraping her yellow, waxy buildup off the linoleum while she waited for deliverers, installers and fixers.

She was musing on all this the day she came home to discover that her daughter and a friend had toasted marshmallows in the fireplace and carefully picked off the burnt spots. She now had a lime-grime, double-dog-spotted rug with Charcoal Fallout. She now was forced to call the Cleaner.

The Cleaner who asked the Working Mother to bring in the rug. Who promised a 10 percent discount, mind you, if she would just jog right on over the 8 miles with the 144-square-foot rug on her back. Who finally agreed to send the Truck.

She thought it was a good sign when the Truck came for the rug at the appointed hour, before she left for work that week. But she was misguided. The fact was that now They Had It. If she ever wanted to see her rug again, she was at their mercy. It was, after all, what you call Supply and Demand.

After they had removed the lime-grime, the double-dog-spot and the Charcoal Fallout, the Cleaner called about delivery. The Working Mother had hoped to negotiate that issue with a sympathetic Working Woman. Someone sisterly like, say, Bella Abzug. But this time, she got the wrong Bella. Bela Lugosi. This Bela would give her a delivery day, but not an hour. This Bela told her that the Truck had a Route and a Route was inviolable and there were No Exceptions. *No Exceptions*.

This Bela suggested that she find a Neighbor, "like other women do." The Working Mother wondered who had these mysterious Neighbors who would spend their days in your house waiting for your yellow rug. Was it a personal flaw that she had no such Neighbor? Was she the only one whose Neighbors also worked?

Next, she tried assertiveness training, which she had learned as a novice reporter from her first city editor. Her first city editor had never dealt with the Cleaner.

So, then, she delivered an ultimatum—"Well, you can bring it on Tuesday, but I am telling you that no one will be home after 10:00 A.M.!" And they delivered a rug at 11:37 A.M. They left her a note instead of a rug explaining that redelivery would cost another $5.

At that point, the Working Mother tried passiveness training, which she had learned from playing victim in her Junior Lifeguard class. She stayed at home for the redelivery.

After all, she reasoned, as she waited for the second coming, if they call this a service industry, it must be because we service it. After all, she consoled herself, they also stand and wait who only serve.

DECEMBER 1976

TAKING THE GOOD WITH THE BAD

Call it gossip, call it character analysis, call it what you will, the demand for private information about public people is running full throttle. We want to know who they *really* are. We want to know what they're *really* like.

We want the warts, and nothing but the warts.

Our reaction, for example, to Joan Mondale is incredulity. She seems to be a bright, friendly, thrifty woman who buys her Christmas presents in July. For which we label her "Too Good to Be True."

That's where we're at. We would never say that someone is Too Bad to Be True these days. We seem to believe wholeheartedly in the bad, and we will only believe that the Real Joan Mondale has stood up when we discover that she rolls burrs into Fritz's socks or kicks cats.

We have come to associate character revelations with Digging Up the Dirt, and we are currently convinced that only the dirt is real. In short, we think the worst of ourselves. We think the worst *is* ourself.

This rampant pessimism comes up in all kinds of little ways. It came up one night when I visited a friend in a state of terminal grubbiness—matched only by the condition of her apartment. She put one hand on her hair rollers and pointed to the laundry with the other hand and grimaced, "Well, now you've seen the Real Me." This woman, who relines her kitchen drawers twice a year, was sure that she had revealed the secret inner soul of a slob.

But why is it that we are all so sure the *real me* is the one with the dirty hair, the one in dire need of a tube of Clearasil, the one who is screaming at the children, the one harboring thoughts of dismembering the driver behind us?

Why isn't the *real me* the one who remembers birthdays, keeps the scale within the limits of self-hate and plays "go fish" with the kids? Doesn't that count? Why are we so convinced that anything good about us is a civilized shell hiding the *real me?*

The *real me* problem is horribly destructive. If one assumes that the truth about ourselves is too bad to be false, then of course we have to hide it from others. They in turn can't truly love us because they don't know the real us. The unlovable real us. It's a Catch '76 in which we assume the worst of everyone else as well.

Our belief in the bad comes from religion on the right and Freud on the left—original sin and original id. Between psychology and theology we've had a double-whammy that's convinced us that way down deep there, in the old subconscious or whatever, we are a mass of grasping, greedy, destructive, angry and rather appalling characteristics.

Abraham Maslow, who was one of the few psychologists to try to help us out of this pessimistic view, once observed that not only do we associate our nature with animal nature, but with the worst of the animals. "Western civilization has generally believed that the animal in us was a bad animal and that our most primitive impulses are evil, greedy, selfish and hostile." He said that we have chosen to identify with "wolves, tigers, pigs, vultures or snakes, rather than with at least milder animals like the elephants or chimpanzees."

Maslow was one of those who tried to convince us that the *real me* is no more angry than loving, selfish than generous. He also tried to show us that people are motivated not just by neurotic needs, impulses and fears, but out of a positive desire to grow, and out of a sense of fun and pleasure.

But we are not yet convinced. The common street-wisdom of the day is that the most successful of us are "compensating" for some lack, and that the happiest-seeming of us are really "repressing" some unhappiness. If we don't see that, then we are told to dig a bit deeper because he or she is just "too good to be true."

Now, I hate to sound like Little Mary Sunshine and I am not advocating that we accept everyone at face value. We've been plagued by masked men. But maybe we can get off the hook by letting others off of it. The things we hate about ourselves—from the roll around the stomach to the bad temper—aren't more real than the things we like about ourselves. The good isn't a fake. Even if we have to dig for it.

AUGUST 1976

THE SMOKING-LAMB-CHOP DETECTOR

As someone who spent long, formative moments of the Cold War huddled in public-school basements under CD signs and who once thought her parents foolish because they refused to stock the cellar with two weeks' worth of canned water and food, I am well aware of the powerful impact of school safety programs. So, over the years, I have tried to be sympathetic, cooperative even, when my daughter has come home from school bearing messages about the Seriousness of one situation or another.

I didn't, for example, scoff during the years of the Halloween Horrorcasts when she arrived with a three-page warning stating that if children absolutely had to trick-or-treat, they must only go out bathed in fluorescent lighting and flanked by two adults carrying buckets of water. Nor did I laugh when, under strictest school orders, the mini-Wonderwoman at my side refused to accept any unwrapped treat, and dissected the brownies at her grandmother's house, looking, as she was told, for razor blades.

In fact, I watched with some interest as schoolchildren were turned into mobile anti-smoking campaigns, human safety-belt buzzers and, more lately, anti-choking rescue squads. I have only recently recovered from my daughter's anti-choking demonstration. My ribs will be unstrapped any day now, but I have, I assure you, learned to chew my food carefully.

All of this is merely background. I want to explain the simple fact that over a year ago a school visit by the local fire-prevention crew ended up with our purchase of two home smoke alarms.

Within a few weeks of owning these round, friendly early-warning systems, I should have known that something was wrong. I had already experienced some strange new facts about home safety.

I discovered, for example, that if there were ever a fire that started from a broiled piece of meat, we would be the first to know it. If there were a spontaneous combustion of a marinated chicken, we would never go unaware. If, indeed, a reheated pizza ever leapt from the oven to the rafters, we would be out of the house before we were overcome by pepperoni fumes.

You see, the sensitive soul of our system was set off by the mere whiff of a hamburger three rooms away. At a hint of bacon frying, it set up an alarm more intense, more judgmental, than the voices of a dozen committed vegetarians.

Never mind the label "smoke alarms": We were the proud owners of two Lamb-Chop Alarms.

If, in a fit of forgetfulness, we attempted something even more offensive than cooking, if we tried to use the self-cleaning cycle on the oven, they would wail out their objections to housekeeping until they were forcibly removed from the wall and buried under a mound of comforting pillows.

Let other alarms be praised for the work of fire prevention. Ours should have been arrested for cruelty to animals. Even a dog which had been stoic through two years of violin lessons retreated, groaning, to another mound of pillows.

Let other smoke alarms go beep in the night when they have to; ours went beep in the night when they wanted to. Without a lamb chop or a puff of smoke, they set up a regular false alarm that raged through the hour of two o'clock. They complained in terrifying spurts if they were dusty, if their batteries were weak, if they were bored, or, I suspect, if they wanted to test our reflexes.

Still, for many months, I considered all these problems to be minor ones—the sort of peculiarities you could tolerate in a hyperactive watchguard, and a small sacrifice to make for safety. Until last weekend.

On that Sunday, we built a first-of-the-season fire. With the flue closed. It took three minutes of shouting and action until the flue, the windows and the door were opened and ten minutes until the heavy smoke subsided. But during this time there had been one noticeable pocket of silence.

Our smoke alarms had slept through it.

These bone-chilling noisemakers, these terrors of the broiler, these champions of dust-free batteries, had actually flunked their only trial by fire.

It is now clear that we own a duet of incompetent, functionally unfunctional eccentrics. Even someone of my own inclination toward safety first, my devotion to paranoia of every kind, is finally faced with the ultimate existential question: Is there any reason to keep my home safe from a broiling lamb chop?

OCTOBER 1978

![] AMERICAN TAXPAYER DAY

It's a day when you wish you owned a piece of the block. H&R.

It's a day when you realize that, instead, you own a piece of a B-1 bomber, and that you are sending the government enough money to just about cover the salary of the IRS investigator who will be after you shortly.

Yes, it's American Taxpayer Day, a day like many others—D-Day, for instance. It comes on April 15, in memory of the birth of Horace L. Tenforty, who, as a small child, deciphered the meaning of phrases like "enter the greater of $2,100 or 16 percent of line 43, but not more than $2,800."

Yes, this is the day when we finally remember how many dollars we have contributed personally to the tobacco subsidy, and try to believe in the significance of a $50 rebate.

But not every American is bitter on deadline day. There are those who look upon this day as an opportunity, a chance to see the sunny side of things—like mortgage payments and root-canal work. Today is a banner day for those who prefer to think deductively and constantly evaluate their lives, hoping for an extra loss or two.

These are the people known as the Tax Deductible Livers. The TDL, prize student of the tax accountant, tries to lead an unblemished 100 percent deductible life. He is, first of all, self-employed and, second of all, obsessive. He puts a low priority on enjoying life, since almost everything self-indulgent has a cost. In fact, his slogan is, "I may not be having a good time, but on the other hand it's deductible."

The TDL never has dinner with friends and lovers. He eats business, the way other people eat Chinese, or Italian. "Business" is a steak-and-salad bar with a client, and a martini in a restaurant that is an imitation Victorian pub and takes credit cards. TDL even puts the tip for the hat-checker on his American Express.

His idea of a helluva-good-time is to take a convention vacation. He would go to Newark for a write-off. Generally he can be found on a Boeing 747 with 346 other chiropodists bound for seven sun-filled days and eight glorious nights in Hawaii. Once there, he will spend the sun-filled days and glorious nights in an imitation Hawaiian pub that takes credit cards. He will also attend the seminar on "Cuticles: To Cut or Not to Cut."

The TDL has a home in his office. He used to have an office in his home, until the IRS cracked down on that. Now he has moved into the office along with a mattress which fits comfortably over two filing cabinets.

This has worked out well for him, because his wife—with whom he hadn't eaten since 1972 (before income averaging)—finally left. The TDL wasn't too upset at losing this exemption, because he had the opportunity to pay alimony, which is deductible.

The same fellow, by the way, sends his mother Candygrams on her birthday and gives his clients' daughters Steuben glass for their weddings. He has a business car which he uses to travel from his business dinners to his home-in-the-office to his little exemptions in the house supported by his alimony payments.

He is a lucky man. He doesn't worry about earthquakes or diseases. His last accident occurred on a surfboard which he bought to entertain clients on. He looks forward to one major piece of surgery a year.

Of course the TDL does have some problems. He has to spend a lot of time keeping records. There is the expense book in his weekly calendar and the mileage record in his glove compartment and the checkbook with the special tax pockets.

He asks everyone, even the drugstore clerk and the toll-booth collector, for itemized receipts. These receipts never turn to lint in the bottom of his pockets and never melt in the washing machine. He arranges them in neat piles. Annotated. For kicks, just for fun, he computes the interest on his home-in-the-office mortgage on his deductible calculator.

The TDL spends most of early April working with his tax accountant, who is very expensive. But he doesn't mind. After all, even the cost of figuring out the deductions is deductible.

APRIL 1977

SEND IN THE CLONES

It seems that all America is wondering whether or not a human being has been cloned and is currently in a crib somewhere learning to call his mirror-image "Da-da."

David Rorvik, the author of *In His Own Image*, is the hottest item on talk shows this side of an erroneous zone. Everyone wants to know whether he is clowning about the cloning of Millionaire Max.

But, concerned as I am about Max's baby, or any other clones we may be feeding, I am more worried about the clones we may be eating.

Even if Rorvik has written science fiction, the agricultural scientists on the West Coast have created a new science fact called the Cloning of an Asparagus. Despite sounding like a horror movie—"The Asparagus That Stalked New York"—this feat was actually accomplished by Ray Dyck and Hsu-jen Yang over three years at a cost of $100,000 at a federal agricultural experiment station in Prosser, Washington.

There is nothing especially new about cloning plants, you understand. But as a longtime vegetable-watcher (nature's equivalent of a China-watcher), I can now safely predict the worst: The Inedible Clone. Every time the agricultural scientists fiddle around with a perfectly decent veggie, they come up with a "bigger and better" product that looks good enough to eat—but isn't.

One need only consider the decline and fall of the tomato for evidence. I consider myself to be an expert on this subject, having nearly completed a text called, "Hard, Fuzzy Tomatoes and Other Aberrations I Have Known."

In this work, I show how the best minds of science and technology—better known as American Know-How, Inc.—have spent decades breeding a tomato that can be picked, packed and transported across state lines for the immoral purpose of saying "Ptui" when it crosses our lips. The only thing we cannot do with this tomato is eat it.

As in so many other dark tales, it wasn't the scientific process that went wrong and created a Frankenstein's Big Boy. It was the goal that was perverted from the beginning: Scientists actually bred this tomato on purpose—for machines rather than palates.

The goal of cloning asparagus—Godzilla the Green Spear—is

equally suspect. Until now, male and female asparagus, left to their own biological urges, tended to shamelessly intermarry with plants which were not, strictly speaking, their own kind. This produced rampant disorder in the patch. Long, short, fat and skinny spears cohabited publicly. Their uneven size and their delicate condition have always required handpicking.

Now, Send In the Clones.

In this brave new world of asparagus, I am convinced that we will be left with rectangular spears of uniform size and a texture which are perfect for a mechanical harvester and disastrous for teeth. Not to mention tastebuds.

The perversion of the veggies feeds our worst fantasies of cloning people. It's bad enough to contemplate a mirror-image of an egotistical millionaire, Max, who doesn't want his precious genes diluted. But consider what would happen if we began producing people like we produce vegetables—not for our egos but for our machines.

The logical climax of this scenario would be to clone people with rectangular mouths, steel teeth and a notable lack of taste. In the end, the only reason for a human clone would be to find someone on earth to eat the vegetable clones.

APRIL 1978

I THINK, THEREFORE I RUN

For the past week I've had what you might call a one-track mind. I have been totally immersed in jog training, which is not to be confused with on-the-job training.

Jog training, as I've experienced it, is a preliminary course designed to help those weak of will and ankle (me), to psych themselves up for actually jogging. It is particularly useful, I have found, for those who come out of a strong ethnic heritage—those whose ancestors, for example, spent so many years running from the cossacks, the English, etc., that when they finally got to America, they looked at each other and sighed, "Now at last, we can stop running."

These people pass on such folk wisdom as, "Sit down or you'll have a heart attack" and "What are you running for? Where's the fire?" Jog training is necessary to help you get over (1) their teaching and (2) your gut feeling that there is essentially no difference between discipline and masochism.

But before I step out into the world on my left heel, rise measurably off my left toe, land on my right heel and get going, I feel compelled to leave behind a small pamphlet which is not available at the Government Printing Office. It's called "How to Jog Train."

The first step, so to speak, in jog training is a full, unrestrained embrace of something technically known in the trade as Self-Hate.

You can experience self-hate in a variety of ways. Taking your blood pressure is useful; so is running upstairs and listening to your shortened life span.

I personally found the cover picture of Farrah Fawcett-Majors in her jogging togs to be most effective, since a detailed investigation of her thighs turned up no—repeat, *no*—wrinkles. But the failsafe method for most people seems to be trying on bathing suits in a dressing room with a three-way mirror under fluorescent lighting. After that encounter with self-hate, those who haven't slit their wrists (there is a slight attrition rate in this course) can move right along to step 2, otherwise known as Seeking Inspiration.

Inspiration, moral encouragement and other positive reinforcements are available from any number of jogging converts. There is the 130-pound weakling who had sand kicked in his face a scant half-year ago; the insomniac who now sleeps like a baby; and assorted former physical wrecks. My own inspiration has been liberally provided by a friend who quit smoking and started jogging in one week and sounds like an escapee from an Ayds ad.

The most inspirational thing about jogging books, by the way, is that they were generally written by someone who started off In Worse Shape Than You Are. The one I picked up was by Kathryn Lance, who modestly admitted that she went from "total slob to track star in approximately nine months."

So much then for Self-Hate and Inspiration and visions of the Boston Marathon. The third step is what is known as Economic Motivation, which is to say: Put your money where your mouth is, and maybe your feet will follow. Or something like that.

Economic motivation is a trick I learned three years ago, when I accepted an advance for a book and spent it. I then realized that I had to do the book or give the money (long gone) back. This time, after reading the book, I went out and bought $30 running shoes. Despite the fact that these days running shoes are the dress code at the local supermarket, I am sufficiently crummy that I feel compelled now to use them. Someone else might try exorbitant designer shorts. But economic motivation only works if you spend more money than you know you should.

This step leads, of course, to the final moment in jog training known as Making the Commitment. Of course, there are private commitments and public commitments, but in this case, a little publicity never hurt. If you tell everyone, casually, with just the right flair, that you're getting "into jogging," you may not be as likely to fink out. At least that is the theory behind this column.

Now that I know How To, now that I have graduated from Jog Training, I am about to put the picture of Farrah's thighs in my pocket, lace $30 worth of Adidas profits to my feet, corral one of my Inspirations as a partner, and actually run. At least, I think I am.

JULY 1977

ALL THE
LONELY PEOPLE

I know a man who has spent this year getting himself in shape. He has taken up self-improvement the way other people take up jogging. In fact, he has taken up jogging the way other people take up dieting, and taken up dieting the way other people take up est, and taken up est . . . well, you get the idea.

In an era when every man is an island, this one is striving to be Bermuda. He has improved the value of his personal property with the zeal of a gardener, covering himself with expensive sod from the local men's shop, feeding himself with proper nutrients from the health store, having the hedges around his ears trimmed biweekly by an expert in topiary.

He has even tried to renovate his interior design with a library of self-help books. Nowadays he talks about the landscaping of his personal space—the number of miles jogged, the inches lost, the psychic paths explored—the way people in Washington talk about Georgetown real estate. Obsessively.

Because of this, his appalled friends have dismissed him as a "New Narcissist" and a Champion of the Me Decathlon.

But I wonder.

It seems to me that there is something too glib about the way we increasingly apply the label of egocentricity to the seventies and something too chic about judging people like this Island-man as self-centered.

Last week I read the *Newsweek* cover story on Calvin Klein, a man in the business of body decoration who has his wrinkles smoothed with silicone injections; who is building a gym in his office; who has tried Transcendental Meditation and est. I thought that his explanation of all this was a revealing one: "I have this thing about health and the body. After all, in the end, that's all you have."

Perhaps inadvertently he had spoken the motto of the Island people—"in the end, that's all you have." Perhaps what we've called a psychological disease, narcissism, is really a social disease, isolation. Maybe this isn't a Me First decade but a Who Else decade. Maybe people aren't hedonistically pursuing their own individual whims; maybe they've been reduced to them.

I know very few people who are so in love with their own images that they eventually drown in them. But in a time when caring seems so transient and connections so fragile, commitment so temporary, I know many more who have come to fearfully believe that the only person you take with you throughout your life is yourself—"that's all you have"—and so, they have withdrawn to the most inner circle.

The Island-man, like Calvin Klein, is divorced. He is divorced once if you only count the legal bonds, and thrice if you count the times he's moved his record collection on and off of shared stereos. By now, like many others, he thinks of marriage as a divorce opportunity, and loss as the finale to any love story.

If there was one thing that struck a terrible core of truth for him and for others in *An Unmarried Woman*, it was the stunning fragility of that "solid" marriage. The movie was believable only because we have seen, all around us, those who invest their years in another person and find themselves suddenly bankrupt.

Today, the emotional-commitment market looks like the 1929 stock market. The Self is the 1978 Real Estate.

So people spend much time glorifying aloneness and denying loneliness, trying to make a fulfilling activity out of solitude and a choice out of a condition. But I wonder if what looks like selfishness, even self-indulgence, from the outside feels like compensation from the inside.

Maybe it isn't egocentrism that's the national ill, but this loneliness and the pervasive sense of impermanence. We haven't chosen this fear. We've caught it like a virus in a splintered society.

It is possible that this man, too, is an island by default—another member of our Outward Bound who has become, in defense, a fearful caretaker of his only acre, grooming and landscaping. And isolated.

MAY 1978

ONCE VERBOTEN, NOW CHIC

The whole thing happened in one of those two-story planes they build to make you forget that you're 5 miles up in the air. I had just settled into a chair and opened a magazine when who should appear but Jo Jo White, standing half-naked in his little white cotton underpants with a towel wrapped around his neck.

Now, let me explain. I am not the sort of person who even fantasizes about encountering strange men in their underwear on planes, trains, etc. The one time I was sent to interview a houseful of nudists, I broke the *Guinness Book of Records* record for maintaining eye contact. I leave the rest to Erica Jong, who has a less conventional fear of flying than I do.

But Jo Jo was not alone. He was to the right of Denis Potvin and above Pete Rose, happily occupying a page in the middle of a respectable national newsweekly which was not called *Viva*. In short, there were eight male athletes posing in their little nothings for a Jockey ad over the cut-line that read: "Take Away Their Uniforms and Who Are They?"

Well, it seems that Ken Anderson is a Fun Top and Jim Hart is a Slim Guy Boxer. The only one who was fit to be seen in public was Jamaal Wilkes, who looked as if he were merely wearing a uniform of a different color. As for Jim Palmer's teeny-weeny green print bikini, his "Skants" were a scandal. Is it possible that he was not raised under the Eleventh Commandment: Thou Shalt Not Go Out of the House in Unseemly Undergarments Lest Thou Get in an Accident.

What were these jocks for Jockey doing—aside from earning a lifetime supply of undies? What were they doing wearing hockey gloves and blue-denim bikinis in front of millions of Americans?

They were being paid to convince the rest of the male population that it's OK to buy items they wouldn't have been caught dead in at fifteen. At that age, the average American male already had a conditioned response to anything that looked fancy or sexy, or smelled good. That response was to the single word imprinted in the playgrounds of their minds: *sissy*.

At the mere sound of sibilant *s*, strong men pulled their bodies into gray flannel like terrified turtles, shaved their heads to within an

222   CLOSE TO HOME

inch of their lives and learned how to remove each other's teeth with a single blow.

But over the past handful of years, men have been urged by women and assorted merchants to adopt a variety of products that were once *verboten*. The more questionable the origin of the product, the more they were sold as maler-than-male.

Pocketbooks were not, gasp, pocketbooks, but tote bags and carry-alls designed to look like saddle bags for the Marlboro Man's horse, or tackle boxes for the fisherman. Men wrote articles to each other about how to carry them—carefully—in a distinctively male over-the-shoulder fashion, as opposed to a female over-the-shoulder fashion.

It was obvious that if you wanted to sell men anything even vaguely neuter, you had to inject it with visual and verbal testosterone. Jewelry, for instance, could be sold either in the garrote-chain style or as medallions heavy enough to double as a mace. Rings were popular in the brass-knuckle fashion; bracelets that looked like recycled handcuffs were also all right.

Perfume—forgive me—Male Cologne, was repackaged and rebaptized. It became things like promise-him-anything-but-give-him—Hai Karate. And then came Macho, a perfume in a bottle the shape of which will never appear in this family newspaper.

But nothing has worked quite as well in the fight against sissy stuff as the jock. No one kicks sand in the face of a superstar. Dave Kopay's efforts notwithstanding, an athletic endorsement is as effective in fighting the old conditioned response as an Anita Bryant seal of approval.

Joe Namath sold pantyhose before he turned brute, or should I say, Brut. Pete Rose took to Aqua Velva before he stripped down to his Metre Briefs. (From the look of him in the briefs, I suspect he was drinking the Aqua Velva when he signed the modeling contract.)

The more things change in male décor, the more they stay the same in the ads. The more androgynous the product, the more macho the role-model. So progress inches forward, or downward, to the Tropez Brief. As a trend-watcher might suggest, it's only a matter of time before we have Doctor Julius Erving, the basketball superstar, selling eye-liner under the brand-name "Sado." In the meantime, I wish Jo Jo White's mother would cover the poor boy up. It must be cold in a Boeing 747 in just a pair of white briefs and a towel over your shoulder.

JUNE 1977

FOIBLES

SPARE ME THE "ME PEOPLE"

If God is good to me, if I always finish my spinach and brush my teeth twice a day, I may be able to get through this life without running into Dawson Wallace.

Dawson is one of the characters in a brand-new $400,000 advertising campaign for *Playboy*. He is featured as a "maturing male adult of the 1970s . . . elbowing his way in, saying I want it all, all of it that's good in all aspects of life." He is a member of what ad director Henry Marks describes rather maniacally as the "New Aristocracy." He is an Experience Collector.

To wit: "He doesn't worry about the future because that's tomorrow and it's not worth a cent today. He's very much focused into today and what he can do for himself today. What a whole generation of young men like him is doing is expressing himself to the world, without denying himself the world."

However, if God is good to me and I do not litter and I wash my hands before every meal, perhaps Dawson will deny himself to my little corner of the world.

To be honest, I thought we might be spared the Me People. I thought, surely they were far too involved in their *ménage à moi* to trouble the rest of us. After all, Blair Sabol wrote in a recent *Mademoiselle* article that she had already met Mr. Right and, "He was me."

A book on the same theme, *To Love Is to Be Happy With*, promised: "By the time you finish reading this book you will be in love with a very special person . . . *you!*" But, alas, it turned out that some of the Me People felt limited in what they knew when they only knew themselves. They have apparently decided to broaden their interests by taking up the chic hobby of the seventies: experience collecting.

The Experience Collector is the Me Person running amok in the world. He fully believes that his mentor was Auntie Mame, the lady who once told her nephew, Patrick: "Life is a big wonderful banquet, but most of the poor bastards are too lazy to get up and eat." He fancies himself Patrick-at-large.

As Henry Marks said of the "new aristocracy" he surveyed: "These were the same kids who in the late sixties were angry and rebellious. Now all of that intensity is focused on pursuing the experiences life has to offer. One of them said, 'I grab life with both hands.' "

But he isn't so much grabbing life as completing his stamp book or his itinerary. He's intent on filling time and space with variety: here a blond, there a brunet, everywhere a left-handed violin-playing Swedish actress.

The Experience Collector can't actually devote too much time or energy to any one item because he has to be out getting more. He refuses to get "locked in" to anyone, or to deny himself "anything." He wants one from column A, one from column B, one from column C. And one from column D.

Needless to say, the Experience Collector regards monogamy as if it were a steady diet of peanut-butter sandwiches. Children are excess baggage. He prefers to have his traveling papers in order; they usually read 31 cities in 31 days.

In defense, Marks says: "He is collecting the experiences of an emotionally maturing adult . . . but I don't want to get into the question of what is an emotionally maturing adult. . . ."

As far as I can see, the fellow isn't eating at the banquet. He's nibbling off the hors d'oeuvres tray.

The one thing he can't collect is an involvement. Involvements take up too much time on the itinerary, too much space in the stamp book. Commitment isn't a hobby, it isn't even something you can "take"; it's something you have to give. If there's one thing experience collectors rarely do, it's give something away.

So if you see this guy Dawson nibbling in my direction, let me know. I'm going off to brush my teeth and say my prayers.

MARCH 1977

TAKE A WINDOW
OUT TO LUNCH

Occasionally, when the barometer of her paranoia about Progress peaks and she is humid with discontent, the woman gets obsessed with one idea. She wants to liberate a window.

You see, like millions of other urban Americans, she spends her days hermetically sealed. The windows of her work-a-day life have lost all contact with their roots—the wind. They do not open, neither do they close. Rather, they sit there on their smug sills, oblivious to her fever of discontent.

So, sometimes she glares insanely at these glasses and regards them as transparent symbols of the hubris of modern times. She wonders: Where is Charlie Chaplin when you need him? What would he have done with these anti-windows?

The woman is, of course, an ingrate. It has taken civilization thousands of years to free people from the ravages of nature, from its temperamental ups and downs, in order to enslave them to the ravages of un-nature with its thermostatic ups and downs.

Now, at all times, her air is conditioned. It is whipped into shape by the most expensive sort of machinery. It is heated when it is cold and cooled when it is hot—and here she is, complaining just because it isn't working right. Here she is, yearning for a breeze.

Who is she, anyway, Ayn Rand? After centuries of being victimized by the outdoors, why doesn't she appreciate the progress that made her a victim of the inside?

Instead, she sits at her desk mumbling suspicions. Working and eating and visiting in what the engineers call a controlled environment, she feels utterly out of control. Freed from the hand labor of opening and shutting windows into the brave new world of centralization, she feels impotent.

She thinks that every time we invent a machine to make ourselves more independent, we end up dependent on the machine. At best, we are now hermetically sealed technology junkies, breathing air from central casting.

It is all quite mad. The most obscene thing she'd ever heard about Nixon was that he turned on the air conditioner in the White

House and lit a fire. It was a ghastly image, worse than the catsup on the cottage cheese. But it was typical.

Americans dump chemicals in all the free water and then spend millions on Perrier Water. We pollute the natural air in order to condition the artificial air.

The biggest office building in her city had windows that fell out, but virtually none of the buildings were now built with windows that opened up. She is told that working windows "leak." They are kinky, and subversive. They throw off the Entire System. So, instead, workers are condemned to be democratically uncomfortable. Each restaurant, each office, has its hot spots and cold zones, its rotating sweaters and passing fans. For want of a genuine window.

Now, just now, there were small signs of rebellion. In the underground of fresh-air freaks, this cranky woman had heard of a graduate student, incarcerated with his Ph.D. thesis in a 10-foot-square room, who had slowly chipped away a hole in the window with his bottle cutter. Like some terrified welfare client, he hid his hole behind a fourteenth-century-French history book.

In a few quarters, the room with the breeze was becoming the new status symbol. It was replacing the room with the view, which had replaced the room with the rug. One Boston building had even broken its rules for a Saltonstall. Could the Cabots, the Lodges, and the masses be far behind?

What she needs is to stop this incessant complaining and organize a Window Liberation Front. The will is there. The overly conditioned inhabitants of controlled environments, the advocates of defenestration—they only need to have their consciousnesses raised before they lobby to have their windows raised.

In the summer of her discontent, she would organize a massive Breathe-In. She would even, yes, Take a Window Out for Lunch.

AUGUST 1978

Part Nine

Social Issues

THE MARY NORTHERN STORY. I.

This is a story about Mary Carolyn Northern, and it's not a very pretty one. It's also about doctors and lawyers, about patients and Saint Augustine, and about how much control we want over our own fate.

The story actually began on January 17, when Mary Northern was carried, struggling, from her house in Tennessee, by the police. Her feet had been frostbitten and then burned while she was trying to thaw them over the open fire. Now they were gangrenous.

At the hospital, doctors tried to convince the seventy-two-year-old woman to have her legs amputated. That would give her a fighting chance, a 50-50 chance. But when she refused the operation, they went a step farther. They had her declared "incompetent"—a ward of the state. They decided to try to save her life, even against her will.

From the low court to the most supreme, the state drew a picture of Mary Northern as a crazy lady. After all, she lived alone with six cats. She was a "spinster." She was reclusive. Her French tapestries had cobwebs, her chair was propped up with catsup bottles, her fireplace was overrun by cigarette butts.

And from the low court to the most supreme, Mary Northern had only one reply: "They are not going to take my legs away from me, you understand that?"

In the end, all of the courts upheld the ruling against this lady. She was judged incompetent for one basic reason: She didn't accept the operation like any "sane" person would have; she didn't choose life.

Now, Mary Carolyn Northern was not a picture of mental health. She was clearly eccentric. But she understood the treatment that was offered and she refused it. And this ruling is a scary one to anyone who wants to retain the power of making choices over his or her own body and life.

Increasingly, the courts are being asked to make the final medical decisions. Not just those of life and death, but those of treatment. Increasingly, they are being asked to rule, not only in cases where the people are obviously incompetent—like Karen Ann Quinlan in a coma —but in situations like that of Mary Northern.

Some of these battles originate with the doctors. As William Curran, professor of legal medicine at Harvard Medical School, sees it, "The patient does something the surgeon considers unreasonable —like refusing some operation or treatment they think the patient should get—and the surgeon wants a psychiatric consultation."

Sometimes the doctors are simply protecting themselves from malpractice suits, but often they really believe that a patient who refuses treatment is "incompetent." The patient's refusal alone is proof.

In the majority of states, when these cases find their way to court, judges are liberal about letting patients decide their own fate. But, in a minority, they step in.

"It's a highly paternalistic attitude," says Curran. "The judges and doctors simply have a philosophical or moral view of what control people have over their bodies."

The *Northern* decision, he suggested, may owe more to Saint Augustine's *Confessions* than to Gray's *Anatomy*. It stems from the idea that individuals hold their bodies in trust, that the body is the vessel of the soul and people have an obligation to sustain that life. In short, they have not been granted the power to decide to die.

Few of us would, in fact, make that decision. Most of us would choose life, even a life without feet or breasts or sight. Most of us also want to "save" another person who is severely depressed or desperate about a temporary condition. Most of us feel a responsibility to help others through a self-destructive time.

But if, like Mary Northern, a seventy-two-year-old woman chooses almost certain death over a 50 percent chance of a crippled life, and if she maintains this choice, then surely she should be let alone. I think all of us want that power over our lives.

The woman's doctors haven't yet exercised the right won in court, partly because her condition has worsened. But the fearful thing is that, for the moment, Doctor's Orders carry the force of law in Tennessee.

MARCH 1978

THE MARY NORTHERN STORY. II.

And now, The Perils of Miss Mary, Part II.

When last seen, Mary Northern, the seventy-two-year-old star of this bizarre saga, was at Death's Door or, at least, in the intensive-care ward of a hospital in her hometown, Nashville, Tennessee. There, you may recall, an array of surgeons, psychiatrists, lawyers, welfare agents and state workers of all stripes were battling over her fate.

In the ramshackle, unheated home where she lived alone, Miss Northern's feet had been frostbitten and then burned. Now they were gangrenous, and the doctors said that to save her life, the feet would have to be amputated. Miss Mary, however, said no to the operation. So, for the next seventeen days, a real cliffhanger of a legal battle was waged through five courts, from Nashville to the U.S. Supreme Court and back, over the issue of whether or not Mary Northern was mentally "competent."

Her state fought to save her life, even against her will. Her lawyer fought to protect her rights, even if it meant her death. The courts tried to draw the line between "eccentric" and "crazy."

In the end, her lawyer lost. But, in a sense, Miss Mary won.

They never did operate on the woman, even after the courts gave the doctors permission. First, she was too ill to withstand the procedure. Then, she went through a highly unusual process known as "auto-amputation"—the flesh of her feet fell off of its own accord. Now, remarkably, Mary Northern is not only alive, but she is quite well, thank you.

As her guardian lawyer, Carol McCoy, put it: "This lady won her own case. She has proved the professionals wrong, the doctors wrong, the judges wrong."

But before you applaud this soap-opera ending, hang onto your cliff a minute. The story isn't over yet.

There is now the matter of paying the costs entailed in fighting the case the state initiated against her. The lady was taken struggling from her home, put through weeks of litigation, declared to have no "capacity" to consent, and now apparently is left with the bill.

The psychiatrists' testimony, the court reporters and assorted legal costs add up to several thousand dollars, before you even consider the lawyer's fee. Her lawyer spent 300 hours and sacrificed most of her private practice for four months defending Mary Northern, and hasn't received a penny.

She says she doesn't want any money that comes from Miss Northern. But the state won't pay legal fees—even when they appoint the lawyer—unless the client is a pauper.

So now the Perils of Miss Mary are financial ones. The lady's only asset is her home, which has been appraised at $16,000 but may be worth substantially more. The state ordered a new appraisal of its value. In a few weeks, they will hold a hearing to decide whether or not Miss Mary should be required to pay legal costs.

The beleaguered assistant attorney general, Bill Hubbard, insists that Miss Northern wouldn't have to sell her house under these circumstances. She could take a loan against it. But she has no income (aside from meager Supplemental Security Income checks) to pay off such a loan.

This complicated tale of woe originated, ironically enough, in a benign state statute designed to help elderly persons in need. It's called Protective Services for the Elderly. But, as they sing on *Sesame Street:* "Some kind of help is the kind of help we can do without." Like the overeager Boy Scout, they have "helped" the old lady to the other side of the street she didn't want to cross in the first place. And left her there.

If she ends up having to sell her house, she will really be a person in need. What will happen when she leaves the hospital? Will the state really have to care for her now? Will she find herself in a state-funded nursing home?

Stay tuned for the Perils of Miss Mary, Part III. It's going to be a humdinger!

MARCH 1978

SOCIAL ISSUES   233

THE MARY NORTHERN STORY. III.

The end, the very end of the Mary Northern story, came on May 1, when the seventy-two-year-old woman died in General Hospital, Nashville, Tennessee.

The autopsy says that she died of a blood clot. The doctors' report intimates that if she had not resisted treatment, including amputation, she might be alive today.

But her epitaph says something else. It was written over a hundred years ago by Charles Dickens, who ruefully observed: "It's a remarkable Christian improvement to have made a pursuing Fury out of the Good Samaritan, but it was so in this case and it is a type of many."

Miss Northern spent the last three and a half months of her life pursued by this Fury, harassed by Benevolence, a victim of Goodwill.

It was caring people, our public Good Samaritans, who chased her, all the while bewildered, because she didn't want their "help." It was social workers who came into her ramshackle, unheated home in January, genuinely worried about her health. It was police who carried her forcibly out of her home to the hospital for treatment. It was doctors who tried to persuade her to amputate her gangrenous feet. Finally, when they all failed, it was the state—the Department of Human Resources—which sued to have her declared "incompetent," in an attempt to save her life, even against her will.

Perhaps James Blumstein, the Vanderbilt professor of law, exaggerated when he said, "These people were killing her with kindness." But they did bludgeon her autonomy, her privacy, her independence, and her legal control over her own body.

Now, the lady—labeled a "spinster" even in the wire-service obituary—leaves us a legacy beyond the ramshackle old house she shared with her cats and her family memories. She leaves a reminder of how often individuals, especially the weak, the sick, the elderly and the dependent, need protection from the powerful establishments. Even the Establishment of Kindness.

Her story is a fitting one for times like these, when we are becoming more sensitive to the problems of doing good.

Once, protective statutes like the one that loosed the Furies on Mary Northern seemed to be entirely benevolent. We had an almost naive confidence in professional need-fillers who had, in turn, naive self-confidence. As David Rothman wrote in a small, intriguing book called *Doing Good: The Limits of Benevolence:* "In their eagerness to play parent to the child, they did not pause to ask whether the dependent had to be protected against their own well-meaning intervention."

Today, while we don't question the motives behind the social programs, we are concerned about the results. We are increasingly aware of the way a vast social services bureaucracy can violate the rights of an individual. And increasingly attuned to the new social problems that arise from solutions to old problems.

In the past week, for example, while Miss Northern lay in General Hospital, the Senate Finance Committee heard a research report which showed a rise in the divorce rate following the government's offer of a minimum guaranteed family income. At the same time, several lawyers expressed concern to me about the zeal with which social workers, following up reports of child neglect, could violate the rights of parents, quite legally, under statutes written without proper procedural safeguards.

In our political life, the conservatives are attuned to these vibrations of anxiety. They offer these examples as proof of the inherent intrusiveness and coerciveness of government. And they broadcast a desire to halt many new attempts to help people.

But it is as cruel to ignore suffering as to force "cures."

The trick of shaping and reshaping social policy is a formula that fills needs while protecting rights, a formula that abides by what Ira Glasser calls the "principle of least harm." We have to distinguish continuously between the times when neglect is benign and when neglect is immoral; when caring is helpful and when caring is coercive.

As Willard Gaylin writes in *Doing Good:* "We can degrade people by caring for them and we can degrade people by not caring for them, and in matters such as these there are neither simple answers nor simple solutions."

There is only the need for constant monitoring, tuning, to create the sort of social planning that neither ignores a neighbor's plea for help nor looses the Furies on an unwilling victim like the late Mary Northern, of Nashville, Tennessee.

MAY 1978

THE CRIME OF SEXUAL DESPERATION

On June 12, the police of Salt Lake City got their man. To be precise, they got their 1,130th man.

Consider, if you will, how much safer the citizens of Salt Lake City slept on the night of the thirteenth, knowing that Allan T. Howe had been apprehended.

On July 23, the courts of Salt Lake City convicted their man. They convicted him of "soliciting sex acts for hire." How righteous, how satisfied and how secure the citizens of the country must have felt on July 24, knowing that "justice had been meted out" and U.S. Representative Allan T. Howe given a $150 fine and a thirty-day jail sentence.

Just think about it. Think about demeaning behavior—"to lower in dignity or debase"—and why we convict the demeaned of a misdemeanor.

Howe, who is appealing his conviction, was the 1,130th man in Salt Lake City to have been arrested under the eight-year-old program to capture the "clients." It is a program in which the city pays civilian part-time police employees at the rate of $4.88 an hour to be bait for men already trapped in their sexuality, sexual mores and sexual morality. These women act as "decoys: one who entices or lures as into danger."

Their "success" rate in Salt Lake City is phenomenally high; 91 percent of the arrested clients are convicted. In Salt Lake, in New York, in Pasadena, in Cincinnati and other decoy cities, we send paid employees in hot-pants onto the streets. We make daring captures of those pursuing "pleasure."

In essence, we pay people to catch others trying to pay for something which is only a crime if, in fact, they pay for it. Why do we deal in this business? What greater good does it serve to round up and fingerprint Allan Howe? We have to consider, if we will, why we want to make victimless criminals at all. It seems that we have enough criminals—the kind who bang other people over the head and embezzle union pension funds and sell heroin to schoolchildren. There is hardly such a shortage that we must go out of our way to make more.

The police of Salt Lake City—and Cincinnati and Pasadena, et al.—are merely upholding the law. We know that. The decoy programs have spread from city to city out of the growing understanding that it is neither practical nor fair to arrest prostitutes without arresting "clients."

It seems likely that more judges will follow the lead of Ollie Marie-Victorie of San Francisco, who threw out charges against thirty-seven women last fall because their male customers went free. It seems likely that, in response, more and more police departments faced with upholding the law will turn to the decoy system.

But the fact is that no matter how "equal" those arrests become, they don't become right. Equality, after all, is not a synonym for justice. Laws can be enforced without regard to sex, race, national origin and the rest and still be totally unjust, impractical, self-defeating and demeaning to the people of the country.

The Howe case, in all its pathos, leads us inevitably to the idea that the only "equal justice" is the decriminalization of prostitution. Neither the buyers nor the sellers are criminals.

It isn't simply the pathetic sight of a strained Howe and his pained wife coming out of the courtroom—the photographs reminded us of our parents' admonitions not to stare at the pained and the crippled in public. It is rather the way in which the pursuit of these "criminals" reflects on all of us.

There is simply no reason to turn demeaning behavior into a punishable misdemeanor, making sexual desperation a crime. It is unseemly for our government to pursue these men.

Consider, if you will, the fact that tonight on some street in some city, there will be a police employee in high white boots walking through the red-light district, trying—in the public interest—to catch the 1,131st, or 2,000th man. How much safer will we feel, knowing that he, too, has been "brought to justice"?

JULY 1976

THE BIRTH-CONTROL GAP

It would be easier if growing up were a more cooperative venture—if our bodies and minds and emotions were fellow-travelers. It would be easier if kids couldn't open a bottle until they were smart enough not to drink the stuff in it, if they couldn't ride a bike until they were more cautious about cars, if they couldn't become parents until they were able to take care of children.

But the route from childhood to adulthood can be dangerously unsynchronized. Because of this, we try to protect our kids. We buy child-proof bottles, appoint crossing guards at the schoolyard, and support driver education to ease them onto the highways.

We do it in an attempt to protect them, even from their own mistakes, because society has a vested interest in helping kids to bridge the most treacherous gaps on the way to adulthood.

And yet, we have made an exception. The adolescents of this country—those who can bear and be children at the same time—have been left unprotected in the area of sexuality. For the past several decades we have chosen to pretend that we can prevent teenagers from being sexually active rather than protect them from the worst consequences of this age gap—pregnancy.

Though half the population of 21 million teenagers between fifteen and nineteen are sexually active, we have continued to make it difficult for them to get information about birth control and to buy contraceptives.

In the name of "sex prevention," this negligence has been at least partially responsible for the rise in teenaged pregnancies. Today one out of every ten teenaged girls becomes pregnant every year, a rate higher than that in eighteen other developed nations.

Last week the Supreme Court took a first major step in removing some of the barriers between teenagers and birth control. They struck down a New York State law that banned the sale of non-prescription drugs to anyone under sixteen years of age. At the same time they ruled against two other provisions in the statute: one that said only licensed pharmacists could sell these contraceptives, and another that prohibited companies from advertising or displaying them. There are similar laws in more than twenty other states that will also be affected by this ruling.

In the decision, the 7–2 majority rejected the old argument of the State of New York that freely available contraceptives would increase sexual activity. They also overruled the dissent of Justice Rehnquist, who fumed about "the right of commercial vendors of contraceptives to peddle them to unmarried minors through such means as window displays, and vending machines located in the men's rooms of truck stops."

Justice Rehnquist's fantasies aside, the point is to bring contraceptives to sexually active teenagers, to turn the old barriers into conduits. Not to promote sex, but to deal with its reality. Short of locking the entire teenaged population in their rooms, the only thing that adults can do is to "help" them avoid the most permanent and disastrous of consequences.

Each year more than 1,000,000 teenagers become pregnant. Of these, 30,000 are under the age of fifteen. Teenagers have one-third of all the abortions in the country (yet how little we hear from the anti-abortion groups about fostering birth control).

Twenty-one percent of pregnant teenaged girls give birth out of wedlock, with 87 percent keeping their babies. Arthur Campbell wrote in the *Journal of Marriage and the Family* about any one of these girls: "Suddenly she has 90 percent of her life's script written for her. She will probably drop out of school. . . . She will probably not be able to find a steady job that pays enough to provide for herself and her child. . . . Her life choices are few and most of them are bad. . . ."

Teenagers give birth to 600,000 children every year, which means that one out of every five American children has a teenaged mother. But more importantly, fewer than one-third of these mothers wanted babies. They became pregnant largely out of ignorance about, and lack of access to, birth-control methods.

Ignorance and inaccessibility—these are issues that the adult population can deal with in terms of protecting the children.

The Supreme Court decision will help. But as Dr. Daniel J. Callahan wrote in a Planned Parenthood study of teenaged pregnancy: "At the very least teenagers should have as much knowledge of sex, as many and as good services available, as do adults. . . . The most we can do is to help them avoid those things we know will hurt them, help to reduce the impact of those acts (even of folly) which they have already done, help them, in a word, to make it through the teenage years with as little lasting harm as possible."

JUNE 1977

STEERING CLEAR OF THE ONE TRUE COURSE

This is the time of year when 2.7 million young Americans can be found chewing anxiously on crocuses while waiting for proof of their acceptability to come fluttering through the mails from some university or other.

Yes, it's college acceptance season, a time to stir the hearts of all those parents contemplating remortgaging their homes, and all those children figuring out a package of loans and scholarships that will introduce them to the glories of deficit financing from now until 1992.

But while they are all riveted on getting in, what are they getting into?

The late philosopher, Alan Watts—a man far too sane to be considered anything but silly—once suggested a new college entrance exam. Instead of multiple-choice questions on the difference between synonyms and antonyms, he thought the applicants should write a twenty-page paper on "What They Want." What they want from college. What they want from life. These essays, he suggested, should be turned over to a tutor. He would examine the applicants closely. Do they know the side effects, the costs, the ramifications of "it"?

At no time would this "test" be more useful than now, with the crop of college students who are in the main so "practical," so sensible, so downright flat-footed about the whole thing.

What so many students today "want" out of college is graduate school. Or, alternatively, a Good Job. Most of them seem to be majoring in initials—embarked on a lockstep course to gain an M.D., a Ph.D. or a V.P.

This is what is called being "hardheaded about life," looking at the "bottom line" and making sure that college is "cost-effective." In accounting terms, they say, a liberal arts degree and 25 cents will get you a cup of coffee.

I have nothing against earning a living, but using college as an employment agency seems like the ultimate extravagance to me. Rather than being "sensible," this notion is motivated by fear—fear of the future—and by a profound misconception that the best armament against uncertainty is a life plan that reads like a Piece of the Rock.

Colleges are urged to "get on with the business of life," as if life were a business, and thousands of families will break the bank in order to prepare their children for a future that is myopically limited to the day after graduation. It's short-term insurance of the most expensive kind.

If I were one of Alan Watts's tutors (and I am eminently qualified, having planned my future once and for all half a dozen times), I'd point out that majoring in what Gail Sheehy labeled "The One True Course" will lead inexorably to a crash.

They can get there by following in the footsteps of professors who are in one stage or other of the midlife crisis, or of parents who are currently feeling locked in. They are being expensively prepared for their own middle-aged discontent, and may end up as the next generation of consumers for self-help books, divorce lawyers and employment agencies specializing in second careers.

The only adults I know who are still merrily marching along their one true course are boring, insensitive or lucky. The rest of us are survivors, survivors of crises, reverses, life changes. What you need to survive is a sense of humor, some joy, flexibility and a philosophy to hang your hat on.

In that case, isn't it at least as practical a thing to teach twenty-year-olds the management of personal transitions as to teach them the management of a department store? Doesn't liberal arts go well with a cup of coffee?

Why not something as sensible as electives in Flexibility 209, Coping 14B (given alternately with Crisis Survival 14A) and Change 143?

They might be antidotes to the sort of practicality that threatens to turn us all into hardheads like the father in *Goodbye Columbus*. He's the one, you may remember, who shrieked at his son, "What's the matter with you? Four years of college and you can't load a truck!"

APRIL 1977

THE DORMITORY TABOO

In the early sixties I lived in a college dormitory that allowed men upstairs once a year as long as you kept your door open and one foot on the floor. At the time, I had a professor whose opinion on the subject of coed housing was, and I quote, "Propinquity breeds. . . ."

Now this erudite soul was reduced to incoherent babbling some years later when his Harvard house began to accept people of, as he said, separate "sexual heritages." He was convinced that this misadventure in people-mixing would lead to sexual impurities of which Mr. Jimmy Carter never even dreamed. In short, there went the neighborhood.

Visions of eighteen-year-old orgies occurring over the pre-med books danced in his head. The word cohabitation came to symbolize all kinds of deep dark "habits" lurking in the hallways of our universities of higher learning.

Of course, he wasn't alone. Battalions of adults, especially alumni, were obsessed with the subject of college sex lives. This was due mainly to the fact that, when they were in college, battalions of adults were obsessed with their sex lives, and instituted rules having to do with parietal hours and keeping one foot on the floor.

Some of us figured, however, that this attitude toward "propinquity" and "promiscuity" would change with the new reality. As sociologist Gordon Allport once said, "Most people do not become converts in advance; they are converted by the fait accompli." As the dorms of hundreds of schools became coed and the parietal hours of thousands stretched to twenty-four, most parents came to accept the fact that the major problem in the dorms was lousy food and not enough hot water.

But not all of them. Take John W. Galbraith of Saddle River, New Jersey. Galbraith had sent his daughter to Wellesley, a single-sex school, only to discover that there were some male exchange students from M.I.T. right there, and that the parietal hours allowed, shall we say, extensive visiting privileges.

A few weeks ago he wrote to the parents of all nineteen hundred Wellesley students that "Our daughters are being taught [sic] sexual immorality . . ." and that "peer pressure will bend them into promiscuous, unhealthy or unnatural sex habits. . . ."

Just as his letter hit the media, along came a new study released by the Yale daily, which said that one out of every three undergraduates was "sexually active." But last week's Yale study suggested that it was the times, and not the rooms we live in, which determine sexual mores. Campus life was not a major factor in these statistics, they said, "even though" the residential units are for men and women.

Putting Mr. Galbraith aside, it seems that coed dorms actually have a dampening effect on relationships. As social scientist Thomas Pettigrew observed about Harvard coed housing, "The most interesting thing that's happened is that the kids have established something like an incest taboo in the dorms."

Instead of promiscuity in every entry, there seems to be a taboo against having romantic relationships with the suite mate, entry mate, and often even the dorm mate. As a senior expressed it in a less Margaret Mead-ish way, "You don't want to get involved with anyone in your entry because if it doesn't work out, you're stuck seeing each other at breakfast for the rest of the year." Which is food for thought for any married couple.

It turns out that closeness is not a great aphrodisiac, and it may still be distance that lets the heart grow fonder. This would corroborate the reputation that men's colleges still have—a reputation best expressed by the song, "Dartmouth's in Town Again; Run, Girls, Run."

When I was a kid, a platonic friend was a guy who was too short for you. Now a platonic friend is the guy who's living under the same roof. Where this will all lead, I'm not sure, but certainly not down the primrose path.

The incest taboo is a testimony to the practicality of the new college generation. They are more concerned with the smooth running of a dorm than with the course of true love. It appears that they have both feet on the ground. And never mind about the floor.

MAY 1976

A BOY FOR YOU,
A GIRL FOR ME

There had been rumors earlier, but they were so hard to believe. A couple aborting their fetus because it was the "wrong" sex? No, it wasn't possible.

But the rumors resurfaced in *Medical World News* last winter, and then again in *Psychology Today*, and finally they broke out into the open at a meeting of gynecologists in Bar Harbor, Maine.

"I am terribly concerned," said Dr. Park Gerald of Children's Hospital in Boston, "about the implications of just obliterating a fetus because it isn't the sex one chooses."

According to the doctors in Bar Harbor, a small but growing number of couples are using abortion as a method of sex selection— the latest, the newest, the ultimate in family planning.

This is a total perversion of a procedure known as amniocentesis, which can detect as many as two hundred birth defects, including Down's syndrome (mongolism), in fetuses. The procedure also reveals the sex of the fetus.

Sometimes, that sex is unwanted.

This news is not (as will be claimed) any "logical" extension of legalized abortion. It is rather the logical extension of a gender-obsessed society. It's the final solution of a world that has long considered masculinity and femininity the most important characteristics of people—far outweighing their individuality on one side or their humanity on the other.

Since the beginning of history, families have practiced "sex selection" by the infanticide and systematic malnutrition of their daughters. More "advanced" societies have so favored male children that a king like Henry VIII committed murder in pursuit of male heirs, and "commoners" all around us have their fourth or fifth or sixth baby in order to "get" (almost always) a boy. Surrounding them are "well-meaning" relatives who peer at baby girls and say, "Well, maybe next time . . ."

But now, we can plan it all medically. The amniocentesis can only be used in the second trimester, but in China a procedure called the "Ashan aspiration" can tell the sex of a fetus as early as 47 days after conception. In the first experimental tests there of 100 pregnant women, 30 were motivated to have abortions. Of those 30 fetuses, 29 were female.

But we can even select our favorite sex with increasing accuracy before conception. Landrum B. Shettles, a gynecologist, has published a method he claims to be 85 percent effective, and at the Sloan-Kettering Cancer Institute in New York they have a selective spermicide that knocks out the Ys or Xs in mice. So far just in mice.

There are some, like microbiologist John Postage of the University of Sussex, who maintain that the largest problem facing the world today is overpopulation and that sex selection is the only method of population control that would be accepted in the Third World. This would at once decrease the number of children for the next generation and the number of mothers for the following generation. What *Psychology Today* called "the manchild pill" would be the central figure of a science-fiction nightmare in which women would continue to be valuable or expendable objects as the reproduction needs vary.

The gynecologists in Bar Harbor said that they have not yet seen a marked preference for one sex or the other. The American ideal is of a perfectly balanced family: Mom and Dad, Dick, Jane, and Spot. Ours is a "Tea for two, two for tea, a boy for you, a girl for me" kind of family. In this prepackaged dream it is almost always a boy first and then a girl. To each girl her own big brother. To each boy his place as the firstborn. And for society the eternal locking in of the sexes in their places.

It still seems impossible for many of us to learn that the differences between individuals are greater than the differences between sexes. Boys will be boys? Don't tell that to the mother of two sons as different as Cain and Abel.

It seems equally impossible for many to believe that what the sexes share—their universal capacity to think and feel, to work and parent—is far more important than their genital differences.

Many egos are so invested in reproducing small versions of themselves, and society has so truly "discriminated" by sex, that they link to their children only by chromosomes. A boy for you, a girl for me.

The questions that come out of Bar Harbor plague us. What kinds of parents are so obsessed by gender that they would abort the "wrong" sex? How will they respond to the child's uniqueness or to the "male and female" characteristics that are fundamental parts of each psyche?

And finally, what about the wanted child of the right sex? Having been chosen exclusively on the basis of his or her reproductive anatomy, what kind of person will that child become?

AUGUST 1976

PARTICIPANTS, NOT PATIENTS

Ten years ago, when Marilyn was twenty-six, she became pregnant with her first child in a midwestern university town. She was excited and anxious when she went to the clinic to ask the doctor what he thought about natural childbirth.

His answer was pretty succinct. She remembers it vividly, and, in truth, bitterly. He said, "I think about natural childbirth the way I think about natural appendectomy." So when Marilyn's son "was delivered by the doctor" (that's the way she talks about it), her role was simple: She was a patient. Her son came into the world upside down and howling at the cold bright light of the operating room. He was, first of all, a patient.

About a year ago, Marilyn's father died. He was, of course, in a hospital, in the cardiac unit of what's called "a major metropolitan teaching hospital." He, too, was a patient, a good one, who took his medicine on time, without complaint. He died during the day shift.

During the months that followed, Marilyn's mother said, over and over, until it became her mantra, "Well, he had the best of care, didn't he? We did everything we could." Since then, Marilyn has been thinking about it, all of it. It seems to come together, these bits and pieces of her life.

She thought about her hospitalized delivery when she read Suzanne Arms's *Immaculate Deception*, a book that reported on the ways in which medicine—with the best of intentions, mind you—has turned maternity into an illness and childbirth into a medical crisis.

She thought about her son's birth when she heard the gentle French obstetrician, Dr. Frederick Leboyer, say that he believes infants should have a "birth without violence," a quiet, warm, bathed entry into the world of the family.

And, of course—how could she help it?—she thought about her father's death during the horrendous Karen Ann Quinlan case. The thing that impressed her about the Quinlan case wasn't whether the girl was legally alive or dead but that she was, she is, indisputably a medical patient. Her existence is a question of medical technology.

So it's not surprising that, this month, when she read a quote from Ivan Illich, the former priest and sociologist, in *Psychology*

Today, she memorized it. "Death that was once viewed as a call from God, and later as a natural event, has become an untimely event that is the outcome of our technical failure to treat a disease."

Marilyn has joined a growing number of Americans concerned about the effect of medical technology on our lives. Not the lack of technology—the intrusion of it. Our well-being is now thought of as a medical question, and the stages of our lives are marked by passages from the pediatrician to the obstetrician to the geriatrician. Through them we avoid pain and treat death pathologically.

Have we given up birth and death to medicine? If they are abnormal, certifiable sicknesses and we send them to the hospital to be dealt with, don't we also lose our emotional involvement with each other and with the critical moments of our lives? If we become passive and patient and seek only the absence of pain, aren't we missing the passages of life instead of experiencing them? What does it do to us when we treat death as a technical error? When someone dies, will we sue for malpractice?

Marilyn is not the type to rail against doctors. She is not for dismantling hospitals and closing down medical schools. She doesn't want to give birth in a rice paddy or have a natural appendectomy. She uses Novocain at the dentist's. But she thinks, as many do, that we have to distinguish between a disease and a process of life. We all are born and die of "natural causes."

She would like the medical establishment to concentrate more on helping us do this in our own time and our own beds. She would like them to use their technology more judiciously, more skeptically. After all, with all the fetal monitors in the obstetrics wards, we are still eighteenth in infant mortality in the world. With all the fancy cardiac units, there is new evidence that home care may be just as effective.

Right now, she says the patients and the doctors conspire in a medical delivery system whereby the patient delivers himself or herself up to be "cured" from life and death. She wants to remind us to be participants, not patients. More and more she has been thinking, just thinking, mind you, that the important questions about the way we live and die aren't medical ones at all.

MAY 1976

THE CHEM 20 FACTOR

When I was in college, there was an infamous course known as Chem 20. Organic chemistry was the sieve into which was poured every premedical student in the university. But only those who came through it with an A or B could reasonably expect to get into medical school.

Chem 20, therefore, became a psychological laboratory of premed anxiety. Every class was a combat mission. Each grade was a life-or-death matter. It reeked of Olympian anguish and Olympic competitiveness. It taught people whose goal in life was the relief of pain and suffering that only the fittest, the most single-minded, would survive.

I remember Chem 20 whenever I read about President Carter's outrage at the medical establishment, or when someone sardonically points out yet another M.D. plate on yet another Mercedes Benz, or when the National Council on Wage and Price Stability points out that the median income of doctors—$63,000 in 1976—has risen faster than any other group. In short, at times when other people talk about the M.D. as a license to make money, I think of the Chem 20 factor.

I know that we regard doctors as altruistic when they are treating us and avaricious when they are billing us. But I don't think we can understand the end result—high fees—unless we understand the process of selection and even self-selection by which people actually do become doctors.

On the whole, doctors made a commitment to go into medicine when they were eighteen or nineteen years old, with the full knowledge that they wouldn't be "practicing" until they were thirty or older. In a "Now Society," they would hold the record among their peers for delayed gratification. The sort of laid-back, noncompetitive person who wants to "live in the Moment" would drop out of Chem 20 with an acute case of culture shock in a week.

It is the dedicated or the narrow-minded (choose one from column A) who go through college competing for medical school and go through medical school competing for a good internship and go through internship competing for a good residency.

Today, residency is not the financial hardship it was when most practicing doctors in this country were young. The magazine *Hospital Physician* says that the average doctor in training earns $12,500 to

$15,000. But it is still basically an emotionalized physical-endurance contest.

It is normal for a young doctor to work an eighty-hour week. It is normal to work every other night and every other weekend. It is normal to be cut off for ten years from anything approaching a rich personal life. It is normal to come to regard the world as a hierarchy and a ladder to be climbed. It is, after all, the Chem 20 factor.

While there are thousands of others who work long hours just to keep a toehold in solvency, there is no other professional training that is comparable in terms of sheer stress. So, many of the doctors are sustained through this training by one vision: the Big Payoff. In this society, the Big Payoff is traditionally translated into dollars.

The end result of the training process is doctors who are often as addicted to work as patients to morphine. And doctors who have come to genuinely believe that they are "worth" whatever fees they can charge because they "worked for it."

I suspect that they are searching—sometimes desperately, and often futilely—for a return on the real investment they have made: their twenties.

So, the government may be right when it says that medical fees are spiraling because there is no free-market economy in doctors. The law of supply and demand doesn't work very well in medicine.

But that is only half of the story. If they want to see the psychological side, they have to go deeper, further, back to where the system begins—back as far as Chem 20.

The course is still being given. Only these days, I hear, there are pre-med students who won't even share their notes.

MAY 1978

■■■■■ "THE RULES
MADE ME DO IT"

The middle-manager was upset. It looked like his company was going to lose mandatory retirement for sixty-five-year-olds, and he didn't like that at all. Mandatory retirement, he said, was neat. No muss, no fuss. It cleaned out the deadwood and put a deadline on the worklife of his employees.

Yes, it was true he'd lost some good workers over the years, but on the other hand, the rule had made life easier for him. It had taken the decision "out of his hands." When it came time, he could just say, "We wish we could keep you, but you know how it is . . ."

The middle-manager wasn't alone in his anxiety. Another executive was talking about the worker he'd been "carrying" on the payroll for three years. And still another manager listed the guys in his corporation who long ago traded in their ambition for long lunch hours and a paycheck, playing the waiting game. He asked, "How are we going to get rid of them now?"

They were all mulling over the effects of extending mandatory retirement from sixty-five to seventy. But in the process they revealed something special, not about aging, but about themselves. Like many of the assorted bosses of our workaday lives, they would, on the whole, rather not deal with people as individuals, one by one, face to face. They prefer a door to hide behind and a rule to do their dirty work. They often acted out of a fear of confrontation, and with the ineptness of those uncomfortable in the business of human relationships.

The workers they were talking about are familiar. There's one in every office. The incompetent or embittered, the stumbler or the coaster. They can be found up and down the age ladder.

Each office develops elaborate dynamics to deal with the problem people by any means except the direct and personal ones. We have seen how often co-workers step gingerly around someone with an emotional problem, and how they work around people who don't perform. Whole conspiracies grow up, to avoid the truth.

In each vast conglomerate there is a fake job and a catalogue of busywork devised to occupy a vice-president. In every company there is an executive who has held onto a title while losing authority. In each division there is at least one worker being humored into impotence under the guise of kindness.

Corporations seem to alternate between ignoring the problem people or summarily firing them, or waiting a bit and retiring them. The employee who has been fired is often genuinely shocked. When he or she says, "They never complained about my work," it's as likely to be truth as a defensive fantasy. The older worker is apt to find his job being removed, memo by memo, while everyone pats him on the back telling him how invaluable his experience is to the company.

The root truth in all these scenarios is how little effort at mutual employer-employee problem-solving goes on in businesses. How little honest encounter.

They prefer to avoid the basic business questions which involve "feelings." How do you reenergize a discouraged employee and recycle a bored worker? How do you deal with someone who isn't performing up to standard? How do you phase people into positions that may require less energy, time or authority without humiliating them?

Only the best bosses can handle the human situations that require understanding and negotiations. The majority shy away from any kind of emotion. They are afraid of a scene, of anger, of tears, or visible pain.

The very same executive who can make a multimillion-dollar decision on steel or importing computers will often go to great lengths to avoid deciding whether one sixty-five-year-old should be promoted and another urged gently into retirement. While comfortable with their power over "things," they are uncomfortable with their power over people, and least comfortable dealing with it in person.

So mandatory retirement has helped those, like the middle-manager. They could blame the policy—"the rule did it"—and avoid guilt and discomfort. They could deal with categories instead of people.

But now, that machete-moment is being postponed from sixty-five to seventy in many places. In its place, perhaps business can develop the more delicate instrument it needs: careful, thoughtful interaction between people—a human relationship.

OCTOBER 1977